TREASURED ISLAND

FRANK BARRETT

Published by AA Publishing, a trading name of AA Media Limited, Fanum House, Basing View, Basingstoke, Hampshire RG21 4EA, UK.

www.theAA.com

First published in 2015. This paperback edition published 2016.

10 9 8 7 6 5 4 3 2 1

A CIP catalogue record for this book is available from the British Library.

ISBN: 978-0-7495-7813-8

Typeset in Bembo Regular 11pt

Printed and bound in the UK by Clays Ltd, St Ives plc

A05417

*To S, and the happy
highways where we went...*

Frank Barrett is Travel Editor of Britain's biggest
selling Sunday newspaper, *The Mail on Sunday*. He has
written several travel books, including *Where was Wonderland?*,
a guide to the real-life locations of classic children's books
such as *Anne of Green Gables* and *The Secret Garden,* and is
the winner of numerous awards for his travel writing,
including the prestigious British Press Award for travel
feature writing.

He lives in Bath with his wife Sheila, has two children,
and once had a dog called Eric. His favourite work of
fiction is Evelyn Waugh's 'Sword of Honour' trilogy.

Contents

Introduction 9

1   Bristol to Georgeham 19
2   Fowey to East Coker 43
3   Jane Austen to Jane Austen 64
4   Steep to Burwash 85
5   Rolvenden to Lydd 105
6   London 123
7   Stoke Poges to Stratford 154
8   Swansea to Shrewsbury 176
9   Eastwood to Whitby 197
10   Heptonstall to Cockermouth 214
11   Burns Cottage to Muckle Flugga 234
Fin. 256

Notes 259
Select bibliography 261
Selected reading 263
Acknowledgements 265
Index 268

Introduction

A young man in front of me paused as we stepped into Shakespeare's Birthplace in Stratford-upon-Avon. He turned to the woman with him: 'Hey, just imagine…this is where the magic happened!'

What magic was this?, I wondered. The magic of conception? The wonder of birth? The mystery of creativity? The enchantment of success? When it comes to The Bard – when you're in Stratford this works better in an American accent as the Bard of *Av*-on – we barely know anything at all: where he was born, when he was born, who he was, what he actually wrote. (We know he has a grave because Stratford's Holy Trinity Church has the cheek to charge you £2 for a quick look.) People have a reasonable idea about Shakespeare's life but nearly everything is just a best guess. None of this lack of precision really matters, however, when a writer is being turned into a tourist attraction.

If politics is show business for ugly people, literary tourism is show business for people who are able to tell a colourful biographical story. This really seems to be most of what literary tourism is all about. Tourism managers are hugely assisted in this effort by the fact that most writers led extraordinary lives – often their real lives were more interesting than their fiction, involving, variously: drunkenness, philandering, bankruptcy, insanity, various degrees of dishonesty and self-delusion, and, of course, tragic early death. You don't have to be a drunken short-lived adulterer to become a successful writer, but it probably helps. Here, then, is the template for a literary tourist attraction: from Burns Cottage to Pooh Corner, these are places that want to tell you an amazing story. And, in the process, it often all goes a bit mad.

The British have always been nice to mad people. This line from Noel Coward's script for *Brief Encounter* kept recurring to me as I criss-crossed the UK looking at the weird and wonderful world of literary places. If a passion to write is some sort of madness then it is a strange obsession, matched in equal terms by the people who feel compelled to create a memorial to their favourite writer. Following close behind in this triangle of insane passion are those who wish to visit these literary memorials. I can understand why writers write; I'm increasingly less certain about what the other two groups of people think they're doing.

It's important to understand that travel and tourism is largely an emotional process: we decide where to go on a day out or even on a three-week walking holiday in the Hindu Kush without the benefit of much careful analysis of available research. We commit ourselves to vast expense and inconvenience, usually on nothing more than a whim. We've heard about Charlotte Brontë, for example; we may know she was a famous writer, we may even know she wrote *Jane Eyre*. We think it might be nice to visit the home of the Brontë sisters in Yorkshire because it sounds interesting: after all, we can't spend the whole of our leisure time in front of the TV just watching *Pointless* and *Homes under the Hammer*. So we get in our cars and drive probably hundreds of miles, suffer the indignity of sub-human toilets in sub-human motorway service stations, and when we reach our destination we spend good money on admission tickets, a brochure and a modest lunch. For all this time and trouble we expect a little entertainment: at a literary attraction, ideally, we want to hear how poor, struggling people heaved themselves out of life's gutter and into the sunlight of wealth and acclaim by imagination and hard work.

The National Trust, as you might have expected given the length of time it's been doing this business, has polished up this turn into a fine art. At a National Trust property, if the house itself or the story it tells disappoint, the cafe and the souvenir shop will surely be magnificent. Other places in the literary tourism business have a less certain grasp of things – this doesn't make them any less interesting (sometimes, if you find yourself in the right place, it can be very entertaining) but it does mean you're unlikely to get a decent afternoon tea or a nice souvenir. But ultimately it's all very British, quite dysfunctional and, in an unexpected way, very uplifting. Britain has produced more of the world's greatest writers than probably any other country on earth; with some major exceptions, we're also rather good at running tourist attractions, even if occasionally visitors get shouted at. I got shouted at quite often – but that may just be the result of me being annoying.

※

My fascination with writers and the places connected with them goes back rather a long way to my childhood home in the Wye Valley. In the 1960s, if you were lucky enough to live anywhere so pretty that it had souvenir shops selling postcards, you might have expected many of the postcards to be of the Donald McGill *double entendre* variety. Sample:

'Did she marry him after all?' asks curious neighbour.

'No,' replies blowzy lady, 'He had a bad accident and it was broken off!'

This is barely even *single entendre*.

I spent the bulk of my growing-up years in a very beautiful place with a ruined Cistercian abbey and a view for which the word 'picturesque' was invented by William Gilpin. Here, the souvenir shop postcards were impressively sober: so serious, in fact, that they came with a slice of 18th-century romantic poetry attached. Printed above a view of our abbey were usually these lines:

> *Five years have past, five summers, with the length*
> *Of five long winters! and again I hear*
> *These waters, rolling from their mountain-springs*
> *With a soft inland murmur...*

This was William Wordsworth's 'Lines composed a few miles above Tintern Abbey'; the poem continues in similar vein, it seemed to my child's eye, for an unfeasibly long time. The poem, I learned later, marked an historic point in English literature. This was the final poem in Coleridge and Wordsworth's jointly produced *Lyrical Ballads,* and it attempted to set out the Wordsworthian belief that God is to be found in natural beauty. Wordsworth was right in one aspect at least: the Wye Valley is one of the most exquisitely beautiful places in the world. There must be something literary in the air. A few miles from the place where Wordsworth contemplated Tintern Abbey stands the childhood home of a writer who, some 200 years later, became the wealthiest novelist the world has ever seen. There is no memorial to J K Rowling in her home Tutshill...yet. Her monument lies in the 400 million books she has sold worldwide.

But, having discovered in Tintern that there was a connection between words and places, my interest inevitably extended to the places featured in the writing that I liked. One of my earliest delights as a reader was Dodie Smith's 1956 novel *One Hundred And One Dalmatians* and its glorious illustrations by Janet and Anne Grahame-Johnstone – especially the drawings of the Dearly residence in Regent's Park. It was my greatest joy eventually to discover that you can stand outside this very house: Number One Saint Andrew's Place on the corner of Outer Circle. It was the London house in which Dodie Smith most wanted to live, and which she instructed the illustrators to draw.

This desire to discover the places behind my favourite works of literature is not one that is new. When Alexander the Great set forth to conquer Asia in the fourth century BC, foremost on his list of 'must-conquer' places was Troy in what was then Asia Minor, now in Turkey. Alexander had been raised on *The Iliad*, Homer's epic tale of the mythical Trojan wars. When the young Macedonian finally reached the place of his dreams, it is written that he celebrated his arrival by imbibing lusty quantities of strong alcohol and then took part in the traditional race – run in the nude – to the supposed 'tomb of Achilles', where he placed a special garland. The locals welcomed the young conqueror with the gift of a shield, said to have been dedicated by the Trojans to Athena. Alexander was also invited to look at the very lyre purportedly played by Paris when he seduced the beautiful Helen of Troy; the conquering hero, presumably badly hungover and sunburnt in tender places, wearily declined this particular exciting excursion opportunity.

This is probably the first recorded example in history of literary tourism. It was a journey which began with high ideals but ended less gloriously, becoming in many ways a template for modern Club 18-30 tourism: young men on the pull, casual sex, too much booze, dubious history, phony pilgrimage, cheap sensation, dodgy souvenirs and eventual ennui. It demonstrated, however, that the act of reading could create a ferocious appetite for travel. You've read the book? Now see the place they've written about. Or – in the case of Alexander the Great – gather an army and conquer it.

※

One of the fascinating things about literature is just how much of it actually exists. What's even more extraordinary is how much there is of it in the UK, and how it shapes where we live.

Look at a map of America and place names sing out to you. 'New York, New York', '(Get Your Kicks on) Route 66', 'Kansas City, Here I Come', 'Long Distance Information Give Me Memphis, Tennessee', 'Highway 61 Revisited', 'Ventura Highway', 'Sweet Home Alabama', 'Oklahoma', 'San Francisco (Be Sure to Wear Flowers in Your Hair)'. You don't need a satnav to guide you round the US; an iPod and a selection of suitable works from *The Great American Songbook* will do the trick. It's a country where there's almost a tune in every road sign. A couple of years ago, heading out of Albuqerque, New Mexico, on Interstate 40, for example, almost immediately a city name on an overhead gantry made me cry out: 'Is *this* the way to Amarillo?' It was.

In Britain, places and roads have never been a major source of inspiration for modern song writers, a shame when you listen to 'Penny Lane' or anything by The Proclaimers. Regrettably, it seems there are few kicks to be had on the A66 and nobody – lyrically, at least – has ever left their heart in Sutton Coldfield. Britain, however, is celebrated in a different but no less compelling fashion: in literature. We may seem a curiously unsentimental race, but burrow down into our souls and poetry lurks. There is scarcely a place in these islands that hasn't been acclaimed in novel, verse or play.

English, as she is spoke here, is riddled with verse; lines of poetry that have simply become part of our linguistic landscape: our everyday conversation littered with verbal ornamentations that firmly display the fact that ours is the language of Shakespeare. A few examples – though I could list hundreds – include: 'strike while the iron is hot' (Chaucer); 'neither borrower nor lender be' (Shakespeare); 'love at first sight' (Marlowe); 'to play with fire' (Vaughan); 'trip the Light Fantastic' (Milton); 'a little learning is a dangerous thing' (Alexander Pope); 'ignorance is bliss' (Thomas Gray); and finally – appropriately, perhaps, in this abbreviated illustration – 'Less is More' (Browning).

Just as our mouths have been filled with their poetry, so writers have similarly shaped our views of the British landscape. No visit to the Yorkshire Moors, for example, can be undertaken without thoughts of Emily Brontë's *Wuthering Heights*; Dorset will be forever glimpsed through the prism of Thomas Hardy's fictional Wessex; the Kent marshes will always belong to Dickens. But it's not just a transformation of the imagination – writers have left physical landmarks too.

Down in England's southwest lies Westward Ho!, the only town in the world to have been named after a novel (by Charles Kingsley) and the only place to have an exclamation mark in its name. In London's King's Cross station you can find signs directing you to Platform 9¾, from J K Rowling's Harry Potter novels. On a September weekend in Bath, thousands travel from as far afield as the US and Japan in order to dress up as *Pride and Prejudice's* Mr Darcy or Miss Elizabeth Bennet – by Jane Austen. The most popular December walk in London takes visitors to see the real-life locations of Charles Dickens' *A Christmas Carol*. The real-life places of a novel? Cynics might justifiably declare: 'Bah! Humbug!'

Around 200 years ago, the poet Samuel Taylor Coleridge, someone we shall meet again very shortly, advanced the view in his 1817 *Biographia Literaria* that if a writer could infuse a 'human interest and a semblance of truth' into an extraordinary story, the reader would be happy to suspend judgement concerning 'the implausibility of the narrative': in other words, we are only too happy to believe that the best novels are all true.

Even if it's only make-believe – does it really matter if we choose to take it seriously? Except that the British take their fiction very seriously indeed. A ferocious debate has raged for decades on the exact location of P G Wodehouse's Blandings

Castle, a fictitious stately home inhabited by the imaginary Lord Emsworth and his prize-winning pig ('the Empress of Blandings'). I've personally been involved in stand-up rows over the likely real-life home village of Richmal Crompton's Just William (hardcore fans have triangulated the position based on the author's passing references to genuine locations such as the A1 and Stratford-upon-Avon).

If Britain is nationally more obsessed with literature than other countries, it may be because we have always been voracious readers – a habit dating back several centuries. In Pepys' diary the author robustly displays four main passions: reading, writing, the theatre and sex. Pepys is wracked with guilt at his endless trips to buy new books; wasting money on books seems to trouble him more than his inappropriate extra-marital dalliances with Mrs Bagwell or Mrs Lane.

It was Britain where the novel established its powerful grip in the 19th century, with literary serials by the likes of Wilkie Collins and Dickens. Dickens' readers in the US were so desperate to know the outcome of *The Old Curiosity Shop* that people stood on the dockside in New York shouting to arriving passengers: 'Is Little Nell dead?' Not everyone, however, was moved by the story – Oscar Wilde remarked: 'One must have a heart of stone to read the death of Little Nell without laughing.'

Countries such as the US, France and Germany may have museums devoted to their Premier League writers: the likes of Mark Twain, Colette and Thomas Mann, who are celebrated in their own lands with due ceremony. Where Britain surpasses the rest of the world is in the eclectic range of this celebration. Shakespeare, Dickens, Wordsworth and Keats, for example, have full-bore museums; several of them each in the case of Shakespeare, Dickens and Wordsworth.

But in the UK there are lavish galleries and museums devoted to those from among the lower divisions of literature:

including – to name but a few – Roald Dahl, Dylan Thomas, Beatrix Potter, George Eliot, J M Barrie, Thomas Hardy, D H Lawrence, Dr Johnson, Virginia Woolf, Rudyard Kipling, Thomas Carlyle and – remarkably – even a museum devoted to a fictional character: Sherlock Holmes. Elementary, my dear Watson. (Sherlock Holmes never said this, of course, but once again we're venturing into the mysterious land of 'who really gives a damn?' – all that matters is for people to believe it was so.)

Today, I estimate that in the UK there are more than 100 attractions and places that you can visit connected with writers. There are dozens of literary properties owned by local authorities, trusts and well-organised enthusiasts. And the number continues to grow. An appeal is underway at the moment, for example, to buy the cottage owned by William Blake in Felpham, West Sussex, where he wrote 'Jerusalem'. We enjoy the magic of great writing, so what is more natural than wanting to see where 'the magic happened', as the Stratford visitor described it.

The National Trust alone has properties connected with 12 writers including Agatha Christie, Carlyle, Coleridge, two Thomas Hardy houses, Kipling, T E Lawrence, Beatrix Potter, William Wordsworth and Virginia Woolf. If the rest of the world doesn't have the range of important literary properties open to the public that we have in the UK, then the answer is that the rest of the world does not have anything like our National Trust.

Political leaders of a certain tinge are always to keen to present Britain as a capitalist country 'red in tooth and claw' (Tennyson). In fact, where we are seen at our best is in an organisation such as the National Trust, which was built largely on the generosity of the wealthy and is run on the enthusiasm of the committed. The museums and literary houses described in this book, which aren't in the possession of the National Trust, are largely run to the same standards of the Trust, such is its extraordinary influence.

There's an argument for claiming that the National Trust has largely replaced the Church of England in the role of caring for the soul of the nation. Where people once went to a church on a Sunday, they now spend the Sabbath contemplating life from a National Trust trail or park. My literary tour of the UK had something of a pilgrimage about it.

I get the impression that the only people who have travelled to the furthest corners of these islands are dogged football supporters who seem to think nothing of driving several hundred miles in a day to watch their team probably lose. Most people these days are happy to jump on a plane to travel a couple of thousand miles when they have no idea what a wonderfully varied and fascinating country we have on our doorstep. If you need an excuse to discover the UK, visiting literary places is as good a reason as any. It needn't be expensive: there are lots of good, inexpensive places to stay, and advance purchase rail tickets can be spectacularly cheap. Take your imagination out for a holiday and who knows where you'll end up?

1

Bristol to Georgeham

In which our intrepid explorer raises a glass to Robert Louis Stevenson, wells up at William Blake, yells 'Watch it' to Samuel Taylor Coleridge and is Otterly bemused in Tarka country.

'OUTSIDE of a dog,' said Groucho Marx, 'a book is man's best friend. Inside of a dog,' he added, 'it's too dark to read.'

In a world ruled by iPads and Kindles, books – along with dogs – appear to have lost their 'man's best friend' status: these days the British pet fish population exceeds the total numbers of dogs and cats combined. Yet, curiously, books – good old-fashioned hardback books – have never been more accessible. With most UK high streets these days seemingly composed of an endless variety of charity shops, secondhand books are on sale at practically every turn and available for amazingly low prices; not just Dan Brown thrillers and copies of *Fifty Shades of Grey*, but highbrow stuff as well, including normally very expensive Folio Society literary gems. Oxfam, for example, now has an 'Antiquarian, rare & collectable books' section on its website which features the thousands of valuable first editions that turn up every day in its shops (current offers include a first edition of Yeats' poems for £250).

I have an iPad and a Kindle and I use both regularly. They are technological wonders, but neither offers the magic, the grace nor the style of a real book with pages. Downloading an album from iTunes, for example, is agreeably easy but, had such a system existed 50 years ago, it would have come nowhere near to matching the tremulous excitement of racing into Chepstow Sports and Record Centre and handing over hard cash – or a record token! – for the latest Beatles LP. The record was brought home on the bus where the album cover was studied in reverential awe – not even a CD offers this pleasure. Real records, like real books, shook the world in a way which – so far, at least – their electronic offspring never have.

But the problem with real books (and real records) is their size. A library's worth of ebooks can be accommodated on a hard drive the size of a Beano annual; in the real world, in our real house, Barrett family books now fill one large garden shed, much of the space in five different rooms and almost the whole of two attics. This summer, when the shed-library showed signs of imminent collapse, we were faced with a brutal choice. Did we swell the shelves of local charity shops with a gift of a couple of thousand books? Or did we bow to the inevitable, and accept that we have inadvertently turned our home into a modest library? (There's a certain irony in the fact that while the Government is busy closing public libraries down, we – people of slender means, I should point out, in case you start getting the idea that we wander around a baroque mansion lighting cigars with £20 notes – seem to have assembled a private one.)

In formulating a plan, I conducted a test examination of the shed-library, whose entrance had, at some time in the past few years, become obstructed with knotweed thick enough for Tarzan to use to swing from tree to tree. I hacked my way to the front door. Torch in hand, like Howard Carter at the entrance to Tutankhamen's tomb, I prised open the door.

'What do you see?' asked my wife.

Wonderful things!

Arrayed on cheap plastic shelving from B&Q and within towers of thin cardboard fruit boxes – acquired long ago by the dozen from Sainsbury's – was the fruit of a lifetime's reading. A 1958 Eagle annual... *The Observer's Book of Cars*... *Swallows and Amazons*... *William Again*... Coles notes for *Richard III*... *John Lennon In His Own Write*... *Animal Farm*... *Sons and Lovers*... *Romantic Poetry: A Guide*... *The Joy of Sex*... the *1980 Red Michelin Guide to France*... *The Brand New Monty Python Papperbok*... *Beatles Monthly*... back numbers of the *Boys' Own Paper*... Here was the story of our lives, literally told in books and publications: each volume a precious memory, not just of the book itself, but of where and when we read it. From childhood towards dotage I was standing amid our history.

Avoiding a toppling pile of 45rpm singles – why did I ever get rid of that jukebox? – a familiar book surfaced from amongst the chaos. A book with a kingfisher-blue hardcover which showed a boy in the rigging of a sailing ship, pointing two pistols down at a pursuing pigtailed buccaneer. *Treasure Island*!

Remember your first record? My brother and I were given our first gramophone in that period described by Philip Larkin in his poem 'Annus Mirabilis' as falling between 'the end of the Chatterley ban and the Beatles' first LP'.[1] The Chatterley obscenity trial ended in victory for Penguin Books in November 1960; the Beatles' first LP was released in March 1963. When I was nine I saw the Fab Four perform live at Weston-Super-Mare Odeon in July 1963, and I was given their first LP for my birthday later in October of that year. But by then we'd already had our gramophone – I think we actually called it a 'gramophone' – for a couple of years.

When we were given the record player, we were supplied with two discs to play on it, a sort of *Desert Island Discs* from Hell: an LP of Tchaikovsky's *Piano Concerto No. 1 in B-flat minor* and an EP of *Treasure Island*. The *Treasure Island* record was a 20-minute 1960 audio version of Stevenson's novel starring distinguished actor Sir Donald Wolfit as Long John Silver; the credits on the sleeve also reveal the involvement of David Croft, subsequent co-creator of *Dad's Army*. The recording was a miracle of miniaturisation, managing to squeeze a 300-page novel onto both sides of a 45rpm record – and, for reasons I can't recall, it was a record made from livid green vinyl. As our only record for a short time, it got played rather a lot. Endless repetition meant that various memorable lines from the book managed to slip into common family parlance: 'The black spot!...You've gone and cut it out of a bible...Them that die'll be the lucky ones...'

So by the time my uncle showed me a copy of the book, *Treasure Island* was already a favourite. He later told me how he found his vintage copy in a NAAFI in Egypt where he was posted during his National Service in the period prior to the Suez Crisis in 1956. (The Suez Crisis, curiously, is one of my first memories – when I was just two and a half years old I remember my father driving me down a long road near our home in Newport, South Wales – parked on both sides were endless columns of military vehicles preparing to be shipped to Egypt for the confrontation with President Nasser.)

When he quietly gave me the book a couple of months before he died, he simply said: 'This book has been a faithful companion.' Over the years he had shared nuggets of information that he had discovered about the book: which real-life people were the probable inspiration of some of the book's characters; the presumed real-life location of the Admiral Benbow Inn.

One of the things that most fascinated him was the 'X marks the spot' map at the very front of the book. 'They say that this was drawn by his father, based on an island in the Shetlands.' He would pore over his AA road atlas, computing the distances involved. Over the years the question, 'Wouldn't you like to go and see it: the Real Treasure Island?' became a saying.

We were children; of course we wanted to go to a real Treasure Island and dig up pieces of eight and bars of gold. Years went by: we continued to talk about taking that trip north to Scotland.

'The real Treasure Island!' we would say. 'I'd love to do that…'

I could have organised it; I should have organised it. I never did.

As I held his talismanic book in my hands again, I felt an acute sense of regret of shared dreams unfulfilled. I flicked open the front cover and looked again at that treasure map. Why not go to the real Treasure Island – and along the way, while I still could, pay homage at other literary shrines? Like my uncle, I had long-fostered ambitions to 'visit' my favourite literary places – this was my chance.

In a week or so I would have to settle the matter of the book-shed. What better time to begin a literary journey that would end in the northernmost point of our Treasured Island.

A real voyage inspired by real books. Wouldn't you like to see the real Treasure Island?

※

Jim Hawkins' journey on the *Hispaniola* to Treasure Island began in Bristol, along with Squire Trelawney, Dr Livesey and Long John Silver. Of course, like any self-respecting pirate, Long John Silver lived in Bristol (the city, after all, was the birthplace of perhaps the world's most notorious buccaneer: Blackbeard). And it was where I, too, decided to begin my own journey in search of Britain's literary landscape and landmarks.

For some 200 years, once upon a time, the city of Bristol was second only to London – a major port which, like Liverpool, built a vast fortune from slavery. In the 16th century it was England's second wealthiest city. It was from here in 1497 that John Cabot sailed west in the *Matthew* in search of Asia but instead discovered America, landing in what he called Newfoundland, a territory claimed for the British Crown. Three hundred years later, it was from Bristol that Brunel inaugurated his epoch-making regular steamship service to New York.

Bristol's literary connections are maybe even more significant. It was at the Llandoger Trow Inn, on Bristol's waterfront, that Daniel Defoe is said to have met the Scottish sailor Alexander Selkirk, who was marooned on an uninhabited island in the South Pacific Ocean for four years. This encounter led to Defoe writing *Robinson Crusoe*, published in 1719 (a book which gave the world the phrase 'Man Friday' – the name of Cruose's helper, encountered on a Friday – and a more recent derivative 'Girl Friday'). Originally published as if it were a real story actually written by Crusoe, *Robinson Crusoe* is credited as the world's first major work of realistic fiction. It inspired – literally – a raft of desert island imitators, from *Swiss Family Robinson* and *The Coral Island* to that perennial secondary school favourite, *Lord of the Flies*.

When Robert Louis Stevenson wrote *Treasure Island*, published in 1883, there were a couple of nods towards Daniel Defoe. The character of Ben Gunn is clearly inspired by Robinson Crusoe. And the story of *Treasure Island* begins in the Admiral Benbow Inn, modelled on the Llandoger Trow.

There ought to be a public house equivalent of the National Trust whose job would be to rescue historic pubs and restore them to their pomp. Few pubs can have fallen so far from grace as Bristol's Llandoger Trow, from the outside a lovely old building situated in a handsome quayside location; it can justifiably lay claim to the title of Bristol's most famous pub. Built in 1664, it takes its name from the village of Llandogo on the River Wye in Monmouthshire, three miles from where I grew up in Tintern. Llandogo was home to Captain Hawkins, a sailor reckoned to be the first landlord of the pub (a 'trow' being the flat-bottomed sailing barge that Hawkins skippered between Llandogo and Bristol).

In theory, the Llandoger Trow ought to enjoy a booming trade, given its location and its links with both *Robinson Crusoe* and *Treasure Island*. However – unbelievably – I arrived to discover that this historic treasure now seemed to be an unloved outpost of the Brewers Fayre chain. How could this have happened? The shock was equivalent to discovering that Jane Austen's home had suddenly become a Little Chef.

Just around the corner was The Hole in the Wall, which no less an authority than the Long John Silver Trust (its aim is to collect enough money to raise a statue of Long John Silver in Bristol) claims as the model for Silver's own fictional Spyglass Inn (a spyglass was used to keep a lookout for pressgangs which operated in this area). Sadly, this establishment seemed to be faring as badly as the Llandoger Trow (both have been tipped the Tripadvisor Black Spot – there must be a pirates' curse in play here). Eschewing both establishments, I retreated to the nearby Cherry Duck Bistro, where I feasted on beetroot and nut roast – not something in seacook Long John Silver's gastronomic repertoire, one imagines. Now all shipshape and Bristol fashion, I spread my maps and plotted my journey. Bristol was the starting point for so many Great Journeys (real and fictional) – what better place to start a trip that combined elements of both?

※

Perhaps it has something to do with the Celtic tradition of bardic tales, or it could be the cider – whatever the reason, the West Country has enjoyed connections with an unrivalled list of writers. From occasional Bath resident Jane Austen to the world's biggest-earning novelist J K Rowling, who was born near Bristol and brought up close to the Forest of Dean, the West Country boasts strong links with an extraordinary range of literary talents, including two Nobel laureates – T S Eliot and William Golding – and ties to five Poets Laureate – Samuel Daniel, Robert Southey, William Wordsworth, John Betjeman and Ted Hughes. Other candidates for a West Country literary First XV might include Slad's Laurie Lee – author of *Cider with Rosie* – Combe Florey's Evelyn Waugh, Exmoor's R D Blackmore – author of *Lorna Doone* – Cornwall's Daphne du Maurier, and John le Carre.

Other striking West Country connections include Bristol's tragic poet Thomas Chatterton, who in the late-18th century began forging phony medieval poetry as a precocious 12-year old and ended up killing himself just five years later at the age of 17 – his short life, however, became an inspiration for Romantic Poets Shelley and Coleridge, and his death the subject of a famous painting by pre-Raphaelite artist Henry Wallis. Virginia Woolf went *To the Lighthouse* when she was a child on family holidays in Cornwall; during the First World War, D H Lawrence and his German wife Frieda enjoyed a brief sojourn near Land's End, which ended in a bizarre episode which might have been taken from Dads' Army.

John Betjeman is buried in St Enodoc's Church in Cornwall near Padstow, but he has what he would probably consider a more glorious memorial at Dilton Marsh Halt station near Warminster. In his poem named after the station, he reflects on its struggle to survive in the post-Beeching world; indeed, a few years after the poem was published British Rail attempted to close the station. A local campaign, which used Betjeman's poem as a central part of the fight, succeeded in keeping the station open. It remains a living tribute to the power of the pen. *Thomas the Tank Engine's* creator, the Rev W Awdry lived as a child in Box, near Bath, and lay in bed at night listening to the steam engines on the nearby Great Western mainline between Bath and Paddington and assigning them personalities. 'Little imagination was needed to hear, in the puffings and pantings, the conversation they were having with one another,' he said later.[2]

In fact, as I pondered all this – and considered a map – I could have spent weeks on a literary pilgrimage through this part of the country alone. For now though, it was time to drain my pint of scrumpy (organic apple juice, at least), slip anchor from Bristol harbour and set sail for the southwest. Or get in the car and take the A39 – the Atlantic Highway – to Glastonbury and all points southwest.

But this way, of course, madness lies…

※

An elderly man at a petrol station in Wells was talking to the cashier about 'that actor blokey off Shylock'.

'My wife just bumped into him outside The Swan,' he said.

The Eastern European cashier betrayed polite yet remote interest. 'Oh, yes…?'

A woman in a green gilet joined the queue and was happy to take the conversation towards more solid ground: 'You mean Benedict Cumberbatch? From Sherlock Holmes?' The man and the cashier looked at her incuriously. She continued: 'He's playing Richard III in some Shakespeare film they're doing outside the cathedral – cast of thousands up there.'

'Lots of young girls there, my wife said,' said the man.

'The girl fans are called "Cumber-bitches", I'm told,' replied the woman.

'Excuse me,' inquired the cashier, 'Are you perhaps collecting the school tokens, please?'

Wells is one of those places in Britain that seems to lie on the border between sense and non-sense. Glastonbury, a few miles away, is firmly in the land of Nonsense; it may even be the capital of that strange country. But once you reach Wells, you are aware that daftness is not terribly far off.

From the petrol station forecourt, the tower at the top of Glastonbury Tor was clearly visible in the bright autumn morning sun. The tower looked like a little lighthouse, for centuries no doubt a comforting sight to those who have lived on the long, flat stretches of the Somerset Levels, a place which had recently suffered catastrophic flooding. The Tor is steeped in Celtic myth and legend, and has strong connections with tales of King Arthur. It was once believed that the Tor marked the entrance to Fairyland. These days, for a new generation of visitors, the Tor merely heralds the way towards the Clarks Village shopping outlet in nearby Street, where there are bargains galore to be had at Timberland, Gap, Marks & Spencer and dozens of other outlet shops.

The elderly man emerged behind me from the shop and paused before returning to his car: 'I don't think Richard III ever really came to Wells. Who cares, though? It's for the BBC probably – they don't care.'

Richard III may never have been to Wells, but there are many people who think that Jesus Christ once travelled this way. Nowadays 'Glasto' is famous for its midsummer pop festival, where the likes of Dolly Parton and The Rolling Stones come to the Somerset countryside and get their groove on. Festival fans probably have little idea that Glastonbury has been a centre of mystery and magic for thousands of years. Actually, few if any of the festivalgoers get anywhere near Glastonbury, since the festival happens several miles away on Worthy Farm, Pilton.

Inhabited since the Iron Age, Glastonbury became more widely known for its abbey, first built in Saxon times. The town has long been a place of myths and legends, the most famous (after Arthur, Merlin and their chums, perhaps) being that it was once visited by Palestinian travelling merchant, Joseph of Arimathea, and his nephew Jesus. You slightly wonder how Mark, Matthew, Luke and John all managed to miss this entertaining chapter from their Gospels. You can almost imagine Jesus tweeting his delight: 'Uncle Joe is just arrived in dad's workshop with Glasto tickets, innit? Miracles! This is well sick, yo!'

It was this legend of Christ in Glastonbury that William Blake was referring to when, in 1808, he published the poem that we have come to know as 'Jerusalem'. The opening lines anticipate a headline style that was to become much favoured by newspaper sub-editors: 'Did Jack the Ripper sink the Titanic?' or 'Does frogspawn cure athletes foot?' – the answer is generally and obviously 'no', but it allows newspapers to ask interesting, if slightly daft or sometimes quasi-libellous questions.

In his poem, William Blake asks if Jesus ever walked on Somerset's hills – he's not saying that Jesus really did but, he's saying, it's worth asking – because the implication is that, what with the growing number of dark satanic mills brought by the industrial revolution at the end of the 18th century, the Son of God would not be very impressed with the way things were going.

Literary research has suggested that Blake was probably not concerned about dark satanic mills in general, but just one satanic mill in particular; the poet lived near the Albion Flour Mill on the Thames in Southwark, which was set up to produce flour on a hitherto unseen industrial scale to keep pace with London's rapidly growing demand for bread. Fearful for their jobs, local independent millers were said to have caused the fire in 1791 which left the five-storey building a blackened shell;

remarkably, poet Robert Southey saw the fire and subsequently wrote about an event that many feared was the first manifestation of the sort of popular uprising which had recently engulfed France.

When I first visited the town in the early 1970s, Glastonbury was a normal, working place with several shops selling the leather goods and sheepskin coats made at local factories, for which the area had become well known. Now these factories have gone and most shops here seem to sell things like scented candles, dreamcatchers and a selection of 'mystical' paintings and sculptures that inhabit the cramped artistic space that lies between 'weird' and 'awful'.

In one of the mystical shops, I asked the lady at the till about the Glastonbury Thorn, which is said to grow from a staff that Joseph of Arimathaea plunged into the soil after arriving in Glastonbury. The tree blooms every Christmas; a blossom is cut from one of the tree's branches in a special ceremony each December and sent to the Queen. It seems I had touched a raw nerve: 'There's been a few thorn trees in Glastonbury and some berk keeps damaging them, snapping off the branches and that. What sort of nutter does something like that?'

As she asked me this I glanced at her bookshelves and spotted a slim volume: *Goblinproofing One's Chicken Coop: And Other Practical Advice In Our Campaign Against The Fairy Kingdom*. Perhaps it's goblins, I suggested.

'Goblins? Yes, you may be right. They're just the sort of nutters who might do something daft like that.'

※

If I had been better organised I would have got the train to Watchet via the West Somerset Railway, the 22-mile preserved 'heritage' line that links Bishops Lydeard and Minehead. Minehead is best known for its Butlin's holiday camp, of which

I have fond memories. I subscribed to the *Eagle* comic in the 1960s which, improbably, ran a Butlin's promotion: collect six tokens and you could enjoy a free day out with a friend at a camp of your choice. So it was that I visited Minehead Butlin's with my school friend Jason Toynbee, son of *Observer* book reviewer Philip Toynbee, half-brother of the *Guardian*'s Polly Toynbee and grandson of Arnold Toynbee, the eminent historian who first coined the phrase 'industrial revolution'. Not even someone as wise as Arnold Toynbee could have predicted the rare delights of Butlin's, with its Olympic-sized swimming pool, onsite Wimpy bar and free fun park rides. Back in the sixties, Butlin's was a cracking day out for two 14-year-olds.

Minehead, however, has a strong literary claim to fame. It was the birthplace of Sir Arthur C Clarke, science fiction writer and father of the geostationary communication satellite. A decade or so ago I interviewed his brother Fred, who died in 2013, and was allowed to browse the huge collection of memorabilia about his brother. Fred was anxious to see the setting-up of an Arthur C Clarke museum. The museum never came to fruition, but Clarke fans will be delighted to be able to rent the author's former West Bagborough home.

Nearby Watchet has two literary claims to fame, the lesser being as the probable model for the seaside town 'Matchet' where, in Evelyn Waugh's *Sword of Honour* trilogy, Guy Crouchback comes to see his father, who is living in slightly distressed circumstances in The Marine Hotel. It is here that Guy meets Jumbo Trotter and ends up joining the Halberdiers.

And the greater claim to fame? It is an ancient Mariner...

I parked in the car park next to the station and lingered, hoping for the rousing sight of a steam train. Before heading to Watchet harbour, I wandered into the station and somehow found myself reading about its policy of 'funeral trains and scattering ashes'.

Amongst them is the option to 'hire a train charter for your sole use, in which the ashes of the deceased will be placed into the firebox at some point along the line. The family can request where and as long as it is a suitable area, this will be discussed with them at the time of booking. The cost for this is £1,850.00.'

What? Almost £2,000 to scatter someone's ashes from the train? (Well, officially scatter. If you wanted to open a compartment window at an appropriate moment and scatter them yourself, one wonders how anybody could stop you.) Other preserved rail lines that lend themselves to ashes scattering include the highly appropriate Eden Valley Railway in Cumbria; the Poppy Line in North Norfolk also has a mournful tinge.

For the more literary rather than morbid-minded, suitable lines might include the West Highland Line in Scotland (which crosses the viaduct made famous in the film version of *Harry Potter and the Chamber of Secrets* – though, if it's just a photo opportunity you're looking for, London's King's Cross station hosts a sign for Platform 9¾ with no ticket purchase necessary), while Knockholt (formerly Halstead) station in Kent is the likely setting of *The Railway Children*; the line runs between Charing Cross and Sevenoaks (scenes from the classic 1970 film version, however, were filmed on the Keighley & Worth Valley Railway in Yorkshire). Sadly, there seems to be no 4.50 train running from Paddington at present; one can't help thinking that '16.49 from Paddington to Oxford' might not have appealed to Agatha Christie as a title quite so much!

Thomas the Tank Engine, meanwhile, seems to do good business touring the heritage railways of Britain for special weekends. Thomas officially ran on the fictional North Western Railway, but the Great Western Railway, running through Box Tunnel, is a fair approximation.

Actually, scattering ashes, it seems, is a business bedevilled by a myriad problems and potential hazards. I stumbled across the website Scattering Ashes – 'celebrating the life of a loved one'

– which deals with the problems of scattering ashes in the UK in astonishing detail, explaining where you can and can't scatter a loved one's remains (mountain tops and beauty spots? No; rivers and sea? Yes, with one or two caveats). Cremated human ashes can 'burn' grass, it seems. In one in five cases, according to Scattering Ashes, human ashes never get scattered; the person responsible keeps putting it off and leaves them on the mantelpiece for someone else to sort out, eventually…

Things in Watchet, therefore, were already a little weird before I got to the quay and discovered a statue of someone who had the look of Iggy Pop in classical shirtless mode of the Bowie and Berlin era. 'Iggy' was looking more than a bit fed up. What accounted for his peeved expression? Had he just been forced to take a visit to the nearby Museum of Bakelite – second only to the Bournemouth Sewage Works in a *Telegraph* rating of Britain's '10 crappest days out'?

The giant statue, a relatively recent incarnation, actually showed The Ancient Mariner with an albatross tied to his neck; this, in fairness, would try anybody's patience. This particular representation of the Ancient Mariner was actually rather lucky, because, while the wings of a fully grown albatross can reach up to 3.5m, this birdy necklace was a tiddler – its wingspan a half-metre at most – but even a mini-albatross around your neck would limit your ability to do most day-to-day activities (washing up, for example, would be a lifeless-winged nightmare).

A visitor to Watchet Harbour would legitimately wonder: who was the Ancient Mariner, what was he doing in Watchet and why was he wearing a small albatross? Welcome to the Land of Coleridge! *The Rime of the Ancient Mariner* is one of those literary works that is much more than a simple poem – it has somehow become part of British life. Even if you don't know it, you probably know of it. It has given the English language the saying 'having an albatross around one's neck';

there's the quotation of 'water, water everywhere, nor any drop to drink' (incorrectly reproduced usually as 'but not a drop to drink'), and the phrase 'a sadder and a wiser man' (again, usually incorrectly said as 'a sadder but wiser man'). The poem is also credited as the father of the phrase 'All creatures great and small' (according to the poem: 'He prayeth best, who loveth best;/ All things great and small;/ For the dear God who loveth us;/ He made and loveth all'.

The real centre of interest for Coleridge fans, of course, lies 11 miles east of here on the A39: Nether Stowey. Real enthusiasts, however, may well want to walk the Coleridge Way, a 51-mile energetic adjunct to the South West Coast Path that connects Nether Stowey with Lynmouth by way of Ash Farm and Porlock. It was at Ash Farm that Coleridge wrote another of his most celebrated poems: 'Kubla Khan'.

Xanadu, or Shangdu, was the summer capital of Kubla Khan's Jing dynasty, visited by Marco Polo in about 1275. His description of the elaborate palace is one of the most complete surviving records of how it looked; less than 100 years later, in 1369, the city was destroyed by the invading Ming army. In recent times the magic of Xanadu has been summoned up by Olivia Newton John in 'Xanadu' and the group Dave Dee, Dozy, Beaky, Mick and Tich in their song 'The Legend of Xanadu'. We'll never know what inspired Coleridge to summon up its delights, but we do know where it happened.

As I approached Ash Farm, a short drive from Porlock, there was a 'wow' moment when I got the first extraordinary view of the coast spread out before me in a vast horizon. It was here, during a break on a long walk, that Coleridge took laudanum to deal with a sudden bout of dysentery; he fell asleep and while he slumbered he had the dream that summoned up a Chinese vision: Kubla Khan: 'In Xanadu did Kubla Khan/ A stately pleasure-dome decree...'

In his drug-fuelled reverie, Coleridge composed in his head hundreds of lines of poetry. However, he was then disturbed by a 'person from Porlock', and subsequently could only remember 54 lines. Ash Farm is certainly no pleasure dome (as described by Coleridge, this sounds more like the giant dome which forms the centerpiece of Center Parcs holiday villages). However, the countryside surrounding Ash Farm was certainly a stirring sight.

It had been suggested that the poem's 'caverns measureless to man' were inspired by Coleridge's visit to nearby Cheddar Gorge. (A visit to Burrington Combe, near Cheddar Gorge, meanwhile, famously inspired Anglican cleric Augustus Toplady to write the hymn 'Rock of Ages' when he sheltered from a storm in a cleft in the rock. The place where he sheltered is now marked by a plaque – and honoured by the nearby Rock of Ages tearoom, where I sincerely hope they serve rock cakes of ages.)

It's not hard to see why Coleridge found inspiration here; you don't need to be on mind-bending substances to have a transcendent moment. This is an experience shared by the army of South West Coast Path (SWCP) hikers who march this way every day, enjoying the sumptuous views of Somerset's coast, the Bristol Channel and South Wales far beyond. The northern end of the 630-mile SWCP starts at Minehead, next to a seafront sculpture of a giant pair of hands holding a map. The trail continues down to Land's End before switching back along the south coast to Poole. This is England's longest national trail: though it's said that a fast walker could complete it in 30 days, more leisurely strollers should set aside seven weeks.

The special charm of the trail is that, unlike many other long distance paths, the SWCP lends itself to being tackled in smaller hits, stretches ideal for a circular weekend trek. Many places along the way have good public transport, making journey planning simpler. But what really draws people to this section in particular are the glorious ever-changing views, vistas so magnificent you can hardly believe you're taking them in. The route up to Ash Farm, for example, takes you through pine and oak trees with the Xanadu touch of tropical jade-green ferns. Along the way are mossy-oaked valleys which nurture sweet sparkling streams.

I opted out of practising what I might preach, however, and drove instead to Nether Stowey and Coleridge Cottage.

In searching for a modern comparison to describe Samuel Taylor Coleridge (1772–1834) and his one-time collaborator William Wordsworth (1770–1850), a guide at the cottage dubbed them the Lennon and McCartney of romantic poetry. Just as The Beatles shook the world with their musical genius, Coleridge and Wordsworth's brief partnership took poetry out of polite Georgian drawing rooms and – inspired by the popular uprising of the French Revolution – handed it to the people (this is more Lennon than McCartney – Wordsworth's McCartney phase was in the future).

The Rime of the Ancient Mariner was Coleridge's *Sergeant Pepper*: a work of staggering genius which set a new benchmark for poetry. And just like *Sergeant Pepper*, *The Rime of the Ancient Mariner* was written on a diet of mind-altering substances. In Coleridge's day, when people felt unwell – particularly if they had a headache, a cough or suffered from diarrhoea – there was a freely available drug which seemed to offer an instant cure. Laudanum was the 18th-century paracetamol: if it didn't actually cure anything, it certainly made you feel more cheerful. This was because its principal component was morphine – actually, morphine in a tincture of alcohol! This may have taken the edge off your toothache, but overuse eventually rendered you a helpless addict.

The worst effects of laudanum addiction were already affecting Coleridge. But in the last days of 1796, when the

Devon-born poet, his wife Sara and baby son moved into a cottage in Nether Stowey on the edge of the Quantocks, he was an emerging talent with a fast growing reputation. During the three years the family spent here, this humble cottage, visited by Wordsworth and poet Robert Southey, effectively saw the birth of the Romantic poetry movement.

Coleridge initially came to Somerset to collaborate with fellow poet Southey on a plan to establish a Pantiscocratic community on the banks of the Susquehanna river in the fledgling US state of Pennsylvania. A Pantisocracy was essentially a prototype hippy community – 'Imagine no possessions' was one tenet of their radical philosophy, which not only abhorred the plight of the common man in Britain, but decried the bloody anarchy produced by the French Revolution. Coleridge and Wordsworth had invested great expectations in the overthrow of the French monarchy, as he wrote in 'The French Revolution as it Appeared to Enthusiasts at Its Commencement': 'Bliss was it in that dawn to be alive, But to be young was very heaven!'

In their haste to get the US colony scheme underway, in 1795 Southey and Coleridge decided that they needed wives, so made arrangements to marry Bristol sisters Edith and Sara Fricker. Plans for the colony, however, quickly fell apart, as did Coleridge's marriage – he went on to pursue a one-sided love affair with Wordsworth's sister-in-law Sara Hutchinson, thinly-disguised in his writings as 'Asra'.

Coleridge also eventually fell out with Wordsworth – his typically manic drug-addict behaviour made him hard to like, it seems. But he survived to find a new career as a literary scholar: his essays and lectures on Shakespeare's plays – especially *Hamlet* – were groundbreaking.

I parked my car across the road from Coleridge Cottage in the car park belonging to the pub called – what else? – The Ancient Mariner. The cottage itself is a gem, recently restored at a cost of over £350,000 by the National Trust. The old part of the house – the original cottage as inhabited by Coleridge – has been returned to its original 18th-century state, looking for all the world as if the Coleridges have just popped out for a stroll with the Wordsworths – who took a more palatial residence three miles away.

This is the new 'immersive' National Trust style, not burdening people with big information-heavy boards, but allowing them to get the 'feel' of the house and its history. It worked particularly well in the cottage's lovely garden, where I sat on a bench and listened to Coleridge's garden-inspired poems, feeling at peace with the world. Coleridge Cottage is a wonderful house marvellously brought back to life and splendidly informative to both Coleridge and non-Coleridge lovers alike.

Despite the success that Coleridge enjoyed during his stay, however, he seemed never to have developed much affection for the cottage, which he tended to refer to as 'the hovel'. A scant two years after moving in, he was off on his wanderings again – and I moved on, too.

※

In America, you can drive for a day and the scenery scarcely changes. The extraordinary thing about Britain is that the landscape can alter in shuddering leaps. Take a detour from the coastal road out of Minehead and scarcely without any warning you've plunged into the blasted heaths of Exmoor. It's as if *Wuthering Heights* has come on holiday to Devon. Forget Coleridge's stately pleasure domes, this is where you will find hard-edged flinty places like the Valley of the Rocks, where the local sheep must look forward to winter as much as central Asia welcomed a visit from Genghis Khan.

Why do so many Americans visit Exmoor, I asked a man in a local tourist information office.

'*Lorna Doone*,' he replied: 'It's on the 19th-century English Literature syllabus for American high schools. If most Americans have one idea of England, it's *Lorna Doone*.'

In 1906, it seems, male students at Yale voted R D Blackmore's 1869 novel, *Lorna Doone,* their favourite book. In truth, the book is less popular now – its whiff of anti-Catholicism doesn't sit well in these more thoughtful times. On the plus side, it gave the world a new name, 'Lorna' (Judy Garland called her daughter Lorna – Lorna Luft – so she was presumably a fan).

Even for those not keen on the book, its settings are well worth a visit. The fictional Doone Glen was set in the vicinity of Badgworthy Water, an area now known as the Doone Valley (life does sometimes imitate art). There is some evidence to suggest that there was at some point a real gang of Scottish outlaws marauding in this part of the country, though Blackmore certainly used plenty of dramatic licence – the real life Exmoor is nowhere near as wild and gloomy as its literary counterpart. There is a waterslide, for example, in Lank Combe Water – but it's nowhere near as steep and terrifying as the one Jan and Lorna escape down in the book.

The highlight for any *Lorna Doone* fan is the Church of St Mary the Virgin in the village of Oare where – spoiler alert – the shooting takes place on Lorna's wedding day. Signs in the church explain the layout of the shooting as if it were a real event, which is sweet but slightly odd, given that this, after all, is a church.

Nearly as famous as Lorna, a furrier friend awaited further away in Georgeham. An exquisitely pretty village buried in the unexpectedly lush North Devon countryside, about 20 minutes drive from Ilfracombe, Georgeham was the place where Henry Williamson – the author of *Tarka the Otter* – lived. One of his Georgeham homes – Skirr Cottage – carries a prominent blue plaque recording Williamson's connection (two doors away, another property, Crowberry Cottage, has a similar plaque showing that it was here Williamson wrote *Tarka the Otter*).

At the garden gate of Skirr Cottage, a blackboard with chalk writing announces that the house is available for holiday lets. I walked up the path and knocked. A laconic young man came to the door. 'I wondered if you knew how much it cost to rent this cottage?' I asked.

'I think we paid £400,' he answered uncertainly.

Noticing children's toys in the garden, I asked, 'Are you all big Henry Williamson fans then?'

'Who?'

'*Tarka the Otter*?'

'Tarka the what?'

This exchange starkly underlines the extent to which Williamson's literary stock has fallen in recent years. It may seem incredible that somebody can claim ignorance of a writer when he is staying in that writer's house with its memorial plaque; and in a region that has branded itself Tarka country (in this part of North Devon there is a Tarka walking trail and even a Tarka railway line, for goodness sake – not to mention the Tarka Holiday Park, Tarka Springs mineral water, Tarka Antiques and Tarka Radio).

When *Tarka the Otter* was published in 1927, this story of the life of an otter in 'the country of the two rivers' – the Rivers Taw and Torridge – became an immediate success, and it has remained in print ever since. Its descriptions of this part of the country are a delight, particularly the river banks, bridges and bogs, which have changed little in the years since Williamson first roamed here. As I sat by the bank of the Torridge and watched hopefully for otters – none, alas, obliged – it was easy to imagine a young Williamson joining the local otter hunt and wading through the shallows as he researched his novel.

Tarka's decline cannot be because we have fallen out of love with animal stories, nor is it anything to do with Williamson's gifts as a writer. His writing influenced a generation. Future Poet Laureate Ted Hughes, for example, spoke movingly of the writer at Williamson's memorial service in December 1977, comparing the lyricism of his writing and his ability to evoke a sense of pathos for the natural world to the finest of English poetry – a sentiment echoed by *War Horse* writer and former Children's Laureate Michael Morpurgo more than thirty years later when he came to write the introduction for the 2010 edition of *Salar the Salmon*. Williamson's fall has almost everything to do with his dubious political affiliations in the 1930s. The writer had performed heroic service in the First World War, seeing active service in Flanders from the very beginning (he was present at the famous Christmas Truce in 1914). After three years' distinguished service he was eventually sent home on disability leave and kept on 'home duties' for the remainder of the war. It seems that the experience of meeting the enemy in no man's land during that famous truce had a profoundly disturbing effect: he came out of the war committed to the idea that Britain should never be involved in such a terrible conflict ever again.

When Williamson travelled to Germany in the 1930s, being present at a Nuremburg Rally of the Nazi party, he became convinced that Hitler's philosophy was the right one for Britain. While there were many who thought this before the Second World War, there were precious few prepared to espouse such a philosophy after 1945. Two who did were Williamson and his friend Oswald Mosley, the British Fascist leader, who had spent most of the war in internment. Williamson eventually parted company with Mosley, but not before irreparable damage was done to his reputation. However distasteful his politics, though, *Tarka the Otter* remains an outstanding work of literature. It remains to be seen whether Williamson's masterpiece can move out of the shadow of history.

✳

Treasured Island

Eighteen miles from Georgeham, near Clovelly, is the small, largely undistinguished town of Westward Ho! It has two claims to fame: it is the only town in Britain (and, some argue, the only town in the world) to have an exclamation mark in its name; and also the only place in the world to be named after a novel. *Westward Ho!* by the Victorian author Charles Kingsley is set in North Devon during the reign of Elizabeth I and tells the adventures of Amyas Leigh, who follows Francis Drake to sea. The story involves kidnap, treasure hunting in the Caribbean, evil Spaniards and the awful effects of freak bolts of lightning. Charles Kingsley is an author best known for *The Water Babies*, but whose work is not widely read these days. That his unfashionability is relatively recent can be discerned by the fact that Kingsley Amis was almost certainly named after the author, whose works must have been a favourite of Amis *mere et pere* (there is evidence to suggest that Amis' mother may have been a cousin of Charles Kingsley). Victorian property developers anxious to find buyers for their North Devon seaside development cheekily named the development after the 1855 Charles Kingsley novel in the hope of drumming up extra trade.

Westward Ho! was where the young Rudyard Kipling was a boarder at the United Services College, an experience which inspired the collection of stories, *Stalky & Co*, published in 1899. It was here that he began a career which led from North Devon to the Nobel Prize for literature.

2

Fowey to East Coker

In which our hero takes the road to Manderley, finds it murder trying to park his car in the Agatha Christie residence and discovers how Ian McEwan found out that he who is without sin casts the first stone.

CORNWALL'S sense of other-worldliness lies in the fact that, until the advent of the railway in the middle of the 19th century, travelling to the far southwest of England was a task not undertaken lightly. Pre-railway, it would not be unusual for the journey to take a couple of weeks or more via a combination of boat and carriage, or mule train (the only train likely to be slower or more obstreperous than First Great Western). When stagecoaches became a feature of life at the end of the 18th century, a fast journey was one that took less than two days. It's worth remembering when the M5 and A30 snarl up with Bank Holiday traffic that things could be worse: you're warm and dry, and you have a satnav.

Sometimes, however, satnavs can be more bother than they're worth. The Old Quay House hotel in Fowey has an online warning for customers using satnavs to guide them: the navigation system will probably want to take you a longer way, via the ferry – or to a different place altogether on the wrong side of the estuary. As instructed, I entered the full address and postcode but, as I approached Fowey, I kept having a nagging feeling that I was in the wrong place. Then, as I began to enter the village, which has an unforgiving one-way system, I realised I was in the right area but heading down a cul de sac.

Fowey is a place full of sudden drops, many of them down scarily steep flights of stairs, a prospect which I was keen not to explore by car. Unable to proceed any further, I pulled across to several empty parking spaces marked 'private'. I realised the hotel was no more than a couple of hundred yards away – I could just walk to the hotel and get their advice on parking.

I was aware that a man loading his estate car on the other side of the small square was looking at me meaningfully. When I shut the door and made for the path down to the main street, he hailed me: 'I say! You're not parking there.'

'No,' I said, 'I'm just going down to the hotel, I'll be back in two minutes.'

'You're not allowed to park there.'

'I hear what you're saying but I repeat, I'm not parking here – I'm coming straight back.'

'What if someone wants to park in their space and your car is in the way?'

'I'll move it.'

'You're not allowed to park there.'

'I understand the point you're making.'

Parking is a Big Thing in Fowey. Where, until relatively recently, there were lots of local residents who probably didn't have their own transport, there are now lots of people from London who have second homes and drive big estate cars and Chelsea tractors, who have turned the place into Parking Hell. If the unnamed heroine of *Rebecca* were to return to Manderley, she would not be obsessed with her husband's wife, she would be worrying about where she was going to park the BMW on her trip into town to buy a spelt loaf and some manchego cheese.

But already, on the journey to Fowey, I'd had a brief encounter with Daphne du Maurier. At a tourist information desk in an M5 service station, two adolescent boys were earnestly questioning the lady on duty. One of the boys was holding out a map: 'We're looking for Brown Willy.'

'Yes,' added his chum struggling to keep a straight face, 'Do you know where Brown Willy is?' Brown Willy is Cornwall's highest peak – no Everest this, it barely scrapes past 1,300ft.

The tourist information lady played a straight bat: 'It's on Bodmin Moor – here,' she dabbed a finger on their map. 'If you stop at Jamaica Inn, you'll probably be able to see it.'

The boys withdrew, disappointed. This, then, was the fabled Jamaica Inn: a stop for bus parties and sniggering school kids.

Yet, as you drive on to Bodmin Moor on the A30, the vista provides a sense of wind-blasted adventure. You're on a dual carriageway but you're staring out at a landscape of dramatic possibilities. Can there be anywhere on a moor more thrillingly named than Jamaica Inn?

Daphne du Maurier had clearly been moved by her visit. *Jamaica Inn* was her 1936 novel of wreckers, smugglers and an albino vicar, where much of the action took place at a remote and fairly desolate public house. The place is still pretty bleak, but now it's more of a bleak service station: a convenient stop for coaches between Bodmin and Launceston.

The low-slung granite building might have looked spooky in the thirties when Daphne du Maurier arrived by horse one rainswept night after losing her way on the moor; now it is mainly a place to pause for a full English – or, of course, a trip to the opportunistically located Smuggler's Museum.

For a time, Jamaica Inn was run more as a literary attraction. The owners spent heavily on acquiring at auction Daphne du Maurier's furniture and other possessions for a du Maurier room. Inside a glass case sits the author's writing table, some family photographs and an ashtray with cigarette ends.

Dame Daphne would not have been amused. In *Vanishing Cornwall* she regretted the transformation of Jamaica Inn, which she admitted that, as a motorist, she passed by 'with some embarrassment' at the shadow her novel had cast. Flattering for an author, perhaps, but there must also have been a sense of sadness that the atmospheric building that first inspired her writing would never quite be the same again.[3]

Thirty years ago, the other string to Jamaica Inn's tourist bow was Mr Potter's Museum of Curiosities, which had then recently been acquired from Arundel. This was the work of an eccentric Victorian taxidermist, Walter Potter, who composed various tableaux of stuffed animals. 'The Death and Burial of Cock Robin', for example, included 98 species of stuffed British birds. If this sounds tastelessly bizarre, imagine 'The Guinea Pigs' Cricket Match' or 'The Kittens' Wedding' – the latter involving 20 stuffed kittens all wearing morning suits or brocade collars with a feline vicar in white surplice; this was actually put on show in London's Victoria and Albert Museum as part of their 2001 Victorian Vision exhibition.

I could have little guessed 23 years ago when I first visited Jamaica Inn that the tourist gold here was not the du Maurier artefacts, but the stuffed animals. In 2003, the Potter Curiosities were put up for auction at Bonham's. Despite receiving a pre-auction bid for £1 million from Damien Hirst, for some reason it was decided to let the auction continue – mistakenly, as it turned out, as the sale raised not much more than £500,000. 'The Kittens' Wedding', for example, sold for £21,150 while 'The Death and Burial of Cock Robin' was knocked down for £23,500.

Fortunately, no stuffed guinea pigs were in Fowey, the real heart of du Maurier country which is one of England's sweetest seaside towns. In 1926, when du Maurier was 19, she went to Looe with her mother and two sisters in search of a house to purchase for family holidays. Du Maurier's father was the famous actor and matinee idol Gerald du Maurier, so money was no object.

Looe was inspected and rejected, and the family moved down the coast to Fowey. Before taking the ferry from Bodinnick over the estuary to Fowey, they stopped for lunch at the Ferry Inn. They noticed a 'For Sale' sign at a house immediately next to the ferry – then called Swiss Cottage but later renamed Ferryside. The house was immediately bought by the du Mauriers and is still owned by the family.

It was here that du Maurier began her writing career in earnest. At Ferryside she largely wrote her first novel *The Loving Spirit*, inspired by the sight of an abandoned schooner in Pont Creek, a short walk from the house. And it was at Ferryside that she first encountered her future husband, Major Frederick 'Boy' Browning, who was sailing with a friend up Fowey harbour. They married on 19 July 1932, shortly after their first meeting. Du Maurier travelled part of the way to Lanteglos church, high above Bodinnick, by boat. They married at 8.15 in the morning, the ceremony arranged early to allow them to catch the tide.

Soon after her arrival at Ferryside, du Maurier became intrigued by an old house called Menabilly, owned by the Rashleighs, an old West Country family. At the end of the twenties, it was the property of Dr John Rashleigh III, who rarely lived there: Menabilly and the surrounding estate had fallen into disrepair. Fascinated by its history, du Maurier would return again and again to explore the grounds and to peer in through the windows of the neglected house. She was fascinated by its solitude, surrounded by trees and overgrown rhododendron bushes, dreaming that perhaps if she won a sweepstake she might live there. It was Menabilly that provided the inspiration for the setting of *Rebecca*.

Du Maurier finally achieved her heart's desire and took possession of Menabilly, albeit on a short lease, at the end of the Second World War. The house is invisible from the road, and you are advised not to stray nearer in search of a closer look.

I stuck to the road. I did not see Menabilly, but I saw Kilmarth, the dower house on the Menabilly estate that du Maurier had to move to when the Rashleighs eventually reclaimed Menabilly. Occasionally, organised tours are admitted on to this hallowed ground. While the house appears to be the main attraction, visitors report that it is the mile-long track down to the sea through tumbled woods, trailing ivy and tangled undergrowth that best evokes so vividly the first page of *Rebecca,* where du Maurier describes her heroine's dream of a return to a Manderley long-abandoned, the grounds shrouded in overgrown woodland, and the drive being gradually encroached upon by nature's 'long, tenacious fingers'.[4]

It's also worth searching out 'Rebecca's boathouse' in Polridmouth Cove: not a boathouse, but a substantial beach-side property; a favourite place for du Maurier and her children, who whiled away many happy hours here, taking a dip in the sea every day, mornings and afternoons during the summer.

One of the sweetest parts of the Cornish coast lies further west than Fowey. I drove an hour to the Lizard Peninsula seeking out the honey-coloured Trelowarren House, first visited by du Maurier aged 23, in 1930. Trelowarren would become one of her favourite places, and its lady, Clara Vyvyan, one of her close friends.

It was on a visit here to see Lady Clara Vyvyan that she first discovered Frenchman's Creek on the Helford River. The secluded creek stirred du Maurier so much it was where she decided to spend her honeymoon with her new husband, and it later supplied the location and the title for her book about a Breton pirate and his love affair with a Cornish woman. Trelowarren House itself appears as Navron House. *Frenchman's Creek* was du Maurier's only romance novel – evidence, perhaps, of her happy memories of times spent here.

※

Travelling east, it was impossible to pass up a chance to make a detour to Dartmoor and the opportunity to meet *The Hound of the Baskervilles*. I headed to the charming Dartmoor town of Buckfastleigh, the starting point for most Baskerville tours.

My appointment with the fictional hound of hell was delayed by a brief stop at Princetown to visit the frightful Dartmoor Prison museum, housed in the old prison dairy; the museum must come close to the prison itself in terms of total bleakness. The man on the ticket desk revealed that the prison, originally constructed to house French prisoners from the Napoleonic war, now hosts less than 600 inmates – Dartmoor actually has the capacity to accommodate ten times that number.

It seems likely that, within a decade, the prison will close completely, at which point it can trade on its grim reputation as the British Alcatraz with hopes that it might become a major tourist attraction. Oxford jail, for example, has become a Malmaison hotel – it can only be a matter of time before Dartmoor hoists the 'vacancies' sign for paying guests. It can certainly cash in on its *The Hound of the Baskervilles* link – an escaped Dartmoor prisoner plays a part in Conan Doyle's narrative. In writing *The Hound of the Baskervilles,* its author was able to call on the research conducted by a friend, a 30-year-old journalist named Bertram Fletcher Robinson. He told Conan Doyle about the 'hell-hounds' legends of Dartmoor, in particular the one involving Richard Cabell, who had been a tireless huntsman and was described as a 'monstrously evil man'.

It had been rumoured that he had murdered his wife – other people suggested that he had sold his soul to the Devil. After Cabell's death in July 1677, there were reports that the night after his burial saw the arrival of a ghostly pack of hounds who came howling across the moor to bay at his grave. On the anniversary of Cabell's death, there were sightings of him leading this grim pack of hounds across the moors.

In an effort to end these ghostly ramblings, the villagers built a large building around the tomb, and to be doubly sure he remained in his tomb a huge slab was placed upon it. Squire Cabell's securely constructed tomb in Buckfastleigh churchyard has become one of the area's main tourist attractions (its creepiness is heightened by the fact that in 1992 the church burnt down after someone broke in and started a fire under the altar; it remains a blackened shell).

It's not certain which of Dartmoor's houses provided the original inspiration for Baskerville Hall, but sinister, misty Grimpen Mire was almost certainly inspired by Fox Tor Mires, south of Princetown. On the grim, lonely moor, scattered with ruins from tin mines and abandoned stone huts, it was easy to imagine that final desperate flight that forms the denouement of *The Hound of the Baskervilles*, pursued by that savage hound – and the awful end amid the oozing mire. As I headed off the moors and a mist begins to swirl in, it was a relief to point the car towards the English Riviera and leave behind hell hounds and escaped prisoners. The road to the coast lifts the spirits once more.

※

Turn up in your car at the entrance to Agatha Christie's holiday home, Greenway, and you may well find yourself subject to an Hercule Poirot-style interrogation. 'Morning, sir, can you give me your name?'

'My name?'

'Yes, sir.'

'You need my name because…?'

'To find you on our parking list, sir. You have pre-booked?'

'I didn't know I had to.'

'It says quite clearly on our website, sir.'

'I didn't know. Sorry. Does that mean I can't get in?'

'It depends if we have space. Fortunately we're not so busy, but normally, as I say, sir, you would need to book an advance.'

'But not today.'

'Fortunately.'

In case I hadn't understood all of this, the gate man then handed me a note before waving me through with the sort of formal flourish accorded to someone on their way in from the cold to West Berlin through Checkpoint Charlie in about 1965. The note picked up where the gate man had left off: 'Thinking of visiting us again? Luckily we had a cancellation in the car park today, allowing us to let you in without booking. However, this is unusual, and we normally expect all visitors to have booked their car in…'

I was exhausted, and I'd barely arrived. I hadn't been subject to such close questioning since I was in the second form and the headmaster's wife thought she had caught me illegitimately 'up town' and not wearing a cap during school hours. (I told her I had been to the opticians and my cap had been stolen. I had to hand her my 'up town pass', which she studied with a wry face as if I had just forged it with a John Bull Printing Outfit.)

'Just because you're married to the headmaster,' I said (or, at least, imagined myself saying), 'it doesn't make you a Gestapo Kriminalkommissar'; actually, I can't imagine that humiliated captured escapees from Colditz were given a more gruelling time.

Have you rung a restaurant for a table and they hum and haw, telling you that actually, they're full and couldn't really squeeze in a two-year-old child, they are so short of space? And then, when you turn up for dinner, you're the only people in the entire restaurant? All evening? I have to say that it was a similar thing at Greenway; after this huge car park space shortage build up, I wasn't that surprised to discover it was actually more than half empty. I should have handed the gate man a note on my way out telling him that 'Luckily this time I decided to continue with my visit, but if you keep on banging on about parking spaces next time I might not bother…'

It may be because there are so many volunteers giving up their time for the National Trust that they are sometimes wont to behave a little officiously. I would have thought that the volunteers offered their services because they had a great love of Agatha Christie. When I suggested this to one of the guides, he chuckled. 'No, she's not my cup of tea – I should guess about half of us have read the books'.

You have an idea of how Agatha Christie must have lived from the world she describes in her books. Something like the world of Wooster, only a little less aristocratic and with a much higher body count. When bad things happen to Bertie Wooster, the worst he can expect is an uncomfortable encounter with one of his aunts or having to fend off unwanted marital talk from Madeleine Bassett or Honoria Glossop. A difficult moment in an Agatha Christie thriller would be finding yourself on the wrong end of a dose of cyanide.

Agatha Christie died aged 85 in 1976 of, we must assume, entirely natural causes. The creator of Hercule Poirot and Miss Marple spent her summers in Devon in palatial splendour at Greenway, situated above the estuary of the River Dart. I can guarantee that, even if you are no big fan of Agatha Christie's whodunnits, you will find her house – its location, at least – enchanting.

When Agatha Christie's daughter Rosalind Hicks first discussed the idea of opening Greenway to the public, she was worried that the house might become a 'Christie theme park'. Mrs Hicks and her son Matthew Prichard, who has since become the guardian of the Christie flame, need not have had any anxieties about whether the opening of Greenway to the public would be the precursor to any sort of tasteless cashing in. Actually, they have firmly remained on the side of sense, merely presenting the house as a reflection of its heyday rather than introducing Miss Marple and Hercule Poirot into proceedings.

This, I think, is a shame. What Greenway is crying out for is a little touch of murder.

Christie herself had been only too happy to oblige. Greenway is easily recognisable as the inspiration for two of her novels, *Five Little Pigs* and *Dead Man's Folly*, with the battery overlooking the River Dart and the estate boathouse doing their respective duties as murder locations. Elsewhere on the estate, the location of the village of Dittisham over the other side of the River Dart could well be the source of a crucial plot point in *Towards Zero*, while the bell that you can ring to summon the ferry to Dartmouth makes its own appearance in *Ordeal by Innocence*. It's now possible for visitors to stay in one of the three holiday cottages on the Greenway estate, but care should be taken: you may find yourself waking up with murder in mind...

For many years the London listings magazine *Time Out* had a one line review for Agatha Christie's play *The Mousetrap*: 'the policeman did it'. As Keats might have said (*The Mousetrap* has had a long run in the West End, but even so, I'm pretty sure it predates Keats): '...that is all/ Ye know on earth, and all ye need to know.'

If I were the National Trust, I would do more to highlight the connections between their various properties. T E Lawrence at Clouds Hill, for example, was on good terms with Mr and Mrs Thomas Hardy (and also, by the by, good friends with

Henry Williamson). Less well known is the fact that T E Lawrence had a connection with Agatha Christie. Lawrence worked with C Leonard Woolley on the excavation of the Hittite city of Carchemish from 1912–14. Agatha Christie's novel, *Murder in Mesopotamia*, was inspired by Woolley's discovery of the royal tombs from 1922–34, and she later married Woolley's young assistant, Max Mallowan. Lawrence of Arabia versus Hercule Poirot: that's a film I'd pay to see.

There are plenty of other real-life settings for Christie's novels: the *Orient Express*, for example, which she travelled on several times when heading to the Middle East. The Pera Palace Hotel in Istanbul has an Agatha Christie room where she is said to have written *Murder on the Orient Express*. One of the best-known locations used in her novels is Burgh Island, just off the coast of Devon – reached by 'sea tractor' – which inspired the novel now known as *And Then There Were None* as well as the Hercule Poirot mystery *Evil Under The Sun*. Due to time constraints, I couldn't make it down to spend a night in the Burgh Island Hotel, where Christie herself stayed (one of the rooms is even named after her) but, for the particularly criminally minded, it's highly recommended.

Agatha Christie had a real-life mystery of her own when, in the wake of learning that her husband had been having an affair, she vanished for 11 days before she was discovered staying in a hotel in Harrogate, booked in under the surname of her husband's mistress. You couldn't make it up – but, of course, Agatha Christie did so for a living.

Christie also played a part in the birth of both Penguin Books and the paperback. Having visited his prize author for the weekend in 1935, Allen Lane, a director of publisher The Bodley Head, was waiting for his London train at Exeter station and anxious to find something to read on the train. All that was available were popular magazines and reprints of Victorian novels. Mr Lane was so appalled by the meagre selection of reading material available that he devised a plan to offer readers good quality contemporary fiction at an attractive price. Under his scheme, these books would be sold not just in traditional bookshops, but also in railway stations, tobacconists and chain stores. To help promote these new paperback books he set about finding a 'dignified but flippant' mascot. His secretary came up with the idea of a penguin – Mr Lane immediately dispatched an artist to London Zoo to make some sketches. The rest is publishing history.

※

Until Dr Beeching wielded his axe, you could take the train from Exeter to Lyme Regis with a change at Axminster. This is a journey through some of the sweetest countryside in England. The Axe valley is home, for example, to chef Hugh Fearnley-Whittingstall's River Cottage. I left the train at Axminster and boarded a bus for the 25-minute ride to the doors of the Lyme Regis Co-op.

We tend to disparage our UK seaside places – the general complaint is that they are too run down and too tacky. We think of charming seaside places in Spain, France, Italy and Greece and wonder why we fare so badly by comparison. Actually, we have a wealth of wonderful coastal places. One of them is Lyme Regis, popular not just with daytrippers, but beloved by writers.

John Fowles lived in Lyme Regis from 1965 until his death in 2005. A prophet is not without honour save in his own country – and it would be fair to say that Fowles, as with his books, got mixed reviews from locals for his neighbourliness. His obituaries described Fowles as 'reclusive' which suggest that he wasn't tremendously keen to mix with his neighbours.

Indeed, when his diaries were published, Lyme Regis residents were somewhat shocked and surprised to discover, in an entry made in 1970, that he had described them, amongst other things as 'the dullest and most abominably retarded community one can imagine'.[5]

Someone who had lived in the area at the same time as Fowles was surprised when they returned to the Dorset town after an absence and discovered that his rudeness had been conveniently overlooked. The town had honoured the author with a footpath alongside Cobb Road near his former home. The complainant wrote: 'I was shocked and irritated to see the new John Fowles Walk. Lyme is a little heaven and Fowles was an arrogant old windbag. Perhaps the walk should be re-christened the Pompous Penpusher's Parade?'

Fowles wasn't quite as reclusive or as misanthropic as either he or the obituarists pretended. While, clearly, he was given to the occasional outbreak of curmudgeoness, he took his job as curator of the Lyme Regis Museum – a post he held for ten years – very seriously indeed. While some may legitimately have taken issue with his occasional lack of interpersonal skills, no one could dispute that his writings presented Lyme Regis to a worldwide audience. Naming a footpath after him was really the least that the town could do.

The controversial footpath was opened in January 2007 by Mr Fowles' widow Sarah, who subsequently found herself in a further row involving her late husband. Fowles' home had been acquired by the Landmark Trust, an organisation which rescues buildings of historical or architectural importance and preserves them by converting them to self-catering holiday accommodation. Sarah complained that Belmont House, an 18th-century Grade II* listed building, had largely been 'destroyed' by the Trust in the rescue process. The Landmark Trust argued that drastic action was necessary as the property had been at 'grave risk'.

All of which goes to show that famous writers and small communities can be a volatile mixture. Any tourist board is keen to cash in on a prominent local literary connection, but tourist capital is often made at the expense of airbrushing out any blemishes. This is clearly a mistake. Even in the best regulated relationships, there are troubles. Cutting them out is not only dishonest, but it also make the writer's story much less interesting. Only a certain type of fairy stories (as filmed by Disney) have phoney happy endings.

Of John Fowles' books, I realise I might be in a minority when I vote for *The Magus* as his greatest achievement. His best-received book, both in terms of reviews and sales, is *The French Lieutenant's Woman,* which has Lyme Regis as its setting.

It was Jane Austen who first put Lyme Regis on the literary map in her last and probably best novel, *Persuasion*; a moment of high drama occurs when Louisa Musgrove leaps off the steps leading from the Cobb and fails to be caught, as she expected, by Captain Wentworth; he has to take up her 'lifeless' body from the pavement.

The Cobb is Lyme Regis' distinctive manmade harbour, an elbow of wall which pokes out to sea far enough to provide ships with a safe port in a storm: actually, even in moderate weather, walkers heading out on the Cobb run the risk of getting the occasional drenching from a rogue wave. It's not hard to see how the Cobb inspired both Austen and Fowles; in *The French Lieutenant's Woman*, as with *Persuasion*, the Cobb has a starring role.

Fowles' book was inspired by a dream he had of a woman standing on the Cobb and staring mysteriously out to sea. According to the local tourist information office, most tourists are drawn to the Cobb to stand where Meryl Streep did her mysterious sea-gazing in the film version, in which she starred with Jeremy Irons. I walked the Undercliff in the footsteps of the French Lieutenant's Woman, and tried to see what remained of Underhill Farm, where Fowles was living at the time he wrote the novel.

Sadly, the coastal area west of the town has been devastated by a slow-moving landslide which has totally destroyed the old farmhouse, and the South West Coast Path, which passes through the Undercliff within 100 metres of Underhill Farm, was partially closed between Lyme Regis and Axmouth. Visitors are not encouraged to walk on what is private land – not an injunction one feels that the iconoclastic Fowles himself would have felt obliged to heed.

※

From Lyme Regis it was a short drive to the wonderful countryside above Bridport – but it was written about in a novel as far removed from the safe Georgian world of Jane Austen as it is possible to travel. *Rogue Male*, published in 1939, was written by Bristol-born, Oxford-educated Geoffrey Household, and tells the gripping story of an unnamed British 'sportsman', who tests his ability as a hunter by embarking on a mission to a country which sounds rather like Germany.

The 'Rogue Male' was on a bizarre self-imposed mission to see if he might be able to get a shot at a European dictator who sounds a lot like Adolf Hitler. He isn't sure whether, even if he gets the opportunity, he will 'take the shot'. He never gets the chance, however, as he is abruptly captured by the dictator's guards, then brutally tortured – but somehow survives their attempt to kill him (as literary heroes are wont to do). He evades capture and manages to return to England, where foreign agents literally run him to ground in a hide he has created deep in the countryside. The unflinching accounts of brutality and the very believable narrative – delivered in a fine stiff upper-lipped clip – set a new style for thrillers that clearly influenced the likes of Ian Fleming's 007 and Frederick Forsyth's *Day of the Jackal*. According to Household himself, he was 'a sort of bastard by Stevenson out of Conrad'.

In *Rogue Male,* Household notes with interest 'how much cover there is on the chalk downs'. He adds that the southwest Dorset countryside with its 'prehistoric pits and trenches, tree-grown tumps, gorse and the upper edge of coverts, lonely barns and thickets of thorn' allows a man to move around unseen. The place where Thomas Hardy's characters eked a hard living from the land becomes in Household's hands a terrifying killing field. The 'Rogue Male' hides from his pursuers in his own fox's earth − 'a safe pit of blackness'[6] − where he is eventually trapped by the foreign pursuer. Passionate fans of the book have triangulated what they believe to be the exact location of this 'earth', based on clues supplied in the narrative, to a Holloway in the area around North Chideock a few miles west of Bridport.

I made a short drive from Bridport, and another huge literary jump, to reach Chesil Beach. This is a pebble beach which stretches northwest for 18 miles from Portland to West Bay. The beach is separated from the mainland for much of its length by an area of saline water called the Fleet Lagoon. The beach has two literary connections. Firstly it provides the setting for *Moonfleet*, J Meade Falkner's popular 1898 children's tale of smuggling. The more recent connection is Ian McEwan's 2007 Booker Prize-shortlisted *On Chesil Beach*. Set in July 1962, the year, according to Philip Larkin, before 'sex began', it tells the sad story of newlyweds Edward Mayhew and Florence Ponting, whose sexual ingenuousness causes their marriage to fall at the first hurdle on the first night of their honeymoon in a small hotel on the Dorset seashore, at Chesil Beach. At the end of the story McEwan writes: 'Edward and Florence's hotel − just over a mile south of Abbotsbury, Dorset, occupying an elevated

position in a field behind the beach car park – does not exist'.[7]
There's a delightful irony in such specific pedantry towards a
non-existent place.

The hotel described in the book actually sounds rather like
Moonfleet Manor, which is a handsome Georgian building
about seven miles from Abbotsbury and which overlooks Chesil
Beach (and provides the setting for *Moonfleet*).

Take only photos, leave only footprints, is a message that tourists
have become familiar with, especially when they're visiting
ecological areas of the world such as the Antarctic that are
particularly at risk from growing numbers of holiday makers. It
is not a warning that best-selling novelists might feel impelled
to heed.

Indeed, in an interview about his book for BBC Radio
Four's *Start The Week*, Ian McEwan admitted taking two handfuls
of pebbles from the protected beach as some sort of lapidary
literary trophy. The resulting howls of protest from aggrieved
environmental campaigners rapidly made McEwan painfully
aware that he had made a grave error of judgement. The area is
designated a site of special scientific interest and anyone caught
removing pebbles could be fined.

'There are plenty more pebbles on the beach,' he might have
stated in his defence, but McEwan wisely opted for a more
apologetic stance: 'I was not aware of having committed a crime,'
he protested in a statement to the press, before undertaking to
return the pebbles as soon as possible. 'Chesil Beach is a uniquely
beautiful place and I'm delighted to return the handful of small
pieces of shingle to it,' he said. It was a moment of sober reflection
for writers; novelists are not above the law, even best-selling
novelists. I took a handful myself and pondered them; some grey,
some blueish, some brown, some tan, a few that curious 'liver'
colour, a few red, or pinkish, or white – pebbles, in fact. Hard to
see what all the fuss was about: I returned them to their fellows.

Woody Allen once said that if he had to live his life again he'd do everything the same, except that he wouldn't bother going to see *The Magus*.

If I had to live my life again, I'd happily welcome the chance to miss out the two awful hours spent watching a touring production of *Cats* 20-odd years ago at the Bristol Hippodrome. Awful not just because of the relentless boredom and the grinding tunelessness of it all, but mostly for the posthumous damage inflicted on the reputation of a great 20th-century poet.

I fear that there's now a whole generation of people who know nothing of T S Eliot's Nobel Prize for Literature nor *The Waste Land* (which secured his nomination). Based solely on their knowledge of *Cats,* they presume Eliot must be just one of the many heroic lyricists that served their turn at the musical coalface at the behest of Andrew Lloyd Webber.

T S Eliot's *Old Possum's Book of Practical Cats* – not Eliot's greatest literary achievement, it has to be said – provided the basis for *Cats* the musical. Of course, all of this happened long after the poet's death; approval for the project first had to be sought by Andrew Lloyd Webber from Eliot's widow Valerie.

Having lighted upon the hapless Eliot, why did Lloyd Webber then choose to hack the Great Poet's poems about? The show's hit song 'Memory', for example, has lyrics provided by the show's original director Trevor Nunn, who 'reworked' two Eliot poems 'Preludes' and 'Rhapsody on a Windy Night'. How or why was it considered necessary for Trevor Nunn, the director (and no Ira Gershwin) to rewrite the work of a Nobel Prize winner? I may be misremembering, but it seemed to me that the cast of *Cats* were either singing or on the point of singing 'Memory' for the duration of the entire bloody show.

T S Eliot's poem 'East Coker', the second of Eliot's *Four Quartets*, offers a largely gloomy overview of the situation of

Britain at war. Written in 1940, the poem was inspired by a visit made to the village a few years earlier to see the place where his ancestors had lived before emigrating to New England in the 17th century (one of Eliot's Massachusetts forebears served on the jury in a Salem witch trial). He was so moved by the experience that he asked for his ashes to be buried in the village church of St Michael.

To reach East Coker from Chesil Beach by car involved a complex circumnavigation of Yeovil's ring roads, a task which taxed my satnav's powers to the max. Given that East Coker is a fairly small place, locating St Michael's church was surprisingly hard, requiring the input of no fewer than three different pedestrians who each gave long and complex instructions from which I mentally tuned out after a few seconds. Men and directions, eh?

The church, however, was worth the journey. It's set on only a modest rise, but it offers a glorious sweeping view of the surrounding countryside. Inside the church, on the wall to the right as I entered, was a plaque which asked visitors to 'pray for the soul of Thomas Stearns Eliot, poet'. I thought about a line from the *Four Quartets* which talks about returning to the place where you started, after life's adventures, and feeling that you know the place for the first time. It's hard not to pause here at Eliot's memorial and contemplate life's journey.

In the years since his death in 1965, it's sometimes been easy to forget just what a huge figure T S Eliot was in the world of poetry during his lifetime. The recipient of the Nobel Prize for Literature and an array of other awards, including the British Order of Merit, he was not just the greatest British poet of the 20th century (and arguably the greatest poet in the world), he was the author of successful plays such as *Murder in the Cathedral* and *The Cocktail Party,* performed both in London and on Broadway. His memorial service, held in Westminster Abbey on 4 February 1965, attracted a huge congregation. Many of his lines have become part of our language: 'Not with a bang but a whimper', the final line of his poem 'The Hollow Men', is among the best-known lines of modern poetry, along with 'April is the cruellest month' – the opening of *The Waste Land*.

Perhaps as a reaction to his greatness, his reputation has come under attack in recent years with accusations of antisemitism – a charge he vehemently denied in his lifetime. Whatever his faults, it seems incontestable that as long as people speak the English language his poetry will be valued, read and enjoyed. And not just by *Cats* lovers.

3

Jane Austen to
Jane Austen

In which our intrepid traveller meets the most photographed man in Britain, pulls out a plum, finds a hill made of clouds and discovers a museum with a ring to it.

WHO holds the accolade of 'England's most photographed man'? Prince Charles? Prince William? Benedict Cumberbatch? The title, apparently, belongs to Martin Salter, who earns his daily bread by standing outside the Jane Austen Centre in Bath and playing the part of Mr Bennet of *Pride and Prejudice*, the paterfamilias of the Bennet girls and long-suffering husband of the redoubtable Mrs Bennet. The *Pride and Prejudice* ladies and gents never actually visit Bath, but this is an apparently insignificant detail.

Do a Google image search of 'Martin Salter' and 'Jane Austen' and a cavalcade of snaps appears: here is Mr Salter with the Duchess of Cornwall, next walking near the Crescent with Rory Bremner and now next to the late P D James. Few celebrities can have come within the orbit of Mr Salter and failed to have a snap taken with him. He is the Jane Austen Centre's jolly public face – though, in truth, more in the way of Dickens' Mr Pickwick than Austen's Mr Bennet; Elizabeth Bennet's dad always struck me as rather sour. In a revealing online memoir Mr Salter confesses his undying thanks for having found himself a starring role in life when a long history of ill-health threatened to keep him on the sidelines for ever. Now apparently permanently standing outside the centre, braving wind, rain and snow, he seems both in the pink and in the prime of life. He maintains a busy dialogue with anyone who passes: waving to passengers in coaches and tipping his hat to traffic wardens.

How many people come especially to Bath for some sort of Jane Austen 'experience'? Nobody is really sure, but former teacher David Baldock sagely judged that many coming to Bath wanting an Austen shrine to worship were disappointed to find barely a mention of their heroine. To make up for this glaring deficiency, in 1999 Mr Baldock set up the Jane Austen Centre not far from the house on Gay Street where Ms Austen was once a resident (she lived in several places in the city at one time or another – Barbara Streisand was said to have been keen to acquire the place where Jane had once lived on Camden Crescent, though it was not Jane herself, but the characters in *Persuasion* who actually lived there. It's a confusing business, literature).

Build it, it seems, and they will come. Americans are the most numerous overseas visitors to the Jane Austen Centre, but there are also substantial numbers from Japan, Australia, New Zealand, China and even the Philippines. The Centre attempts to steer a line between sober study and fun – there's lots of fascinating information on Austen's life and works – but you can also dip into a Georgian dressing up box, have a look at a forensically produced waxwork of Austen, and dine at the centre's own tearooms. All the staff dress up in period costume.

And all the time, Mr Salter is out there on the doorstep channelling the spirit of Mr Bennet and giving it his all. I, of course, took his photo.

Pride and Prejudice may be the most famous of Austen's novels, but it's *Northanger Abbey* that truly has its roots in the city; it is to Bath that the heroine, Catherine Morland, is invited by her wealthier neighbours for the winter season, and in Bath that she forms the acquaintances and entanglements that propel the rest of the novel. Catherine's Bath is a place of action, excitement and the merest hint of scandal. She and the Allens lodge on 'Pultney Street', where the famous Great Pulteney Street Bridge can be found, socialise at the Pump Room, walk on the Royal Crescent and take in the view of Bath from Beechen Cliff – exactly the same sights that today's tourists can be found heading for. Some things, it seems, never change.

※

I took the road south out of Bath up Wellsway and soon found myself entering the strange real-life world of nursery rhymes. There is a surprising amount of sense in what are commonly thought to be nonsense rhymes. 'Sing a Song of Sixpence', for example, is reckoned to be about Henry VIII's dissolution of the monasteries (Catharine of Aragon is the 'queen' in her parlour while the 'maid' in the garden is taken as a reference to Anne Boleyn); it's popularly believed that 'Ring a Ring o' Roses' is about the Black Death.

Other rhymes with a real-life location include 'Pop Goes the Weasel' and a reference to The Eagle pub in London's City Road: it was near the original offices of *The Independent* newspaper when I worked there. 'Ride A Cock Horse to Banbury Cross' is the story of Lady Godiva riding without a stitch or a report on Queen Elizabeth I's visit to Banbury –

whichever, someone was wearing bells on their shoes. 'London Bridge is Falling Down' is not more bad news about over-running engineering works, but probably an account of the sacking of the real London Bridge by Olaf II of Norway in 1014. Tourists, eh!

A final hat tip to the city of Gloucester is name-checked in 'Dr Foster' – one interpretation claims that the rhyme tells the story of Edward I, King of England, who visited Gloucester during a storm, rode his horse through a stream which was deeper than he thought and had to be pulled out. There's an entire episode of *Casualty* right there...

You probably imagined that the Little Jack Horner of the nursery rhyme, who 'put in his thumb and pulled out a plum', was entirely fictitious. The lovely village of Mells has several literary claims to fame: war poet Siegfried Sassoon, for example, is buried in Mells churchyard, but its greatest claim comes, so legend tells it, via a rhyme.

Thomas Horner (presumably the nursery rhymer changed the name for legal reasons) discovered nursery fame due to the popularly attributed fact that at the time he worked as the steward for the last abbot of Glastonbury. The abbot had concealed the deeds in a pie created for King Henry VIII; en route to the capital, Mr Horner helped himself to the property. The manor became the home of the Asquith family – with links to Asquith the prime minister and a more recent connection to Helena Bonham-Carter. After the First World War, Mells Manor attracted the likes of Evelyn Waugh, who was a regular visitor, and wrote parts of three of his books whilst staying with friends in the village.

Nearby Kilmersdon, by curious chance, claims to be the place where Jack and Jill went up the hill to fetch a pail of water. Apparently, in 1697 (never say a nursery rhyme can't be precise about the details), an unmarried couple were said to have done their courting on the hill. Jill ended up pregnant but, before the baby was born, Jack was killed by a rock that fell off the hill. Jill is then said to have died in childbirth! *EastEnders* eat your heart out. There is a nursery rhyme walk that you can follow up the hill. Really.

I confess, I did not take it. Every man has his limits.

※

It's a 60-mile drive from Kilmersdon down to the heart of Hardy Country around Dorchester. En route, I paused in Shaftesbury to enjoy the view down Gold Hill – described as one of the most romantic sights in England, but best known for providing the setting for one of Hovis' most famous bread commercials, which also famously features a brass band version of Dvorak's *New World* symphony. Near Dorchester I encountered one of the strangest places in England – Prince Charles' bizarre new town, Poundbury, which has a touch of Disneyland about it. A place less suited to the works of Hardy can hardly be imagined.

A recent literary investigation carried out by *The Guardian* came to the conclusion that Thomas Hardy has good claim to the title of the world's gloomiest author. P G Wodehouse, for example, gazed out on a country scene and saw jolly larks involving slow-witted police constables, braying toffs and dyspeptic peers; Hardy looked out and saw death and despair. If his literary world is an external manifestation of his state of mind, you would have to say that he probably had a bit of a tendency to let things get him down. The Hardy 'gloom-o-meter' hits maximum in *Jude The Obscure,* which can probably lay claim to be the most relentlessly depressing piece of fiction ever produced; not far behind are *Tess of the D'Urbervilles* and *The Mayor of Casterbridge.* By comparison, *Far From The Madding Crowd*, which has its share of death and disappointment, is a bit of a romp.

But while his books may not exactly be full of shiny, happy people, the settings are always pretty uplifting: bad things happen in a nice world. Hardy, I can understand, may not be everybody's cup of tea. Just before form trips were banned by my school for a continuing pattern of bad behaviour – nothing to do with me, I hasten to add (though of course, I would) – our fourth year outing to see *Far From The Madding Crowd* at the Bristol ABC cinema in autumn 1967 stands out as a special memory. I don't think any of us had read Hardy, but we knew it was 'literature' and therefore, as the basis for a film, likely to be very dull stuff (*The Great Escape* was probably the brightest cinematic star in our firmament at that time). When we discovered that the Hardy film was just shy of three hours long, we feared the worst.

In fact, the film proved to be a transformative experience. As a piece of cinema it had a sort of documentary style in which the director attempted to portray Victorian rural life exactly as it might have been; a level of verisimilitude the like of which we had never seen before. We had certainly seen nothing like Julie Christie. In the hands of director John Schlesinger and cinematographer Nicolas Roeg (who was to work as director with Julie Christie in the stunning *Don't Look Now*), Dorset becomes a visual feast. The reviews were less positive: one critic described the film as 'an under-dramatised postcard' another merely described it as 'sluggish'. But just as David Lean neatly captured Dickens world in his film of *Great Expectations*, Schlesinger's *Far From The Madding Crowd* is arguably the most successful adaptation of Hardy's works to date.

Hardy is the gift that keeps on giving for Visit Dorset. A new *Far From the Madding Crowd* movie starring Carey Mulligan and adapted for screen by *One Day* author David Nicholls was released in 2015. There have been recent adaptations of *Tess of the d'Urbervilles* (also, interestingly, adapted by Nicholls; clearly he has an affinity with Hardy) and *Return of the Native*.

Hardy's creation of his fictional Wessex, in which real places were made over as facsimile towns – such as Dorchester and Oxford, for example, which became the thinly disguised 'Casterbridge' and 'Christminster' respectively – provided a new sort of literary interest for readers. When the books became successful at the end of the 19th century, there was inevitable interest from people who were keen to see the real places where the fictional events had taken place. This was an idea taken seriously by public institutions: at 10 South Street in the centre of Dorchester, for example, a blue plaque appeared on what is now the local branch of Barclay's Bank with the inscription 'This house is reputed to have been lived in by the Mayor of Casterbridge in Thomas Hardy's story of that name written in 1885.'

By the end of the 19th century, literary tourism was already well established. Publishers A&C Black, for example, by 1904 had published special 'Pilgrimages' guides to literary places, with books devoted to travelling in the footsteps of Sir Walter Scott, Robbie Burns, Charles Dickens, William Thackeray and Chaucer's *Canterbury Tales*. Their newest guide that year covered a modern writer who was still very much alive: Thomas Hardy, who at that time was 63 and would live for another 24 years. He had, however, published all of his Wessex novels, and by then was concentrating on poetry. In his foreword to *The Hardy Country: Literary Landmarks of The Wessex Novels,* Charles G Harper describes 'Hardy Country' as 'a land literally flowing with milk and honey'.

Hardy was no doubt flattered to be given so much attention, but he was writing about Dorset as it had been many decades earlier when the industrial revolution was beginning to affect rural Dorset. So he was probably only too aware that travellers may have been coming to view a Dorset that was no longer quite the picture of the land of milk and honey that guidebook writers had been painting.

For the modern visitor – and for me, certainly – the fascination of coming to Hardy Country lies partly in seeing the places of the books and partly in seeing where Hardy was born and where he lived. 'Birthplace' museums are often something of a disappointment; seeing where a writer was brought up as a child is interesting, but usually not that informative. In the case of Hardy, however, the National Trust has two Dorchester properties – one is the birthplace cottage in Bockhampton, three miles northeast of Dorchester; the other is Max Gate, the house that Hardy had built for himself on the edge of town when he became successful. Hardy wrote in both, producing his first published novel in the modest cottage in the woods.

In her foreword to the excellent National Trust guide to the Hardy homes, Claire Tomalin, author of *Thomas Hardy: The Time-Torn Man* (a book I strongly recommend for any fans of Hardy), describes a visit to the cottage at Bockhampton as 'an emotional experience for anyone who loves Hardy's work'. It's Tomalin's view that Hardy's imagination was shaped by the landscape of his childhood, from cottage to heath, meadow and woodland – this is a place full of meaning.

Anyone visiting the cottage now enjoys an enhanced experience: next to the car park I found a large visitor centre with a cafe, shop and ticket office. From here it was a longish walk to the cottage down a lovely lane with a view that has probably changed little since Hardy's time.

It has long been common for artists of all sorts – and their advocates – to exaggerate the lowliness of their birth. There is nothing we like more than to hear how someone has brought themselves, Cinderella-like, out of extreme poverty to become famous and prosperous. It is worth noting that, of course, Cinderella was only sweeping the kitchen because the Ugly Sisters made her do it – the family was, actually, very well off. The same is often the case for those whose humble origins are often laid out for our inspection. Hardy wasn't born with a silver spoon in his mouth but, compared with those of the lumpen Dorset proletariat, he was positively middle class. Which isn't to say that the Hardy family home would have been a candidate for inclusion in a late-Victorian issue of *Dorset* magazine.

When I reached the cottage, it offered an impressive sight – chocolate-box pretty with overhanging thatch and uneven windows with roses, japonica and honeysuckle growing up the walls. The cottage was surprisingly tiny, a handful of rooms up- and downstairs with a terrifying staircase connecting the upstairs bedroom with 'Granny's Kitchen', once occupied by Hardy's grandmother Mary, who must have pretty fit to have got up and down that vertiginously steep flight to her bedroom. Of most interest, probably, was Thomas' bedroom, where he used to write on a small table under the window (the original table can be seen in the Dorset County Museum). This is where he wrote his first novels: *Desperate Remedies* (1871), *Under the Greenwood Tree* (1872) and *A Pair of Blue Eyes* (1873). From his place next to the window, Hardy could look west towards the Hardy Monument (this was constructed to honour the 'Kiss Me' Hardy – no relation – who famously held the dying Nelson in his arms at the Battle of Trafalgar), which is ten miles away on Blackdown Hill.

If you follow in Hardy's (and my) footsteps to visit the cottage, make sure you wait for the briefing in the parlour from a National Trust volunteer, whose talk can bring the house to life – reminding visitors of the musical evenings in the cottage when Hardy's father on the bass viol would join Thomas and his brother Henry on their violins. Spare time too for the garden and orchard, which cover an acre now full of lovely flowers. Also worth a look is the earth closet of the sort which, incredibly, we had at the primary school I attended in the Wye Valley in the 1960s. Not a place to spend any time on a hot, sunny summer's afternoon.

Parking at the second Hardy house, Max Gate, can be difficult, so if you have the time and the energy you can make the three-mile walk which Hardy made frequently, from Bockhampton to Dorchester – a clear map in the official guidebook, which covers both properties, shows the way. A walk through the Hardy countryside is an excellent way of getting inside the minds of the characters for most of whom walking was the only way of getting around. On a surprisingly hot October Sunday afternoon it was a real pleasure for me to leave the busy roads behind and plunge into the lush places that lie between Bockhampton and Dorchester.

Thomas married Emma Lavinia Gifford in 1874, and then lived in different properties in London, Somerset and Dorset. In 1883 he purchased a plot of land from the Duchy of Cornwall in the southeast of Dorchester and, using his architect training, designed his own house, which he commissioned his father and brother to build. The couple moved there in 1885 and Hardy remained until his death in 1928. It was in Max Gate that he corrected the proofs of *The Mayor of Casterbridge* and wrote *Tess of the d'Urbervilles* and his final novel, *Jude the Obscure* – and here that he wrote the poetry which he considered his greatest work. The birthplace cottage is small and charming; Max Gate by contrast is large and rather ugly. It was the house that Hardy wanted and so, we must suppose, it is the property that he wanted the world to judge him by. He thought it said: I have arrived. The visitor today might say: Where did you think you were going, exactly?

The house is much less than the sum of its parts – it has lots of rooms and all the mod cons of an early 20th-century house – but what it doesn't have is any of the atmosphere of the modest Bockhampton cottage (this, however, doesn't make Max Gate any less interesting). It also has to be borne in mind that, while the property has been in the hands of the National Trust since 1940 when it was bequeathed by Hardy's sister Kate, with the stipulation that the house should be lived in, it has only recently been open to the public as a significant attraction in its own right. After Thomas Hardy's death, the contents of the house were sold at auction. At Dorchester's Dorset County Museum a replica of his last red-painted study can be seen, including a calendar stopped on the day of his death, pens lying in a tray with names of the novels they wrote engraved on their backs, and his boyhood fiddle. This museum exhibit – 'A Writer's Dorset' – has been created to celebrate Hardy and tell the story of his life and work; it looks at the part-real, part imaginary Wessex of his books, 'their settings inseparable from the places that inspired them', as the museum itself puts it.

Originally, it was never intended to open Max Gate to the public. Hardy's sister bequeathed the house so that its rental income could fund the eventual purchase and upkeep of the birthplace cottage when it became available; she considered this humble property much more significant in the story of her brother's life. The cottage was the home presided over by their mother, who had worked as a servant but made schoolteachers of both her daughters and arranged for her talented firstborn son to train as an architect instead of joining the family trade of building.

It was once at Max Gate, meanwhile, that Thomas and Emma's marriage began to break down. The estrangement became physical as they began to live apart within their own house. Emma moved into the attic rooms – a bitter retreat for someone who felt that she played no small part in Thomas' extraordinary rise to literary fame and fortune. Visitors to Max Gate reported that Hardy was less than gallant to his unfortunate wife, peremptorily ordering her from the room if he wanted to continue conversations with friends. Emma was suddenly taken ill in 1912 and died, leaving Hardy to regret his treatment of her for the rest of his life. His memory of her inspired some of his finest poetry.

Thomas failed to die of a broken heart, however, and two years after Emma's death he married Florence Dugdale, 39 years his junior, who had been working as his secretary. The second Mrs Hardy installed a telephone, which her husband refused to answer, in the hall, and a bathroom with hot water that he also refused to use. Hardy made it clear that when he died he wished to buried in the same grave as his first wife in the local churchyard at Stinsford. His executor, Sir Sydney Carlyle Cockerell, however, was keen that Hardy should be buried in Westminster Abbey's Poets' Corner – an idea strenuously resisted by his wife and close family. Eventually, a compromise was reached: his heart was buried at Stinsford with Emma, and his ashes were laid to rest in Poets' Corner.

Something of an urban myth has arisen about Hardy's heart. After removing the heart, the local doctor is said to have placed it on the table before temporarily leaving the room; he returned, it is said, to discover the cat eating it – some claim that the unfortunate cat was thus condemned to the grave alongside its meal. Hardy would no doubt have been delighted.

At the ceremony in Westminster Abbey, the principal mourners included his widow, his sister, the Prime Minister Ramsay MacDonald, Sir James Barrie, George Bernard Shaw, Rudyard Kipling and A E Housman – a surprisingly stellar lineup, given that Hardy had largely kept himself out of the limelight in rural Dorset. The grave was elaborately lined with purple, and the Dean of Westminster sprinkled a handful of Wessex earth during the service. Whether all this makes up for the earlier pantomime cannot be said, though it's hard to imagine the general public being so accepting of divvying up body parts in this fashion in the present day.

Fans of Hardy novels who visit Dorset will be delighted to discover that many of the places he describes in his books are still just as he wrote about them. Several buildings and places in the Puddletown area (renamed 'Weatherbury' by Hardy) are reckoned to appear in *Far From The Madding Crowd*. For example, Waterston Manor, just off the B3142, is reckoned to be Bathsheba's 'Weatherbury Upper Farm'; Gabriel Oak's cottage is also said to be on the same road. It is on Toller Down ('Norcombe' in the book) that Oak loses his flock. To the east of Kingsbere (Bere Regis) is the site of 'Greenhill Fair', where Sergeant Troy re-enacts Dick Turpin's ride to York, and gallops around the tent in his highwayman disguise.

※

It was a 20-minute drive from Max Gate, the house of Thomas Hardy, to Clouds Hill, the house of Lawrence of Arabia – so close together in distance, yet worlds apart in style. The more you see of writers' houses, the more you understand – and this in no sense a criticism – that they are places which belonged to slightly bonkers people, managed by slightly bonkers people, for the pleasure of slightly bonkers people (I'm more than happy to include myself in that category).

In the early 20th century, Britain seems to have been a place of natural eccentrics, but even in this glorious world of oddness T E Lawrence – or Lawrence of Arabia as he became known – was a very unusual man. And I was delighted to discover that he was the owner of quite the oddest house in the National Trust collection. Clouds Hill in Dorset took a little bit of tracking down and I wondered if, in the words of the Michelin guide, it would be worth the journey. I needn't have worried.

If we know anything about Lawrence, it is based on David Lean's film *Lawrence of Arabia,* with Peter O'Toole cutting a dash as he races through the wide desert expanses on his camel. While they had a reasonable physical resemblance, Peter O'Toole was 6ft 2in while the real Lawrence was just 5ft 5in, a little smaller than, say, Tom Cruise.

The film *Lawrence of Arabia* offers only a relatively restricted view of Lawrence's achievements, though. He was primarily a scholar and a man of letters. He read constantly, translated Greek works, advised publishers and kept a busy correspondence with many of the country's leading literary figures. *Seven Pillars of Wisdom*, the book on which *Lawrence of Arabia* is based, is a significant work of literature in its own right.

Story boards at Clouds Hill tell the extraordinary tale of Lawrence's progression from an academic working on the architecture of crusader castles to his role as a key agent in the Arab rebellion against the Ottoman empire which culminated in the 1918 capture of Damascus. The room steward was also a fund of fascinating facts, including the one about Lawrence's actual height. 'I don't think Peter O'Toole would have managed very well in this house, do you?'

Indeed, Clouds Hill is Hobbit-cosy – an elaborate man-cave with no kitchen, but a nice bath. The steward said that probably more people came to see the house because it was so interesting than because they wanted to find out more about Lawrence. Which is a shame, because both are absolutely fascinating.

Clouds Hill is a tiny tumbledown Dorset cottage rented by Lawrence in 1923 as a place to escape from his military service. Unusually for a National Trust property, it has no garden – Lawrence didn't think much of them. It is compact and modest: a basic two-up and two-down. In the Middle East he had dined with kings and princes; here, in his bolt-hole away from life in the Tank Regiment, he wanted somewhere he could relax. It wasn't somewhere he intended to live, more a place to read and write and enjoy the company of friends. So there was no kitchen and, initially, no bathroom; the steward explained that the downstairs bath was an addition in 1933, the year before Lawrence's death in a motorbike accident. Lawrence's friend E M Forster later recalled that despite the lack of home comforts for himself, however, Lawrence was anxious that his guests would not suffer the same; 'one would find a hot bottle in the bed…in case his precious visitor's feet should be cold.'[8]

Lawrence arranged the large upstairs room as a place to listen to music (he had a fine gramophone) and the small room next door as a tiny bedroom lined with tin foil to keep out the damp. He was proud that there was no wallpaper, plaster or paint at Clouds Hill, just exposed timber and brick. The ground floor was a library, with a large bed covered in brown cowhide.

Shortly before his death, it seems that T E Lawrence had been flirting with fascism. On the day of his fatal road accident, Lawrence was returning from Bovington post office after sending a telegram to *Tarka the Otter* author Henry Williamson confirming lunch arrangements at Clouds Hill the following day: Williamson was keen to recruit Lawrence to the Moseley cause. That lunch would never occur.

There have been suggestions that his motorbike death was suicide; according to the room steward, however, he crashed while attempting to avoid two young boys on bicycles – exactly, in fact, as shown in the movie *Lawrence of Arabia*. The cinema gets things right sometimes, it seems.

※

From Hardy Country, I continued east into Wiltshire, and the cathedral city of Salisbury – a place captured in literature by a number of writers over the centuries.

William Golding (1911–93) was awarded the Nobel Prize for Literature in 1983 and knighted in 1988. The author of *Lord of the Flies* taught English at Salisbury's Bishop Wordworth's School, which was founded by a great-nephew of William Wordsworth. His 1964 novel *The Spire* tells the story of the building of Salisbury Cathedral's spire. The story often uses symbolism to enhance and dramatise issues raised within his narrative: the spire serves as a symbol both of obsessive lust and the quest for Heaven – and its cost. From 1958 to 1985 Golding lived at Bowerchalke, about nine miles southwest of Salisbury, where he is buried.

In *An Autobiography*, posthumously published in 1883, Anthony Trollope describes how a visit he made to Salisbury in 1852 when he was 37 years old proved to be a literary epiphany. He was wandering around the cathedral precincts one midsummer evening when he conceived the story of *The Warden*. As well as *The Warden,* the series went on to include *Barchester Towers*, *Doctor Thorne*, *Framley Parsonage*, *The Small House at Allington* and *The Last Chronicle of Barset*. Trollope was quickly able to give up his job – he had been working for the Post Office in the West of England – and become a full-time novelist. His Barchester novels have not stood the test of time as well as Dickens' works – 19th-century ecclesiastical politics are a slightly *recherché* field – but Trollope still enjoys a substantial following.

Thomas Hardy must have been impressed by Salisbury Cathedral and Close as he features them in both *Jude the Obscure* and *The Hand of Ethelberta,* as well as describing them in two poems: 'The Impercipient' and 'A Cathedral Façade at Midnight'. His sisters Mary and Kate went to a training college for schoolmistresses at the King's House in the Close; in *Jude the Obscure*, this was used as the college that Sue Bridehead attends.

Most tourists, however, are brought to Salisbury by the lure of Stonehenge, eight miles north of Salisbury. One of the world's most famous sites, it has a standing stone circle which archaeologists believe was built between 3,000 BC and 2,000 BC. Stonehenge appears in several novels: in Fanny Burney's *The Wanderer*, Peter Ackroyd's *Hawksmoor* and most memorably in Hardy's *Tess of the D'Urbervilles*. In the novel, Tess and Angel walk through the Wiltshire countryside at night, stumbling upon Stonehenge by accident. Tess falls asleep on an ancient altar and wakes to find that the police have surrounded them.

At dawn she is taken away to prison where she faces execution. Sadly it's no longer possible to wander amongst the standing stones (attempt to recreate Tess's nap these days and you may well suffer her fate…).

※

Bath isn't the only place to lay claim to Jane Austen, and I ended this leg of my journey at another shrine for fans of the author: Jane Austen's House Museum in Chawton.

Over the years, the works of Jane Austen have become more than simply words on a page. To her band of most devoted fans, they're a sort of holy writ. J K Rowling's relationship with her first husband, Portuguese TV journalist Jorge Arantes, began in a cafe in Porto when they found they had a shared love of Jane Austen. When Rudyard Kipling began researching real life behind the lines in the First World War for a history of the Irish Guards he was writing, he found that reading was a common means of escape from the horrors of fighting. He discovered that the six novels of Jane Austen were particularly popular with the troops. Austen devotees, who glory in the name 'Janeites', had their own front-line literary freemasonry, according to the Kipling short story *The Janeites,* first published in 1924. Kipling reported that, while the lower ranks were happy to benefit from proclaiming a passion for Austen, they found the phenomenon a little hard to fathom, as one of the characters Humberstall explains:

> Jane? Why, she was a little old maid 'oo'd written 'alf a dozen books about a hundred years ago. 'Twasn't as if there was anythin' to 'em, either. I know. I had to read 'em. They weren't adventurous, nor smutty, nor what you'd call even interestin'—all about girls o' seventeen (they begun young then, I tell you), not

certain 'oom they'd like to marry; an' their dances an' card-parties an' picnics, and their young blokes goin' off to London on 'orseback for 'air-cuts an' shaves. It took a full day in those days, if you went to a proper barber. They wore wigs, too, when they was chemists or clergymen...[9]

Kipling had become an Austen fan too. He visited Bath in March 1915 with his wife, a visit that inspired him to re-read the works of Jane Austen. 'The more I read the more I admire and respect and do reverence... When she looks straight at a man or a woman she is greater than those who were alive with her – by a whole head... with a more delicate hand and a keener scalpel,' he wrote to a friend. According to Mrs Kipling's diary, Kipling spent part of January 1917 reading Jane Austen's novels aloud to his wife and daughter, 'to our great delight'.

My satnav suffers occasional mad moments when it suddenly decides it wants to go to an address it seems to have plucked from the air. Since these moments tend to occur when I'm heading, say, west on the M25 and it decides that I should effect a U-turn 'wherever possible' and turn east, I usually know that I need to turn the satnav off and on again. This always does the trick. The satnav digitally blinks and wonders: 'What happened there, then?' and patiently gets to the job of counting down the miles again. This time, however, the satnav went off-message a couple of miles out from Chawton, and for some reason suddenly sent me on a diversion to Selborne. As this is the location of the home of the naturalist Gilbert White and features a gallery devoted to tragic Antarctic hero Captain Lawrence Oates, the satnav was displaying an impressive interest in both the natural world and Edwardian pluck. My true destination, however, was Jane Austen's House Museum in Chawton, a few minutes away.

Some attractions immediately get on your wrong side by offering parking difficulties. Either you can't find the car park, or when you do there aren't any spaces, or there are spaces but you discover that you are in the 'overspill' car park and face a huge hike to the attraction. Jane Austen's House, like the author's writing, immediately charms the visitor: I drove into a big, nearby car park that levied a reasonable charge.

Kipling himself, I am sure, would have been delighted to visit here; the presentation of Austen's work and life was thoughtful and bright, and the welcome warm and genuine. By chance, I noticed an ad in the local paper for volunteers to act as house stewards at weekends. According to Janet Johnstone, volunteer manager: 'Our aim is always to give all of our visitors a memorable experience of visiting Jane Austen's home. A friendly face as you come through the front door always makes our visitors feel welcome.' (I would have to say that, in many other similar attractions around the UK, friendly faces are at a premium.)

At the museum itself you really do enjoy a polite, friendly welcome. The person on the till told me that attendance fluctuates according to whether a Jane Austen book has recently been dramatised on TV or the big screen (the Internet Movie Database records more than a dozen TV and movie versions of *Pride and Prejudice* alone). At the moment, the museum is still enjoying a boost in visitors brought about by its purchase of a turquoise and gold ring that belonged to Jane Austen which had originally been bought at auction by US singer Kelly Clarkson – who knew that the *American Idol* singer was a closet Janeite? When Clarkson purchased Austen's ring at auction for £152,450 in 2012, hopes of keeping it in the UK seemed lost. However, Culture minister Ed Vaizey issued a temporary ban preventing the ring from being exported, giving time for a UK purchaser to match the price. A 'Bring the Ring Home' campaign in 2013 resulted in it being bought for Jane Austen's

House Museum, where it is now on permanent display. Clarkson was magnaminous in defeat, announcing that she was 'happy to know that so many Jane Austen fans will get to see' the ring at the museum.

Also worth a word or two of praise is the museum's guidebook, a model of concise clearly set out information and invaluable insight into Austen's world. The gift shop matches the thoughtful style: as well as new copies of Austen's books, you can also buy valuable vintage editions.

'How are you enjoying your visit so far?' asked one of the volunteer house stewards, a rehearsed move, perhaps, in an attempt to engage visitors – but well done! I asked her if she was a Jane Austen fan: 'I wasn't until I started to work here – I've been here two weeks and already I'm onto my third book. I'm now a big fan. I didn't realise the books were so readable and so funny.'

And I hadn't realised the Jane Austen museum would be so interesting. What it does – and what so many similar museums fail to do – is offer a fascinating narrative which not only tells the story of the author's life but places it in historical context, explaining where her work fits in to the social and political events of the period. You can see the table Austen sat at to write, you can read family letters and look at the family's Clementi pianoforte. Austen's fondness for describing balls and other social events lends itself to light and amusing presentations – it's an open goal that the museum doesn't fail to hit.

After visiting a place that is practically a shrine to the life and works of Jane Austen, it would be easy to imagine that the writer is a universally adored star in the literary firmament. What sort of person would fail to find her work a delight? Strangely enough, that person turned out to be the American humourist Mark Twain; in fact, Twain seems to have harboured quite a grudge (whether this was genuine or pretended is hard to tell). He often admitted being surprised, for example, that Austen had been allowed to die a natural death rather than face execution for her literary crimes. 'Her books madden me so that I can't conceal my frenzy,' Twain remarked in a letter to his friend Joseph Twichell in 1898, complaining 'I have to stop every time I begin. Every time I read *Pride and Prejudice* I want to dig her up and beat her over the skull with her own shin-bone.'

Mr Twain doth protest too much, methinks.

4

Steep to Burwash

In which our literary sleuth goes for a Steep walk, finds cold comfort on the downs, is not afraid of Virginia Woolf and plays Pooh sticks in Ashdown Forest.

IN a surprising amount of the literature of the First World War, it's interesting how often comparisons are made between the horror of the trenches and the glorious pristine English countryside that lay on the other side of the English Channel. From Kent and the South Downs, for example, much of the Western Front was close enough that people could lie in bed at night and hear the sound of artillery bombardments; the noise must have been like an ever-present distant thunder.

Sometimes, the comparisons hark back to the golden summer before the outbreak of war. In an affecting passage from Alan Bennett's 1968 play *Forty Years On* – a moment in which the author is being entirely serious – the narrator describes a late-night motor car trip down to the English countryside in the summer of 1914, taken by Edward Horner, Julian and Billy Grenfell and Patrick Shaw-Stewart (all of whom were to perish in the First World War) to hear nightingales sing as dawn came up. A year later, observes the narrator, from the same place listeners would be hearing the sounds of death and destruction from France.

Perhaps the most poignant literary trail in the south of England is the walk around the village of Steep, in east Hampshire, in the footsteps of poet Edward Thomas, whom Ted Hughes described as 'the father of us all'. Thomas is classified as a war poet not so much because his poems are about war, but because he died in battle, and his work summons up the idyll of English life that was lost forever when war broke out (most famously in the spirit evoked in his most anthologised poem 'Adelstrop'). Nowadays, Steep is known as the location of Bedales, a progressive co-educational public school that has attracted starry pupils such as Lily Allen, Sophie Dahl and Minnie Driver, and has boasted some famous parents too – including Mick Jagger, Jude Law, Jeremy Paxman and Boris Johnson. But while its country lanes these days may boast more than their fair share of high-end Range Rovers and BMWs, you can still recognise the charming village as the place which Thomas fell in love with over 100 years ago.

I stood outside All Saints church where Thomas is commemorated by two engraved windows, and could see at a glance what made the village so attractive to the writer. Berryfield Cottage was his first home in the area before he moved to the Red House. His final home in Steep, No. 2 Yew Tree Cottage – one of a group of semi-detached cottages – must have seemed like the perfect haven, a place safe and remote from the growing danger emerging from the continent.

It was here that Thomas lived with his wife Helen and three children between 1913 and 1916, when he wrote most of his poems. The house – and two others he lived in here – form part of a Thomas Trail that takes visitors up to the wooded hanger known as Little Switzerland. Thomas' own favourite spot was the climb up the Shoulder of Mutton Hill, where there is a memorial stone to the poet; I lingered for a few meditative moments in the evening stillness and drank in the glorious views to the south, Thomas's 'Sixty miles of South Downs'. He describes the hillside in several poems, including 'When First' (written in July 1916):

> …*Fast beat*
> *My heart at sight of the tall slope*
> *Of grass and yews, as if my feet*
> *Only by scaling its steps of chalk*
> *Would see something no other hill*
> *Ever disclosed.*

Returning to the village, I paused at the memorial to the fallen of the First World War at the junction of Mill Lane and Church Road, which lists Thomas's name. He died at the Battle of Arras in 1917, before the first poetry collection under his own name was published.

※

Much of my journey for this leg of my literary tour bore a remarkable similarity to the time I drove to Glyndebourne – to the opera, for a spot of corporate hospitality and *Don Giovanni*. Along the way I found myself driving through the setting of the final stages of *The Day of the Triffids*, the land of *Cold Comfort Farm* and into *Winnie-the-Pooh* country: this time round, I was lucky to have the chance of exploring each of these in more detail.

All three books are, socially speaking, out of the top drawer – the writers were people who talked about 'dinner' and genuinely meant the last meal of the day. Given that this literary mix also includes the likes of Jane Austen, Virginia Woolf,

Treasured Island

Anthony Trollope and John Fowles, the south of England emerges as the high-born heartland of English letters.

In truth, until the middle of the last century, books were almost exclusively written by the socially advantaged and the well off (until the 1950s, university education was largely the privilege of the rich). For the humblebums who made it against the odds, from the Brontë sisters and Dickens to Thomas Hardy and D H Lawrence, it was nearly always a painful struggle. And even when they'd 'made it', there was the ever-present feeling that they would never be properly accepted, as they were plainly 'oiks' who didn't know which knife to use or which way to pass the port. Despite what *Downton Abbey* says, the landed gentry were generally not nice to know – especially if you were unlucky enough to be of the servant class.

The democratisation of poetry, with more poets emerging from more humble backgrounds, had the effect of making verse more hard-edged. The prototypical poet in popular imagination used to be the effete Fotherington-Thomas in the Willans and Searle classic *How to be Topp,* which painted a wonderfully crazy view of prep school life at St Custard's. Fotherington-Thomas would spend most of his time like a junior Keats or Shelley, skipping around crying: 'Hullo clouds, hullo sky.'

After the brutalities of the First World War, poetry became a more general reflection of people's lives. Philip Larkin was a skilled commentator on modern life and its disappointments. He's not a writer usually associated with the south, yet one of his best-loved poems, betraying a more upbeat side to his character, was inspired by a visit to Chichester.

I, also, had something of an epiphany on the road to Chichester. I have long abhorred the fold-up bicycle. There is an aura of smugness which attaches itself to all cyclists – that 'look at me, I'm saving the planet' self-regard which they think gives them the right to bowl over innocent pavement dwellers or permits them blithely to ignore the red signal at traffic lights. This uber-vanity is displayed tenfold in the cyclists who bring their awful toy bikes onto my train, which not only blocks up the precious luggage section at the end of the carriage, but delays a speedy exit as the folding cyclists struggle to offload them.

When a friend invited me to borrow his folding bike for the five-mile run from his home near West Dean down the Centurion Way cyclepath to Chichester, I told him I wasn't keen. I look a prat on a bike at the best of times – on a folding bike, I feared I would look deranged.

'It's only five miles…it's downhill,' he insisted.

I relented. After all, this cycleway was a Sustrans project, established by an organisation which has imaginatively turned many disused railway lines into cycle paths (the late-20th-century equivalent of beating swords into ploughshares). Insisting on a cycle helmet, I climbed aboard.

'You're right,' he said, 'You do look deranged.'

On a fresh sunny morning, the cycling was glorious. As a boy I practically lived on my bike – cycling was freedom. This run towards the beckoning tower of Chichester Cathedral smelt of teen spirit; I was rejuvenated.

Appropriately enough, Philip Larkin was a great cyclist, and even managed to include a reference to his cycle clips into his poem 'Church Going'.

Unlike contemporaries John Betjeman or Ted Hughes, Larkin largely shunned the limelight as a poet. But despite his reclusiveness, his poems, such as 'This Be The Verse' and 'Annus Mirabilis', have insinuated themselves into our consciousness.

Perhaps his best-loved poem, 'An Arundel Tomb', was written in 1956 after a New Year tour of the southern counties that Larkin took with his friend and occasional muse, Monica Jones (Jones, incidentally, was also said to have been the inspiration for Margaret Peel in Kingsley Amis' *Lucky Jim* – rather less flatteringly). They went to Winchester, where Larkin mentions visiting Winchester Cathedral 'where Jane Austen is buried', and attended evensong at Salisbury Cathedral.

They also visited Chichester Cathedral and saw the medieval Arundel Tomb, which shows the figures of Richard Fitzalan III, 13th Earl of Arundel, and his second wife Eleanor – who, by his will of 1375, wanted to be buried together 'without pomp' in the chapter house of Lewes Priory. The most striking thing about the tomb is that the two figures are holding hands – it is this which inspired Larkin's poem, declaring that ultimately 'what will survive of us is love'.[10]

After 'An Arundel Tomb' was published, it was claimed that the two figures were made to hold hands in a 19th-century restoration – news which helped convince the author that the poem was not one of his best works. The cathedral, however, now believes that the hand-holding was an original feature, noting in a plaque:

> If so, the monument must be one of the earliest showing the concession to affection where the husband was a knight rather than a civilian.

Critics, however, are divided about whether Philip Larkin, a famous curmudgeon, was being ironic when he suggested that love will be all that survives of us – or whether he was being quite serious.

One thing is clear: the various guides who bring groups around the cathedral are not entirely sure who Larkin was. One man bringing a party of Chinese students around in my hearing told them that the Arundel tomb was well known 'for reasons you needn't be interested in. It was a written by a bloke called Philip Larkin who was Poet Laureate and he wrote a poem which has sort of become well known about the tomb. But you don't need to worry about it.' There were lightning flashes from a bank of mobile phone cameras held aloft – but nobody was worried.

Philip Larkin should have been Poet Laureate perhaps, but he never was. When John Betjeman died, Larkin was asked if he would like to take up the role; he declined, saying that he no longer wrote 'meaningful' poetry of any sort. It's doubtful, it has to be said, whether any Poet Laureate has ever written a meaningful poem. 'An Arundel Tomb', however, is a beautiful tomb and a moving poem (whatever it actually means).

By the way, apart from the Arundel Tomb, there is a lot to like about Chichester Cathedral: it's a beautiful cathedral in a very pretty location in an attractive part of Sussex. The cathedral has stoutly refused to levy an admission charge – not even in the guise of a forced donation (you are, however, invited to donate – in these circumstances it would be churlish to refuse). It seems an unlikely thing to make anybody angry, but I have to say that I blaze with fury at the whole issue of charging people to go into cathedrals. I have no religious faith, but if the New Testament is about anything, it strikes me that it is about letting people into places of worship without being strong-armed at the entrance.

※

In the final section of John Wyndham's *Day of the Triffids*, protagonist Bill Mason searches for his lost love Josella:

> By midday the clouds had gathered, and the rain began once more. When, at five o'clock, we pulled up on the road just short of Pulborough it was still pouring hard.
>
> 'Where do we go now?' inquired Susan.
>
> 'That,' I acknowledged, 'is just the trouble. It's somewhere over there.' I waved my arm towards the misty line of the Downs, to the south.[11]

Treasured Island

Just as in the First World War when it was almost impossible to imagine a greater contrast between the mud-soaked nightmare of Flanders fields and the sweet English countryside, Wyndham brings the terror of the triffids to inoffensive little Pulborough.

Barrister's son Wyndham published *Day of the Triffids* in 1951: the story of how triffids – effectively giant killer stinging nettles – conquer Britain after a meteor shower blinds all those who watch it (hey, it could happen!). The book ushered in a new era of post-apocalyptic fiction. The blokey stiff upper lip of the hero Bill Masen and his awful patronising attitude towards female survivor Josella was never likely to win it The Woman's Book of the Year – but then, it is a book very much of its time, where men fought triffids and women turned the triffids into nettle soup (actually, nobody attempts triffid soup, which I think is a bit of an oversight). Giant killer stinging nettles, it has to be said, are much more terrifying as an idea on paper than they can ever be as giant plants on the movie screen, where they tend to look a bit daft.

I'm not entirely sure why, but I get more pleasure from re-reading this Wyndham novel more than almost any other book in my possession. Much of the narrative takes place in London; a key location is the University of London Senate House building, which I had cause to visit often as a London student. Taking my exams near here, it was hard not to keep thinking about rogue triffids at large. The Senate House tower would have looked as monumental as New York's Empire State Building 60 years ago; now, it is more of a dot on the landscape.

When Bill escapes the capital he heads to a community that is being planned near Devizes in Wiltshire, then to Beaminster in Dorset, before ending up on a farm near Pulborough on the Sussex Downs, where they are left hoping that the world will one day recover from its blindness/killer stinging nettle situation. The extraordinary thing about the Downs is that, in places, they seem remote and sometimes eerily deserted – perfect for that post-apocalyptic vibe. Yet even in this remote fastness you are little more than an hour from central London. If, like Bill and Josella, you had to find somewhere to set about rebuilding civilisation, this would be as good a place as any (in the wilds of northern Scotland, every day you'd be fighting the rising impulse to hurl yourself into the sea).

Bill and Josella should have been grateful they didn't end up on *Cold Comfort Farm*. In 1930, 28-year old doctor's daughter Stella Gibbons, while working for *The Lady*, 'the magazine for gentlewomen', began writing a novel. It was conceived as a parody of the 'loam and love child' novels popular at the time, a curious trend for bleak rural fiction that combined folk wisdom with earthy D H Lawrence passion, including Mary Webb's best-selling *Precious Bane* and Sheila Kaye-Smith's *Sussex Gorse* – as humorous magazine *Punch* put it, 'the kind of story in which peasants have babies in cowsheds and push each other down wells'. As a work of literature, Gibbons' novel transcended mere parody: the book's confident, carefully managed humour was so impressive that a rumour began circulating that *Cold Comfort Farm* was actually the work of Evelyn Waugh, writing under a pseudonym.

The book tells the story of young orphan Flora Poste, who imposes herself on her estranged distant family at the remote Cold Comfort Farm, near the village of Howling on the Sussex Downs. The inhabitants of the farm include Aunt Ada Doom, who has been driven mad by having once seen 'something nasty in the woodshed', the Starkadders, and various rude mechanicals, who feel an obligation to accommodate her in an effort to make amends for some unexplained wrong once done to her father. The whole family, as seems to have been the tradition of a certain genre of romantic 19th-century and early 20th-century literature, are each cursed by some terrible character defect which needs to be resolved by Flora in her brisk commonsense way.

It was probably no coincidence that the Starkadders' Cold Comfort Farm is set in a part of Sussex that at the time was famously also home to artists Vanessa Bell and Duncan Grant and their circle of literary friends. During the period of the 1920s and 1930s, Charleston, their famously eccentric home, became the country retreat for the Bloomsbury Group, which numbered writers E M Forster and Virginia Woolf amongst them. The Downs at this time were seen as the very essence of rural England, summoning up a John Major vision (partly borrowed from George Orwell) of cricket on the village green, 'old maids bicycling to Holy Communion through the morning mist' and warm beer – so this was somewhere clearly ripe for satire.

Howling, Beershorn and Godmere, the places which are located in the vicinity of Cold Comfort Farm, are all invented. However, Stella Gibbons cleverly intersperses several real towns into her narrative. For example, Flora Poste expresses concern that Elfine might become 'all arty-and-crafty' and 'keep a tea-room in Brighton'; indeed, Elfine herself declares that if she does not marry Richard Hawk-Monitor, she could always 'get a job in an arts and crafts shop in Horsham'.[12] Did Horsham even have anything like an arts and crafts shop? It seems doubtful. From my brief pass through the centre, these days it seems to consist of little more than a station (a surprisingly splendid 1930s building), a Beefeater pub and a jarringly modern Premier Inn (Elfine, thou shouldst be living at this hour; Horsham hath need of thy arts and crafts!).

It would be a shame to come to the Sussex Downs and fail to visit Brighton, if only to take a stroll on its pier and raise a glass of warm beer to Graham Greene, author of 1938 novel *Brighton Rock,* a story of small town gangsterism that succeeds in making Sussex-by-the-sea's best known resort look about as alluring as a punch in the face.

Brighton is also clearly the faded resort that John Osborne had in mind as the setting for *The Entertainer*, the play – which saw Britain as a run-down music hall – he wrote for Laurence Olivier. Osborne had lived in Brighton and he was a big fan of Brighton's own Max Miller, the music hall artiste, and clearly the inspiration for Archie Rice, the character played by Olivier both on stage and in the film version of the play.

Sadly for the Brighton tourist board, nobody seems to have written a book which offers a more upbeat account of the resort – a surprise for a town so beloved by those of an artistic, or alternative, bent. One day, perhaps?

※

One Southern England resident who never had to resort to keeping a tea room in Brighton or seeking a job in a Horsham arts and crafts shop was Virginia Woolf. She wrote much about London in *Mrs Dalloway* and Cornwall in *To The Lighthouse*, but it's in Sussex, at the National Trust-owned Monk's House in Rodmell, that her flame is most conspicuously kept alive.

Virginia Woolf is a bit of an acquired taste: her books may seem difficult at first, but her fiction proved groundbreaking. Her 1925 novel *Mrs Dalloway* is credited with transforming the English literary landscape: an astonishing story, like James Joyce's *Ulysses*, it is set in the course of a single day. Whether you like her writing or not, though, everybody seems to agree that Monk's House is a gem and well worth seeking out.

Situated four miles from Lewes, the property was acquired in 1919 by Woolf and her husband Leonard in an auction – they paid £700. Monk's House seems to have been unimpressive at the initial viewing – Woolf noted in her diary that the rooms were small, the kitchen was bad, there was no hot water and no bath and, as she had never even been shown the Earth Closet toilet, so she presumed that it must have been terrible. But they decided to bid nevertheless and, by the time the house was acquired, she was more enthusiastic: 'That will be our address for ever and ever.'[13]

And so it was, serving as their country retreat for weekends and holidays – and for long stretches in the summer. As Woolf became more successful as a writer, money was spent on improving the property: the kitchen was rebuilt and a bath and hot water were installed. Money from *Mrs Dalloway* and *The Common Reader* bought two new water closets; and in 1929 they added a two-storey extension – which, in truth, looks a bit flimsy and out of character. By 1931 there were even electric fires in the bedrooms. Woolf was very pleased with it all, and no doubt their visitors were extremely grateful for the modernisation – when E M Forster came to stay, he had been so cold that he stood too close to the solid fuel 'Cozy Stove' installed in his bedroom's chimneyplace trying to get warm, and burnt his trousers (A Room With a Flue, you might say).

The feeling I got from a visit was that Monk's House was a real house that had real people living and working in it. The National Trust has done an exceptionally good job in maintaining both house and garden in the way that the couple had known them while they lived at the house. Woolf particularly loved the garden, and, after her suicide by drowning in 1941, her husband buried her cremated remains here beneath an elm tree. On a warm summer's day, it would be hard to imagine a more beautiful place to linger. Woolf's Lodge, her writing 'shed', is a particular joy: in the house there's a lovely picture of Woolf sitting in deckchairs outside the shed with a group that includes John Maynard Keynes, arguably one of the most influential economists of the 20th century, who looks so happy and relaxed that I imagined that he was about five seconds away from putting a knotted handkerchief on his head.

※

There is no evidence that Virginia Woolf and A A Milne ever met, though Woolf's brother Clive Bell was a contemporary of Milne's at Trinity College, Cambridge, where Milne studied on a mathematics scholarship. Woolf got very cross about the success achieved by Stella Gibbons' *Cold Comfort Farm*, so one imagines the popularity of *Winnie-the-Pooh* was not likely to have given her much pleasure.

Winnie-the-Pooh is the Marmite of children's fiction. For its legions of fans it is among the most deeply revered works of English literature, reckoned to be the book which best recaptures the innocent world of lost childhood. Despite Walt Disney's ham-fisted cartoon version of the stories, in recent years the idolisation has been ramped up several notches: efforts have been made, for example, to claim that Pooh's attitude to life embodies the positive life-guiding principles of the Taoist philosophy; there are some who even claim the books rework potent bear myths from Celtic mythology.

On the other side of the divide sit those such as American wit Dorothy Parker who, writing as Constant Reader, lacerated A A Milne's *The House at Pooh Corner* in a 1928 review in *New Yorker* magazine. She had already savaged an earlier Pooh tome, *Now We Are Six,* the previous year, accepting in the process that 'to speak against Mr. Milne puts one immediately in the ranks of those who set fire to orphanages'.

Parker took particular exception to the passage of *The House at Pooh Corner* in which Pooh confessed that he was wont to add the words 'tiddely pom' to his Outdoor Song in order to make it 'more hummy'. This was a tweeness too far for Parker: 'And it is that word 'hummy,' my darlings, that marks the first place in *The House at Pooh Corner* at which Tonstant Weader fwowed up.'

Before I had children of my own, I have to say that I sat on Dorothy Parker's side of the fence. Most of children's literature, up until at least the 1960s, was predominantly middle-class, depicting people who inhabited a world of affluence and comfort of which I knew little: they were worlds that included nannies, nurseries and endless treats. I'm not saying we drank tea out of a rolled up newspaper, but growing up it was hard not to notice a vast gap between the haves and the have-relatively-little rest of us. Reading about posh kids having fun in books was an over-rich diet you had to enjoy sparingly.

When you have children of your own, however, it means you have to find ways of keeping the little darlings entertained, if only to hold on to your sanity on long car journeys. Of all the audio cassettes that filled the glove box of our car, the most frequently played was probably Alan Bennett reading *Winnie-the-Pooh* (runner-up was Alan Bennett reading another middle-class kids fest: *The Wind in the Willows*). Gradually, we reached the point where we knew entire passages almost by heart: the wit and wisdom of A A Milne had entered our lives. Brainwashed? Perhaps. Fans? Certainly.

In 1926, when he wrote his first Pooh book, Milne would have expected to be remembered as a successful playwright, with works being performed simultaneously in London and on Broadway. Today, however, his immortality rests on a toy bear purchased from Harrods for Christopher Robin, his only son. The bear was named 'Pooh' after a swan Milne and his son had once encountered in Arundel. 'Winnie' came from a bear kept in London Zoo (and loved by Christopher Robin), so called because it had been brought by a First World War soldier from Winnipeg in Canada.

Christopher Robin and Pooh made their first appearance in the volume of poetry *When We Were Very Young*, published in 1924, which contains the famous and much-parodied 'Vespers'. *Winnie-the-Pooh* came two years later, followed by another book of poems, *Now We Are Six* in 1927 and *The House At Pooh Corner* in 1928. The first literary pilgrimage we ever undertook as a family was in search of Christopher Robin country. Pooh's fictional Hundred Acre Wood is easily located; it's the Five Hundred Acre Wood in Ashdown Forest in East Sussex. Milne lived at nearby Cotchford Farm until his death in January 1956. (The house was subsequently bought by Rolling Stones guitarist Brian Jones, who drowned in its swimming pool in 1969.)

That Pooh Pilgrimage was made on a bitterly cold December day, when we had a guided tour of the forest and discovered that while *Winnie-the-Pooh* may have been the product of the imagination of the author A A Milne, the world his characters inhabited was real enough – and what most pleased us all was that everything looked pretty much as artist E H Shepard drew it for the books. Here, fiction really was drawn from a decent amount of fact.

Today, the Ashdown Forest, two-thirds heathlands and the largest open access space in the southeast, is well geared up for Pooh visitors. Two walks are downloadable from the Ashdown Forest website: they both start in Gills Lap ('Galleons Lap' in the stories) car park – the shorter walk, at about half a mile, is ideal for smaller children and includes The Enchanted Place and the Sandy Pit; the longer walk – about two miles – visits the North Pole and Eeyore's Sad and Gloomy Place.

Returning and taking the walk to the North Pole revived happy memories of our family visit 20 years ago. Christopher Robin came up with the idea of a trip to the North Pole, although he was not quite sure what it was, beyond the fact that it was something that could be discovered. It was Pooh who called the trip an 'expotition'. Along the way they came across a stream into which Roo manages to fall. Pooh pulls him out with the aid of a stick which they conclude must be the North Pole – so Pooh discovers the North Pole and Christopher Robin places the pole in the ground and ties a notice to it recording Pooh's achievement.

I looked out for the memorial which commemorates both A A Milne and illustrator E H Shepard. Christopher Robin said this was where his father sat and where Pooh sat too; now I could see what they saw. This is a place that generates genuine emotion – it was here, among the pine trees, that Milne bid farewell to Christopher Robin and Winnie-the-Pooh at the end of *The House At Pooh Corner*. The story comes to an end: Christopher Robin has grown older and it is time for him to go to school. But, as the author observes, the story never really ends; in this Enchanted Place in the Forest a little boy and a bear will always be playing.

One of the highlights of a visit to Pooh Country was the chance to play Poohsticks on the real Poohsticks bridge; I dropped a Pooh stick into the water for old time's sake and, like Christopher Robin, accepted that life moves on. (Though, sadly, the real Christopher Robin found himself stuck in perpetual childhood – the curse of being written about in a best-selling book.)

※

My final stop on this stage was Bateman's – the East Sussex home of Rudyard Kipling, near the village of Burwash.

It is difficult now to grasp just what a national phenomenon Kipling was during his lifetime. He was born in Bombay in 1865, the child of imaginative and loving parents who had moved to India to seek a new life. After dark years separated from his parents while he attended school in England, Kipling eventually returned to India, where he was employed on a local newspaper and wrote stories about the lives of the English in India. These eventually formed the basis of *Plain Tales from the Hills*, the first of the books which would quickly establish his name around the world.

There has probably been no other writer who has added quite so many phrases to the language: 'East is East, West is West', 'The White Man's Burden', 'What do they know of

England who only England know?', 'The female of the species is more deadly than the male', 'He travels the fastest who travels alone', 'It's clever, but is it Art?' and '...if once you have paid him the Dane-geld you never get rid of the Dane'. He wrote one of the most famous political quotes of the 20th century, which was spoken by his cousin, Prime Minister Stanley Baldwin, in an attack on the owners of the *Daily Express* and the *Daily Mail*: 'What the proprietorship of these papers is aiming at is power, and power without responsibility — the prerogative of the harlot through the ages.' If he had written nothing else, his poem 'If' would have been enough to ensure his name was remembered as long as the English language endures (it was rated Britain's favourite poem in a BBC poll).

With the First World War, Kipling played a substantial part in national life. His son Jack found it impossible to enlist because of his poor eyesight, but Kipling was able to pull strings to enable him to join the army; sadly, Jack died during the Battle of Loos in 1915. Partly as a response to the death of his son, after the war Kipling joined the Imperial War Graves Commission and advised on the choice of words for memorials. He selected the biblical phrase 'Their Name Liveth For Evermore' for the Stones of Remembrance found in larger war cemeteries; he also suggested the phrase 'Known unto God' for the gravestones of unidentified servicemen; and he chose the inscription 'The Glorious Dead' on the Cenotaph in London's Whitehall.

His body of work is extraordinary: he was the author of 'If', 'Gunga Din', *Kim*, *The Jungle Book* and *Just So Stories,* which were dedicated to his daughter Josephine who died of pneumonia aged six. The level of success achieved by Kipling was extraordinary: by the age of 32 he was reckoned to be the highest paid writer in the world. In 1907, at 42, he became the first British recipient of the Nobel Prize for Literature – still the youngest person ever to receive this award.

Kipling's reputation, however, has since suffered, especially in recent times. It is claimed that he was an apologist for the worst excesses of the British Empire. Though he may use racist terminology, many would argue – including George Orwell and Salman Rushdie – that Kipling's intentions were honourable. He was a writer of his time who knew India well – he felt that Britain had achieved many good things with its Empire, but he was also well aware of the bad things done in the name of Britain – a point often made so ironically in his writing that his true intention is sometimes mistaken. The generally held view is that Kipling may not have been a great poet, but he was certainly an unforgettable one, whose felicitous knack for a phrase deserves a place in the front rank of Britain's literary greats.

By the time he received the Nobel Prize, the Kipling family had been living in Bateman's for five years. The magnificence of the property bears eloquent testimony to the elevated position in life that the writer had achieved – a place in the world probably reached by no other writer before or since.

Visitors to the National Trust-owned Bateman's may be familiar with *The Jungle Book* or the poem 'If', but most people are astonished that Kipling had written quite so much and climbed so very high. 'I knew he made exceedingly good cakes, I didn't know he'd made an exceedingly big fortune,' joked one awestruck visitor I passed in Bateman's grand hallway. (I'm assuming this was a joke; however, it wouldn't surprise me if there was a survey somewhere in my inbox – carried out by an online hotel booking agency – which has discovered that 70% of British people think that Rudyard Kipling was primarily a baker...)

A chance to visit Bateman's offered the sort of experience that would convince me that I should be a National Trust member – if I weren't already. I can wholly understand Kipling's immense joy when he took possession of this fabulous house. He wrote in a letter to his friend C E Norton in November 1902:

> Behold us lawful owners of a grey stone lichened house – A.D.1634 over the door – beamed, panelled, with old oak staircase, and all untouched and unfaked. Heaven looked after it in the dissolute times of mid-victorian restoration and caused the vicar to send his bailiff to live in it for 40 years and he lived in peaceful filth and left everything as he found it.
>
> It is a good and peaceable place standing in terraced lawns nigh to a walled garden of old red brick, and two fat-headed oast-houses with red brick stomachs, and an aged silver-grey dovecot on top.[14]

Bateman's is a 17th-century sandstone house which was hidden away in a wooded and 'secretive' weald – the Kiplings were keen to maintain their privacy from the prying eyes of any sightseers. The Kiplings made many improvements made to the property: a turbine was installed to provide electricity to light ten 60-watt bulbs for four hours every evening. And, with the money from the Nobel prize, they created a pond and a rose garden in the grounds. The Kiplings, however, never troubled to install a telephone.

Bateman's has remained just as Kipling described it when he moved in, over 100 years ago. It was, he concluded: 'a real House in which to settle down for keeps.' And they did, staying for 34 years until Kipling's death in 1936 at the age of 70. The house passed into the hands of the National Trust after his wife's death three years later, and here it has remained ever since. Long may it continue to be so.

Kipling's concerns about modern life are reflected in his writing at Bateman's. His best known works here were *Puck of Pook's Hill* and *Rewards and Faires*, two of his finest short story collections. Puck takes children Dan and Una back into the English past so that they may 'claim it as theirs'. On this journey, they encounter a veteran Norman knight, a young Centurion of a Roman Legion which had been stationed in England, and a builder and decorator from the time of Henry VIII. The books are fondly loved and remembered by those who read them as children – and, as I drove away from Kipling's home, I found myself thinking just how beautifully the stories meshed with the surrounding Sussex countryside.

5

Rolvenden to Lydd

In which our intrepid explorer discovers the secret garden of Kent, has great expectations for his visit to Cooling, pursues Goldfinger down the A2 and discovers how many steps John Buchan really had in Broadstairs.

AT the end of the 19th century, successful writers – if they chose – had the money to leave the city and live in rural splendour. Many headed south: Kipling lost himself in a quiet Sussex valley, and not far away were Virginia Woolf and the Bloomsbury Group writers. Others chose Kent, which was much more accessible to London, but lacked none of Sussex's rural delights. Kent, after all, was known as The Garden of England – what better place to imagine one of the most famous literary gardens of all time: *The Secret Garden*?

Near the border with Sussex, in the village of Rolvenden, stands Great Maytham Hall, where from 1898 to 1907 lived the writer Frances Hodgson Burnett. Burnett had an extraordinary life; after the death of her father, a prosperous Manchester ironmonger, her family were forced to emigrate to America, where her mother took them to live with her brother in

Tennessee and they struggled to make enough money to survive. When her mother died, Burnett became the breadwinner. She wrote and eventually sold stories to magazines, in time becoming a successful writer. Her major success was the book *Little Lord Fauntleroy,* which launched her as an international celebrity. She began to spend more and more time in England, eventually renting Great Maytham Hall; apparently she had high hopes of striking up a close relationship with American writer Henry James, who lived about 10 miles away in Rye on the Sussex coast. When she took on the property she wrote to her son Vivian telling him that the house was:

> ...a charming place with a nicely finished park and a beautiful old walled kitchen garden. The house is excellent, panelled square hall, library, billiard room, morning room, smoking room, drawing and dining rooms, seventeen or eighteen bedrooms, stables, two entrance lodges to the park, and a square tower on the roof from which one can see the English Channel.[15]

It must have seemed a long way from Tennessee.

After she had moved in, like the young heroine of *The Secret Garden*, it seems that Burnett was alerted by a robin to a door hidden behind a mass of tangled ivy that covered one of her crumbling garden walls; forcing open the old door she found a concealed garden. Excited by her discovery, she set about restoring the 'secret garden', planting hundreds of flowers, and creating a rose walkway. She visited the garden every day to write under a gazebo while her friendly secret garden-discovering robin perched nearby.

The Secret Garden was inspired by Great Maytham Hall, but it wasn't published until four years after Maytham's owners sold the house, and she was forced to leave. She wrote to her sister

Edith, in September 1908, 'It was living at Maytham which meant England to me, in a way,' continuing in a later letter:

> That place *belongs* to me—it is the only place I ever felt was *home*...It seemed a sort of outrage that I was not living there. It seemed so what one needed—that sense of being able to go out of one big room into another—to go down corridors into room after room—to go upstairs & walk about...[16]

I called ahead and made arrangements to visit the garden at Great Maytham (the hall has been converted to private flats, but the garden can be visited) and found my visit to the 'secret garden' strangely moving. It's one of those moments when you feel you've stepped, Narnia-like, into another world. Here is one of the great literary landscape experiences, all the more exciting because it is truly a hidden delight.

It's interesting to note that, at around the same time as Hodgson Burnett was writing, in another part of Kent Edith Nesbit was working on another classic Edwardian children's novel: *The Railway Children*. Published in 1906, it was inspired by her childhood spent in Halstead and the railway which ran near the family house. You'd be forgiven for associating this particular story far more with Yorkshire, however – the famous 1970 film version used the Keighley & Worth Valley Railway line for its location shots.

Yorkshire, of course, is where Mary Lennox's Misselthwaite Manor can also be found – another parallel.

※

It took me less than half an hour to drive from Great Maytham down to Rye, but in the process the scenery changed completely, from the Weald of Kent's Garden of England to the sort of seaside place that seemed more familiar from French impressionist paintings: wide, flat coastal plains with huge skies.

The American novelist Henry James was another giant of the southeast's literary scene. James had stoutly resisted Burnett's strenuous campaign to make him her bosom companion, pretending he wasn't home when she chose to call unexpectedly. Although they had been friends when they had lived in London, he clearly felt that proximity to her in the countryside might become onerous.

Rye is an extraordinarily well-preserved historic town, standing above Romney Marsh, with level green pastures stretching down to the sea. The hilltop fortified town was once surrounded by sea, and had a key role in the defence of the south coast of England. Full of timbered buildings and terracotta roofs, this is somewhere that would hardly look out of place in Tuscany. There are cobbled streets and a network of secret passages, once used by smugglers.

The town, and Lamb House, were discovered by James rather by chance when he called on an architect he knew who lived here. Lamb House delighted him; he quickly decided to lease the property in 1897 and, when the house became available to buy two years later, he avidly snapped it up. Among the novels he wrote here were *The Wings of the Dove*, *The Ambassadors* and *The Golden Bowl*. Henry James had a very wide circle of literary chums, such as H G Wells, Joseph Conrad, Rudyard Kipling, Max Beerbolm, Hilaire Belloc, G K Chesterton, Compton Mackenzie and Ford Maddox Ford, and all of them visited him here.

E F Benson's much loved *Mapp and Lucia* novels were set in Rye; Lamb House has a starring role, appearing as 'Mallards', the home of Miss Mapp. The property is owned by the National Trust; be warned, it has very limited opening times – two days a week. A number of visitors have expressed disappointment at the fact that there are just a couple of downstairs rooms to see – fans of Henry James and *Mapp and Lucia*, however, seem to find the limited experience entirely delightful.

※

From here I headed north again, into the territory of one of my great literary heroes. Charles Dickens bestrides the narrow literary world of the southeast like a Colossus.

Judging by the number of Odhams Press collected editions always available for sale on eBay, it seems that it wasn't just my family that grew up with a shelf-full of Charles Dickens novels. Most of these online Dickens collected edition sellers also claim that these books are 'like new', which suggests that these were works of literature bought primarily for display rather than study. 'Books do furnish a room,' to quote Anthony Powell, and nothing said 'well educated' quite like a load of Dickens. In my childhood home we had a line of Dickens, a complete works of Shakespeare and the complete set of Arthur Mee's Children's Encyclopaedias – throughout my entire childhood I have no memory of anybody troubling to look at any of these improving volumes. The Arthur Mee books struck me as a bit odd, all very 'the sun never sets on the British Empire' and 'Britannia rules the waves' – a sort of UKIP Bumper Fun Book for Boys and Girls.

It would be good to report that my introduction to Dickens came when, aged seven, I plucked *Dombey and Son* off the shelf and read it at a single sitting. Actually, my acquaintance with the author began with 1960s black and white TV dramatisations of *Great Expectations* and *David Copperfield*, and subsequently with the Classics Illustrated versions of both books (you could read the Classics Illustrated version of *David Copperfield* in the bath in a single go!). It wasn't until I'd left school that I read a whole Dickens novel: I took down our untouched (unabridged) copy of *David Copperfield* and took it on an Interrail trip around Europe. When I try to remember what I did during those three weeks, my clearest memory is night-time sliding-door compartment trips through middle Europe while, by flickering train light, I followed Copperfield's troubled journey through life. Whenever I reached a particularly gripping part – Dickens' novels were originally written for serialisation so are built on regular cliffhangers – I would often decide that I couldn't be bothered to get off in Copenhagen or Milan; I would simply board another train and stick with the book. When I eventually finished the book – it's 360,000 words – it seemed like a good time to go home. (Twenty years ago, when I flew around the world in two-and-a-half days to see what the experience would be like (interesting but exhausting), I took Victor Hugo's *Les Miserables* – 1,463 pages and 530,000 words – and couldn't get beyond the first few chapters.)

Dickens stands with Shakespeare as someone whose works have become part of British life, with characters and stories which most of us think we know – thanks largely to TV and cinema – even though we have often never read them. And probably many people will never read them: a 2013 survey showed that a third of those questioned had no idea who wrote *Great Expectations*.

Of all the British writers, though, Dickens works provide us with a host of actual places that can still be visited. There are Dickens museums, certainly – but the real pleasure is going to the places that he wrote about almost 200 years ago and finding that many of them are still there.

I began my Dickens pilgrimage in Cooling, on Kent's Hoo Peninsula. Soon, I was heading down country lanes that in Dickens' imagination once led to prison hulks and childhood terror. In Cooling, as I entered through the church lychgate, a man in bright cycling gear must have identified me as a fellow literary pilgrim and called across the graveyard, pointing down to the spot at his feet:

'Are you looking for the Dickens graves?' he asked.

Not Dickens' actual grave, I should clarify; the writer was controversially buried in Westminster Abbey, contrary to his expressed desire to be laid to rest nearer his Kent home (the Dean of Rochester Cathedral got as far as having a vault dug for him before the prestigious body was purloined by the Dean of Westminster). The man who had hailed me was one of two cyclists taking their ease near the church door; here, they had a packed lunch spread out on a tomb. Near their feet were two rows of pathetically small stones marking the graves of 13 children.

This is the affecting sight at St James' Church in the Kent village of Cooling that inspired Charles Dickens in his description at the very start of *Great Expectations*:

> To five little stone lozenges, each about a foot and a half long, which were arranged in a neat row beside their grave, and were sacred to the memory of five little brothers of mine – who gave up trying to get a living, exceedingly early in that universal struggle – I am indebted for a belief I religiously entertained that they had all been born on their backs with their hands in their trousers-pockets, and had never taken them out in this state of existence.[17]

The cyclist pointed again at the stones: 'Infant mortality was quite dreadful in Dickens' time. I've been telling Thomas here that this is why Victorians had such big families, they wanted to be sure some of their kids survived out of childhood. Queen Victoria had nine children, I told you that, didn't I, Thomas?'

Thomas nodded.

'He's from Poland, he's being putting in a new boiler for us so I promised him a little outing around some of our famous sights. We had a look at Cooling Castle – have you seen it? That's owned by Jools Holland – he's a pop star, Thomas. Thomas wanted to go on to Bluewater shopping centre but we're finishing up at St George's Church in Gravesend, which is where they say Pocahontas is buried – died of tuberculosis aged 22 on a ship as she was sailing back down the Thames to Virginia in America. They have a statue of her. Thomas thought she was just a Disney character. He now knows all about Dickens – he'll soon know all about Pocahontas.'

'Do you know any Dickens?' I asked Thomas.

'I am the ghost of Christmas presents,' he replied in a ghostly voice. 'Is that correct?'

'Sort of,' I said.

Remarkably, St James' Church is among the most popular Dickens attractions in the UK. According to the Churches Conservation Trust, which manages the property, each year it attracts around 15,000 visitors. In David Lean's lovely 1946 movie version of *Great Expectations* starring John Mills, the opening churchyard episode provides one of British cinema's most memorable scenes (this was actually filmed in the studio with a six-foot high model of the church). This is the scene where young Pip encounters the terrifying escaped convict Magwitch, played by Finlay Currie. Much of the opening parts of the film were shot on location not here in Cooling but in nearby St Mary's Marsh, on the River Medway. In 1946, the Medway setting had probably changed little since Dickens' day. Not so the view from St James' Church, which would have been windswept and remote in the middle of the 19th century – now, looking towards the Thames from its graveyard, I could see the oil refineries and terminals at Thames Haven and Shell Haven; also visible was the sprawl of Canvey Island and the more distant tower blocks of Southend-on-Sea. Once, the surrounding countryside here was marshes, but these have long been drained to create valuable farmland. But on a quiet windswept Sunday morning, it wasn't hard to imagine Magwitch suddenly leaping up from behind a nearby gravestone, desperate for nourishing 'wittles' and a file to release him from his leg irons.

Outside London, this area of Kent provides the most fertile territory for Dickens enthusiasts. Visit nearby Rochester and Chatham and you can see where Dickens spent some of the happiest times of his childhood. When I first visited Gad's Hill, some years ago, I parked in the car park of the Sir John Falstaff public house – Falstaff talks about 'Gadshill' in Shakespeare's *Henry IV Part One* when he sets out his plan to rob travellers on the Pilgrims' Way, the road to Canterbury and Dover which ran along here. I knew that Dickens' Gad's Hill Place was now occupied by an independent school and assumed that it was off-limits to visitors. It was only when I visited the Dickens Museum in London's Doughty Street that I saw a reference to the plans that were being made to open up the old Gad's Hill house as a museum, and to mount an annual exhibition in Gad's Hill Place during the school's summer holidays allowing the public regular access into the main house of Dickens' life. The museum had already returned Dickens' writing desk, where he composed his novels, to the study there.

And, in the meantime, it is possible to arrange a visit on several days of the year. For this trip, I made immediate arrangements. Holy ground for literature fans, Gad's Hill Place became Dickens' home in 1856; it's the house where he wrote *Great Expectations* and *A Tale of Two Cities* (in his Swiss chalet in the grounds); and the house where, finally, he died following a stroke – in the house's dining room – in 1870. For Dickens' fans, Gad's Hill would represent the ultimate outing – the snug ground floor room which he used as his study has been restored to look how it was when he wrote here. Although no longer on the main road between London and Dover as it used to be, the road outside Dickens' house remains busy, especially with lorries. As I arrived, a Norbert Dentressangle articulated lorry had somehow jammed itself right across the road as it tried to make an ill-advised turn in front of the property.

Given Dickens' withering account of privately owned Dotheboys Hall school and its terrible headmaster Wackford Squeers, I should imagine that it was with some measure of nervousness that the Gad's Hill independent school opened its doors in Dickens' old home. The school, however, seems to have gone from strength to strength, building a substantial new development which meant that the older part, which belonged to Dickens, has now become surplus to requirements – hence the plans to turn it into some sort of museum. Impressively, the basic fabric of the house has remained largely in place, so that it could easily be restored to the way it looked when Dickens lived here. Dickens' restored study is the main attraction. The door famously features a mock bookshelf which, when closed, looks indistinguishable from the shelves that line the walls. The titles of the dummy books shown in the door display Dickens' wry humour; as a cub reporter who spent long, boring hours covering Parliamentary debates, he suggests, for example, *Hansard's Guide to Refreshing Sleep*; there is also *Cat's Lives* in nine volumes, the series *The Wisdom of Our Ancestors: I Ignorance, II Superstition, III The Block, IV The Stake, V The Rack, VI Dirt,* and *VII Disease, History of a Short Chancery Suit* in twenty-one volumes, and *King Henry the Eighth's Evidences of Christianity*, and, next to these a very narrow dummy volume entitled *The Virtues of Our Ancestors*. This was a room that was always kept locked when Dickens was not occupying it and no servants were allowed inside.

In grounds he owned across the main road from the house Dickens installed a miniature Swiss chalet, a present from an actor friend (and early example of flat-packed furniture – it arrived in multiple boxes), which is where he wrote in good weather. In order to reach his little park, known as the Wilderness, Dickens had a tunnel built under the road; you can still see the tunnel's Wilderness entrance from the road. On either side of the tunnel are two plaques which were bought by Dickens in Italy and brought home – they depict Comedy and Tragedy. While Dickens probably went to the expense of building his underground walkway to avoid the unwelcome attentions of curious fans, he wasn't altogether standoffish. He was at pains to maintain popularity among the locals, allowing them to have cricket matches in his meadow and famously arranging Boxing Day sports each year.

During their first month at Gad's Hill Place, the Dickens family had Danish fairytale writer Hans Christian Andersen as a guest. He had been invited to stay for a fortnight, but he proved to be a nuisance by extending his stay to five weeks – Dickens was not amused. He left a sign on the mantelpiece of the room used by the Danish writer which read: 'Hans Andersen slept in this room for five weeks — which seemed to the family AGES!'

Serious Dickens fans might want to visit the birthplace museum in Portsmouth but, in truth, this is not a significant place in Dickens' life. Dickens was born here, but the family moved away in 1815 when the writer was still a toddler and it is unlikely that he recalled very much about the experience. Portsmouth is attempting to leverage its slender Dickens connection for all that it is worth: in 2014, it unveiled a statue of the author, ignoring the writer's well-known stipulation that there should be no statues of him – he believed that the books should be his sole monument. Portsmouth Council begged to differ.

※

One of Dickens' favourite journeys was down to the Kent coast; the sweet seaside air must have been a tonic for anyone long-confined in the fetid air of insanitary London. But even well into the 20th century, the Kent seaside was a popular escape for wealthy city dwellers for whom cheap flights to Europe were still a gleam in a no-frills airline pioneer's eye.

One of those sometime city dwellers was Ian Fleming, who had a house in St Margaret's Bay and spent a lot of time in Kent. Remember the line in *Goldfinger*? 'Ah, Mr Bond – welcome to Whitstable.' No? Likewise, you probably won't recall 007's arch-enemy plotting the seizure of America's gold deposits (and the downfall of world capitalism) from his villainous bunker built beneath a caravan park near Broadstairs. But neither of these examples are that far from the truth.

Unfortunately, when it came to the silver screen, the makers of the best-loved Bond films chose to omit the wilder shores of Kent from the Hollywood version of the stories. Yet much of the early part of Ian Fleming's *Goldfinger*, published in 1959, actually unfolds within about 30 minutes' drive of Dover. In the book, when Bond is instructed by 'M' to pursue Goldfinger, he points his Aston Martin DB Mk III (in preference, Fleming tells us, to the office Jaguar 3.4) down the A2 ('in preference to the A20,' adds Fleming, with his apparently inexhaustible appetite for spurious detail).

To follow Bond's journey to Kent in *Goldfinger*, you would need to begin in London, and from Rochester you could follow 007's footsteps on the arrow-straight A2 from Sittingbourne down to Faversham. Unlike Bond, I was starting slightly further east and, again, unlike 007, I didn't have a long-barrelled Colt .45 in a trick compartment under the driver's seat, nor reinforced steel bumpers fore and aft. This is an eternal disappointment, though perhaps for the best.

From Faversham, the A2 heads on to Canterbury. While Dickens is a dish that I'm happy to feast on again and again, Chaucer may be a taste I've yet to acquire – though there's still time!

Although I appreciate the historic value of Chaucer guiding his pilgrims down the medieval equivalent of Old Kent Road to Canterbury, he is someone I can only associate with English Literature examinations. What even I can't argue against, though, is his deserved place in Britain's literary pantheon – due to his government work he was buried in Westminster Abbey, and unwittingly created Poets' Corner.

As Chaucer is one of Britain's best known writers (certainly one of its most assiduously studied authors), I expected the city to have a major Chaucer museum of some sort, linking him with the story of Canterbury as a place of pilgrimage. What Canterbury actually has – and the city should really hang its head in shame – is The Canterbury Tales, an attraction which is billed as 'Medieval Misadventures with Geoffrey Chaucer and his band of bawdy travellers'. Really? I like a laugh as much as the next man, but The Canterbury Tales is a sort of 'Carry on Chaucer'. Now, there is much in the *Canterbury Tales* which has a 'Carry On' element to it. But only an element: Chaucer's work is proper literature which deserves a dignified setting.

I was not alone in my disappointment. 'Not Worth the Visit,' reckoned one, clearly very unimpressed, online reviewer: 'Just boring, both for kids and adults alike – there are plenty of things to do in Canterbury to fill each day without having to suffer this.' Sarah H, Manager at The Canterbury Tales, responds (full marks to all who respond to criticism) with admirably tight-lipped reserve: 'Thank you for your review'.

Bond hadn't paused for Carry on Chaucer. Neither should have I. Time to move on.

※

In the book, Auric Goldfinger lives in Reculver, at the eastern edge of Herne Bay. The approach is through the unprepossessing suburban sprawl of doner kebab shops and curry houses ('Do you expect me to talk?' 'No, Mr Bond, I expect you to enjoy this excellent chicken tikka with basmati rice, spiced chutney and pappadums'). Hard to see where Goldfinger might have had his desirable residence in which he entertained Bond to dinner. These days Reculver seems mostly a tangle of holiday caravans. Over it all presides the lovely Saxon facade of St Mary's Church, much of which was long ago damaged by coastal erosion, before the decision was taken to demolish the main part of it in 1809.

Before coastal erosion and the silting up of the waterways, Reculver sat at the northern end of the Wantsum Channel; a watercourse that separated mainland Kent from the Isle of Thanet. No longer an island, though it retains the name, this is the home of some of Kent's great seaside towns, including Margate and Broadstairs.

Ian Fleming was happy to acknowledge the big influence that sometime-Broadstairs' resident John Buchan's sparely-written work had on him when he began work on his 007 novels. One of the most influential novels of the 20th century, a style of thriller that led directly to Ian Fleming's 007 series, *The Thirty Nine Steps* was a literary game changer. While much of the action takes place in the wilds of Buchan's native Scotland, where hero Richard Hannay is pursued by ruthless Prussian agents, the final action of the novel takes place in the town of Bradgate – a thinly disguised Broadstairs.

The title was inspired by the a visit made by the Buchan family to the seaside here in August 1914 to help daughter Alice recover from a mastoid operation. No sooner had they arrived than Buchan began to suffer from a duodenal ulcer; forced to stay in bed, he began to work on what he believed could be a new style of thriller. The cousin of Buchan's wife, Susan, was renting a large villa at nearby North Foreland, where the family made use of a set of steps cut into the chalk leading down to a private beach.

Even though I was equipped with my satnav, I was surprised at how hard it was to pick my way along the coast to Broadstairs; it was slow going along a series of small roads which bent their way around new out-of-town shopping developments. When I reached the turn off to Cliff Road from North Foreland Road, it became a private road, resembling the sort of gated communities which are such a feature of American life. But here there are no gates and you can drive down to the grassy strip that separates the grand houses from the cliff and the beach.

Opposite the house called St Cuby, where Buchan recovered from his ulcer, I found the famous steps. Entry is now controlled by a gate accessible only to residents, but I could still look down this very flight of stairs – almost. The truth is that there aren't, and never were, 39 steps.

When Buchan was here, there were actually 78 of them, which zigzagged through two shafts and three tunnel sections. Buchan family legend credits the title of the novel to six-year-old Alice, who was learning her numbers at the time, and counted each step as she went down one of the flights. Whether true or not, the tale resonated; when, in the 1940s, the wooden steps were replaced with concrete ones, a builder is said to have saved a chunk of the 39th and sent it to the family as a keepsake.

Buchan wasn't the first novelist to enjoy Broadstairs – it had been a favourite of Charles Dickens. For 14 years from 1837 to 1851 it was his holiday place of choice – and Dickens has long been a favourite of the people of Broadstairs. There is a sizeable slab of Dickens here: the Dickens House Museum celebrates his connection with Broadstairs, and the town holds a festival in his honour every June.

On his first visit here, Dickens wrote to a friend marvelling about how he had seen 'ladies and gentlemen walking upon the earth in slippers of buff' – that is, walking on the beach in bare feet. These same ladies and gentlemen were also 'pickling themselves in the sea in complete suits of the same'[18] – swimming naked in the sea; not quite how one imagines staid Victorian life.

The museum was situated in the cottage that provided Charles Dickens with the inspiration for the home of Betsey Trotwood in *David Copperfield*. Dickens' son Charley wrote that they frequently had tea here with one Miss Mary Pearson Strong. Miss Strong thought she had the right to prevent the passage of donkeys in front of her cottage, an obsession which Dickens gratefully wrote into the character of Betsey Trotwood – did Dickens ever have to make anything up, I wondered, with this sort of raw material to work from? In the museum, among the Dickens items on view, were letters he wrote about Broadstairs, a mahogany sideboard, his writing box and a collection of prints by one of Dickens' principal illustrators, H K Browne (Phiz). Another property in Broadstairs – Fort House – is said to have been the inspiration for *Bleak House* – though, in Kent, it's hard to throw a stone without hitting a house that claims some sort of connection with the Master.

Leaving Broadstairs, I was back on my Fleming trail. I popped in for a quick look at Ramsgate (Bond stays here at the Channel Packet Hotel – reckoned to be the Foy Boat pub, according to the Foy Boat pub, at least – before heading down the coast.

One of the best-remembered episodes of the film of *Goldfinger* sees Bond and Goldfinger pitted together in a no-holds-barred game of golf (with Oddjob in his killer bowler hat acting as his boss's caddie). In the movie, the match is played to the west of London at Stoke Park (handier for Pinewood Studios, one presumes). In the book, the action happens at the 'Royal St Marks' in Sandwich – a thinly disguised Royal St George's club, the often-used venue for the Open.

Novelists are famously advised to write what they know about. Fleming took this to heart. He knew the Sandwich course well (and most of the other good golf courses in the area). He served at St George's on the handicap and other subcommittees, and had a flat in Sandwich. For a golf club with an international reputation, St George's is surprisingly tiny (practice grounds at American clubs have a far grander presence).

Fleming had lunch at the club the day before he died of a heart attack, aged 56, in August 1964. He had been nominated to be club captain, a role he was due to take up the day after he died. Inside, the clubhouse barely looks as if it has changed since the day that Fleming had his final lunch – it is as if time has stood still. If you play golf, and can obtain a letter of introduction, you can arrange to play here on certain days; it's worth doing so in order to be able to enter the clubhouse and enjoy an authentic 007 experience. Go to the bar and order a martini – shaken, not stirred.

From Sandwich, it was on through Dover and Folkestone and down to Lydd. In the book (and the film), Bond follows Goldfinger to the airport on Romney Marsh. It was from here in the 1950s and early 1960s that Silver City ran its air ferry service to Le Touquet. I remember coming here in the early sixties as a young boy, watching with delight as the ungainly planes lumbered in and out of the airport on their regular 20-minute runs to Le Touquet. Now the airport (bearing a sign that grandly claims it to be 'London Ashford' airport) is as quiet as a graveyard. I could almost feel the ghosts of the past crowding its now-empty departure lounge. Diana Dors, Dirk Bogarde, Sir John Mills and Lady Docker, with her famous gold-plated Daimler, were all regular users of the air ferry service. Sir Winston Churchill is said to have sent his limousine ahead via the Le Touquet run, the boot full of paints and easels, in readiness for his annual holidays in the South of France. All who used it claim that Silver City represented the high point of cross-Channel travel.

Now, of course, the Channel Tunnel has swept all before it, revolutionising not only travel to Paris, but travel from the Kent coast to London. In Fleming's day, he could probably have beaten the slowcoach South-Eastern railways train to London in his Bentley. Nowadays, thanks to the Channel high speed line to St Pancras, trains can make the journey to London in 54 minutes. Which was where I was about to head for next.

6

London

In which our hero goes back to school with P G Wodehouse, please sir has some more Dickens, is enchanted by Peter Pan, is disappointed by Poets' Corner and has a moment of Zen in Hampstead.

JOHN Ruskin was a Victorian genius: a leading art critic, art patron, key social thinker and famous philanthropist. But, like many people labelled 'genius', he seems to have found everyday life a bit challenging. He agreed to marry famous beauty Effie Gray but clearly wasn't keen on the basic concept of marriage, particularly not the most intimate part of a relationship. The main problem – well, one of the main problems – as far as Effie was concerned was that Ruskin loved his mum and dad with a devotion unusual in a 29-year old, and he loved living in their house in Denmark Hill. As soon as Effie discovered that Ruskin's family home was south of the river – that place to which no London black cab driver will want to take you – maybe alarm bells should have been ringing.

The problem of going to and from Kent by road is that I had to pass through south London and its endless traffic jams that reduced my progress to a crawl through the *terra incognita* of New Cross, Peckham and Camberwell. To someone largely familiar with north London, south London is an incoherent tangle of anonymous back streets and insignificant villages. But no, genius has flourished on these unregarded byways.

Dulwich College, for example, a public school some 15 minutes by train from Victoria Station – and within brisk walking distance of Denmark Hill – has memorials which honour two famous old boys, both of whom have become internationally famous writers (both can seen by prior arrangement with the school): Chandler and Wodehouse.

Novelist and screenwriter Raymond Chandler is author of the Philip Marlowe hardboiled private eye novels (Marlowe is one of the House names at Dulwich College). In 1988, the centenary of Chandler's birth, the school honoured the writer with an exhibition; in 2009, the 50th anniversary of his death, the school renamed the lower school library as the Raymond Chandler Library.

The school has a much more lavish tribute to P G Wodehouse, who attended Dulwich College from 1894 to 1900, a period which the writer described as 'six years of unbroken bliss'. It seems that Wodehouse was a model pupil and top of the class in Classics, hence the many classical references in his writing. He was a good singer and performed in school shows, served as editor of the school magazine, *The Alleynian*, and turned out for both the 1st XV rugby and 1st XI cricket teams. During his final term at school, he wrote an essay called 'Some Aspects of Game Captaincy' which was published in the *Public School Magazine*, and for which he received the princely sum of half a guinea. The Wodehouse writing business was up and running.

Wodehouse is best known for the character Jeeves, inimitable valet to Bertie Wooster; Jeeves made a very brief appearance in a short story in 1917, before becoming a star in his own right in a series of short stories first published in 1919; he continued to appear in Wodehouse's fiction for nearly sixty years.

Wodehouse's literary output was surprisingly broad; by the time of his death aged 93 in 1975 he had written 43 novels, 10 books for boys, 300 short stories and was author or part-author of 16 plays and 23 musical comedies (his first love was musical comedies – he was a self-confessed stage door Johnnie). The college library, which bears his name, (fortunate, with two writers to honour, that Dulwich College has two libraries with which to do so) has a permanent Wodehouse display of his desk and memorabilia, and also possesses a collection of his books, letters and manuscripts.

Just as it is surprising that Mark Twain had no time for Jane Austen, it is also slightly shocking to learn that the prolific Wodehouse had an active dislike of the equally abundant Charles Dickens.

'Do you hate Dickens's stuff?' Wodehouse once wrote in a letter to Denis Mackail, a longtime friend. 'I can't read it.'[19] (Evelyn Waugh, meanwhile, said that Bertie Wooster and his valet, Jeeves, inhabited 'a world as timeless as that of *A Midsummer Night's Dream* and *Alice in Wonderland*'[20]). There is a sort of strange other-worldliness about Wodehouse's rarefied diet of butlers, stately homes, manicured lawns, top hats and monocles. The world that Dickens described is also to some extent an invented sphere which tends to focus on hard childhoods, cruel parents and grasping capitalists – with a huge dose of general good humour in the face of terrible adversity. Given Wodehouse's preference for a somewhat sanitised presentation of the world, Dickens' depiction must all have seemed a bit too much like real life.

To understand Dickens, you need to explore the world that he knew in London. Charles Dickens is probably the writer most closely identified with London; he grew up, lived and worked in the city. It was in London that he quickly found huge, international success. His novels are mostly about the city and what were then its villages: Southwark, for example, the home of the Marshalsea debtors' gaol, where Dickens' father was once incarcerated – a major location in *Little Dorrit* – or Highgate, the home of Steerforth in *David Copperfield,* or Camden Town, the home of the Cratchit family in *A Christmas Carol* and the Micawbers in *David Copperfield*, and also the home of the Dickens family when he was growing up.

Dickens lived in several places in London. It is, however, his house at 48 Doughty Street where he resided from 1837 until 1839 – the terraced Georgian dwelling Dickens described as 'my house in town' – that has become the Dickens Museum in London. Fortunately, when it was threatened with demolition in 1923, the Dickens Fellowship acquired it and opened the museum in 1925. It is certainly a key attraction for all lovers and students of Dickens. I would have to say, however, that it is quite a 'cold' place. One less-than-enchanted visitor posted an online review describing the Dickens museum as 'a house with stuff in it'. This is true, of course, of many 'museums' dedicated to famous figures, but clearly I am not alone in occasionally wishing for something more.

On one recent visit, I encountered paparazzi armed with small ladders, long lenses and hunted expressions lurking near the entrance to the Dickens Museum. It was not Dickens that had brought them here, but Amal Alamuddin, the then soon-to-be-wife of actor George Clooney, who was working as a human rights lawyer for Doughty Street Chambers a couple of doors along from the museum. Dickens, who was fascinated by the law and passionate about defending the downtrodden, had a special fondness both for acting and attractive young ladies – he would have enjoyed the opportunity to doorstep George Clooney's lawyer fiancée. Dickens, after all, was first and foremost a reporter: he began his writing career as a freelance court reporter, and went on to cover Parliamentary debates before quickly becoming a magazine editor, as well as setting up and helping to set up several successful magazines in which he published his novels as monthly serials.

By the time that Dickens moved to Doughty Street with his family in March 1837, he was already well on his way to unparalleled international success. It was here that he wrote *Oliver Twist,* and it was here that his 17-year-old sister-in-law Mary Hogarth died in his arms – a traumatic event for the writer. Given the huge popularity he enjoyed in his lifetime, I was surprised to discover that the Charles Dickens Museum has been in existence here since just 1925. The property has recently undergone an extensive £3 million refurbishment, but in my opinion it still lacks the interest and excitement of other writers' houses: the Hardy houses, for example, or Jane Austen's Chawton home. It is probably more of a place that recreates the look of a house at the time Dickens lived there rather than trying to offer an in-depth look at Dickens' career as a writer or examining his work campaigning for social reform. It would probably be best to visit during an 'event' – such as Christmas, when people dress in Victorian outfits and provide more of a Dickensian atmosphere.

If you want to see the world of Dickens' novels, the best place to go, in my opinion, is to the streets of the city that he was so passionate about. Within 20 years of the publication of Charles Dickens' second novel *Oliver Twist*, London council archives show that people had already identified the fictional home of Bill Sikes on the notorious Jacob's Island, located near Shad Thames in a place 'used by thieves of the area'. Within a decade, books were published to help tourists discover 'Dickens' London'. Dickens had written *Oliver Twist* with the serious intention of highlighting the plight of orphans and the way they were being sucked into criminality. Readers, however, were as interested in seeing the place on London Bridge steps where Nancy betrayed Bill Sikes.

Charles Dickens himself was something of a 'dark tourist'. Not far from London Bridge, he attended the public execution of Marie and Frederick Manning, at Horsemonger Lane Gaol, on November 13, 1849. (The prison, the largest in the country, was closed in 1878 – part of the prison site was turned into Newington Gardens.) Dickens joined some 50,000 people gathered outside the prison; many had been happy to stay up all night to be sure of the best spots for this special occasion: the first husband and wife to be executed for more than 150 years. Like other better-off sightseers, Dickens had taken the trouble to rent rooms to guarantee that he would enjoy a grandstand view.

He was obviously intrigued by Marie Manning: she provided the inspiration for the sinister French ladies' maid Hortense in *Bleak House*. But even though he had a fondness for the macabre, Dickens was appalled by the atrocious behaviour of the mob who attended the hanging, writing in a scathing letter to the Editor of *The Times* that same day that the crowd, which included many children, displayed:

> every variety of offensive and foul behaviour...
> inexpressibly odious in their brutal mirth or callousness
> that a man had cause to feel ashamed.

There was a football-crowd feel to the occasion: as they waited, people amused themselves by singing 'Oh Susannah', substituting the words: 'Oh Mrs Manning, don't you cry for me.' Those with money eagerly bought the printed sheets which told the gory story of the murder for which the Mannings faced execution.

The hanging, when it finally took place, was judged to be something of a disappointment, as Mrs Manning was allowed to keep her head and face covered to the last. Dickens' letter to *The Times* condemning the behaviour of the mob that day marked the first steps towards the ending of public executions in Britain, which were finally stopped 19 years later (the last man to be hanged in public, in May 1868, was Michael Barrett – no relation to me).

After the success of Lionel Bart's *Oliver!,* Dickens was increasingly seen in the late-20th century less as a sharp social commentator and campaigner and more as the creator of colourful characters, a bastion of Old England. How much is left of Dickens' London? When I gazed over the skyline bristling with new shiny towers, it was easy to suppose that the Victorian city which Dickens endlessly prowled had been swept away by the rising tide of Starbucks and Sainsbury's Locals. While the Square Mile of the City, however, has many big new buildings, a surprising number of old, small ones remain. With a Dickens book in my hand, it wasn't hard to follow the action in the places that the author described.

If Scrooge were to return today to his old office on Cornhill in the City of London, he might find that an Abokado shop occupies the ground floor.

How can we know where Scrooge actually did business? At first glance *A Christmas Carol* seems vague about the exact setting. In fact, Dickens sprinkles enough clues through the story to allow us to identify several locations. For example, we are told that Scrooge's counting house was on a court in the vicinity of Cornhill (after the office closes, Bob Cratchit merrily goes down a frozen slide on Cornhill 20 times 'in honour of its being Christmas Eve'). Opposite the counting house, writes Dickens, was 'the ancient tower of a church, whose gruff old bell was always peeping slyly down at Scrooge out of a gothic window in the wall'. Opposite the ancient tower of the Church of St Michael's on Cornhill is Newman's Court – this, it seems, is the possible site of Scrooge's office. It's a very Dickensian place. Standing in it, it was very easy to imagine a foggy Christmas Eve afternoon with 'candles flaring in the windows of the neighbouring offices, like ruddy smears upon the palpable brown air'.

Out in the street beyond, 'the brightness of the shops, where holly sprigs and berries crackled in the lamp-heat of the windows, made pale faces ruddy as they passed'. A few minutes' walk down Cornhill 'the Lord Mayor, in the stronghold of the mighty Mansion House, gave orders to his 50 cooks and butlers to keep Christmas as a Lord Mayor's household should...'

Scrooge, however, didn't keep Christmas at all. While Bob Cratchit raced home to his family in Camden Town, Scrooge took 'his melancholy dinner in his usual melancholy tavern'. Behind St Michael's Church, down St Michael's Alley, stands the Jamaica Wine House, built on the site of Pasqua Rosee's, which opened in 1652 as London's first coffee house. Nearby is Simpson's – the oldest chophouse in London established in 1757, whose address is, curiously, 38½ Cornhill. Could this have been Scrooge's melancholy tavern?

My own choice, around the corner from the Jamaica Wine House, would be the George & Vulture, which is where Mr Pickwick lodged in Dickens' first major book, *Pickwick Papers* – and where Dickens himself had stayed. The building that you see today is just a small part of the original coaching inn, but retains much of the atmosphere of former times. Upstairs is what is reckoned to be the room where Dickens slept when he stayed here – take that with a large pinch of salt – but the winding stairs up to it are very Scrooge-like. I wouldn't have been surprised to meet the old miser coming down them, 'bah, humbugging' as he went. Serving City workers, the George & Vulture is open only at lunchtimes from Monday to Friday, and I timed my visit to take a meal here; I bet even Scrooge would have had the pork chop. (Another London pub with a strong Dickens association, for the interested, is the similarly named George Inn in Southwark. On the wall of its downstairs restaurant, next to the fireplace, is Charles Dickens' life insurance policy – he was insured with Sun Life for the princely sum of £1,000.)

As I sat in the congenial atmosphere, it was a good opportunity to flick through the pages of *A Christmas Carol* and reflect on the extraordinary effect this small book had on the world – an impact probably greater than anything else Dickens wrote. 'I have endeavoured in this ghostly little book to raise the ghost of an idea,' wrote Dickens modestly in the preface. 'May it haunt their house pleasantly and no one wish to lay it.' Its story of a mean old man who discovers the pleasure of giving has become as much a part of Christmas festivities as crackers and streamers.

Dickens' story is so powerful that it successfully defies all adaptations and, in the century and a half since it was written, it has become almost as familiar as the tale of the Nativity. In fact, many argue that this book 'invented' the way we have come to celebrate Christmas. Dickens gave us what we now know as 'the Christmas spirit' and, shortly afterwards, Prince Albert married Queen Victoria and is popularly credited with bringing the Christmas tree with him from Germany. British shopkeepers have given thanks ever since.

If Dickens' story moves our emotions today, it is, perhaps, because Dickens felt so strongly about the story it told. In writing it, he is said to have wept over it, 'laughed, and then wept again'. As the story took shape in his mind, he tramped alone through London's streets at night, covering as much as 15 miles at a time. The story harks back to the troubled times of Dickens' own childhood. The poverty-stricken Cratchit family in a small terrace house in Camden Town bear a striking resemblance to Dickens' family, who also lived in Camden Town when Dickens was a young man. Dickens' mother and father had a child known not as 'Tiny Tim' but 'Tiny Fred'. And Dickens' sister Fanny had a son, Henry, who was crippled from birth.

Despite his popular success, however, at the time he came to write *A Christmas Carol* in 1843 at the age of 31, Dickens was very hard up. He hurried to complete the book in just six weeks so he could have it published in time for Christmas (Dickens couldn't be faulted for his marketing acumen). He made lavish plans to publish it in a handsome cover with gilt-edged pages and full-colour etchings – and all at the relatively modest price of five shillings. But while the story sold well – it was the best-selling book of the Christmas period – Dickens, unhappily, saw little profit. As was all too common at the time, a 'pirated' edition was published. Dickens sued for breach of copyright and won. But the pirate publishers and printers declared themselves bankrupt, leaving him with a bill for £700. As a result, his hoped-for profit of £1,000 turned out to be nearer £130. Dickens immediately feared that he – as had his father – might end up in the debtors' prison. 'I shall be ruined past all mortal hope of redemption,' he wrote mournfully.

It was a brief setback. As we all know, he went on to produce his greatest works. Towards the end of his life, he earned more money – and became probably more famous – for the public readings of his books, particularly the ever-popular *A Christmas Carol*.

After my meal at the George & Vulture, I wandered back up the alley to Cornhill and walked west for a few minutes down to the Royal Exchange, where the Last of the Spirits led Scrooge:

> ...amongst the merchants, who hurried up and down, and chinked the money in their pockets, and conversed in groups, and looked at their watches, and trifled thoughtfully with their great gold seals and so forth, as Scrooge had seen them often.

It was here that Scrooge heard his fellow merchants discussing his death in a cold, off-hand way. Across the road from the handsome Exchange building stands the Mansion House where, according to Dickens, the Lord Mayor 'gave orders to his 50 cooks'. The Lord Mayor still lives here but, presumably, he has to make do with a smaller kitchen staff now.

Heading back up Cornhill to Leadenhall, I turned off to the right to Leadenhall Market. After his visit from the last spirit, Scrooge found himself back in his bed on Christmas morning with a chance to make a fresh start. One of the first things he did was to instruct a passing boy to go to the poulterer's 'in the next street but one'. The boy was to buy the 'prize turkey' – which Scrooge would send to Bob Cratchit's house. The turkey would almost certainly have been bought at Leadenhall Market, which Dickens knew well. Once at the centre of the Roman Forum, the market now sits in the shadow of the extraordinary Lloyd's building, one of London's most famous pieces of modern architecture. Leadenhall is a handsome covered market with attractive cream and maroon cast-ironwork. In *Nicholas Nickleby,* Dickens wrote that there was no point in living in the country when you could get newly laid eggs each morning at Leadenhall – in Dickens' time, Leadenhall Market would probably have boasted several poulterers.

Today, for those of a carnivorous persuasion, just one purveyor remains: A Butcher. The Butcher family has sold turkeys in the market for most of this century. On my visit, above the sawdust-strewn floor of the shop hung a rail heaving with plucked turkeys, their heads discreetly bagged.

It's not far from Leadenhall Market to Fleet Street – I headed for St Paul's Cathedral, then strolled down to Ludgate Hill. When I first worked on Fleet Street, all the major national newspapers were clustered around here. At lunchtime the pubs and wine bars would be full of journalists and newspaper production staff who still created pages from hot metal type. Though now just a few decades ago, with the switch to digital production which began in the mid-1980s, the world of Fleet Street seems positively medieval.

In a hard-to-find square, a couple of minutes walk up an alley from Fleet Street stands a house which belonged to one of the most revered names in the history of English writing. Samuel Johnson was a lexiocographer, essayist, poet, moralist, literary critic, biographer and editor. In the century before Dickens' success, Dr Johnson had dominated the London literary scene. The 19th-century world of London, as presented by Dickens and the Dickens Museum, is largely a grim picture of grime, deprivation and misery. Even the pleasure of being one of the 'haves' was mitigated by the dangers of being cheek-by-jowl with the legions of 'have nots': spreaders of disease and potential snatchers of your valuables.

In Johnson's time, London seems to have been an altogether more agreeable place – if you had money, of course. The affluent Georgians had more than a whiff of Bertie Wooster and the Drones Club about them. I read in the museum an account by the French writer La Rochefoucauld, who discovered that:

> the conduct of an Englishman's day in London leaves little time for work. He gets up at ten or eleven and has breakfast (always with tea). He then makes a tour of the town for about four hours until five o'clock, which is the dinner hour; at nine o'clock in the evening he meets his friends in a tavern or club and there the night is passed in play and drink.[21]

That seems like a reasonable daily plan to me.

In his 1791 biography, *The Life of Samuel Johnson LL.D.*, his friend James Boswell wrote that he generally visited him at midday and reported that he 'frequently found him in bed' and the Great Man spent his day pretty much as La Rochefecauld reported.

Born in 1709 in Lichfield, Staffordshire, Samuel Johnson was the son of a bookseller; after attending the local grammar schools in Lichfield and nearby Stourbridge he went on to Pembroke College, Oxford, but was forced to leave after 13 months because his parents could no longer afford the fees. After a marriage and a failed effort to set up a school in Edial, near Rochford, he walked to London and worked as a writer and journalist (just like Dickens). In March 2009, to mark the 300th anniversary of Dr Johnson's birth, two men dressed in 18th-century costume made a re-enactment of Samuel Johnson's walk, taking 11 days to complete the journey from Lichfield to London, The walk was largely completed using canal paths (suddenly, it almost feels like my own literary pilgrimage isn't trying quite hard enough…).

Dr Johnson's big opportunity came in 1746, when he was commissioned to write his famous dictionary. The house where he was living when he worked on the dictionary, in Gough Square, a short walk from Fleet Street, has been preserved as a museum devoted to the life and works of Dr Johnson.

It's something of a miracle that the house has survived at all – it certainly needed divine providence to survive the London Blitz, somehow remaining standing despite being struck several times, including necessitating the replacement of the roof. The fact that such strenuous efforts have been made to preserve the property is a testimony to the love and regard in which Johnson was held by his contemporaries and the recognition by later generations of writers who appreciated his work both as a compiler of his famous dictionary and as a patron of the arts.

Johnson seems to have been something of an enigma: kind and generous, but also prone to terrible fits of rage. One imagines that compiling his dictionary of over 40,000 words almost single-handedly (he hired six assistants, who would copy out Johnson's definitions onto slips of paper and file them), a task conducted seven days a week for just over eight years in the house's attic, would have taken a mental toll on anybody.

The house offers a remarkable picture of an extraordinary man – it deserves to be much better known.

✳

From Fleet Street I headed on to the Strand and took the Number Nine bus, described as not only Britain's oldest bus route, but also the 'very best and least expensive tour of London'. Its route runs between Hammersmith and the Aldwych travelling via Hyde Park, Hyde Park Corner, Green Park, Trafalgar Square, the National Gallery and the Strand. Getting off at Kensington Palace, I was in the part of London most closely associated with *Peter Pan* creator J M Barrie. I wandered down the very road and stood outside the very house where 100 years ago Peter Pan first flew into the nursery of the Darling family.

But Peter Pan didn't exist, you cry. You probably don't believe in fairies either (no, don't say it out loud!). Yet behind this evergreen children's fictional favourite, there is a surprising degree of fact. The true story behind J M Barrie's tale of the boy who didn't grow up, first performed as a play at the Duke of York's Theatre in London on December 27, 1904 (Daphne du Maurier's father Gerald played the role of Captain Hook), is stranger and, perhaps, more poignant than the fiction.

Painfully shy and married to a woman with whom it is doubted that he ever had what is coyly described as a 'full' relationship – their marriage was childless – Barrie found pleasure in friendship with other people's children. He was barely 5 feet tall, and, with his large walrus moustache, must have cut a curious figure – he also usually wore a bowler hat and very large overcoat. Children, however, warmed to him almost immediately. Margaret Henley was one of the first children with whom he struck up a friendship; she referred to the writer as 'my friendy' which, in her childish lisp, emerged as 'my fwendy'. Margaret died when she was only five and, no doubt as a tribute to her, when Barrie needed a name for his *Peter Pan* heroine he called her Wendy – he is sometimes credited with inventing it as a Christian name.

If you're visiting London, you can track down many notable Pan places with the aid of a street guide. Start at 133 Gloucester Road, a short walk south from Gloucester Road tube station. It was here in this solid Victorian residence that J M Barrie was living in 1897 with his wife Mary and a large St Bernard dog, Porthos. Although just 37, Scottish-born Barrie had established himself as a significant figure in London's literary scene, a playwright with a reputation both in Britain and America. But no one could then have guessed the extraordinary success that would soon make him a household name around the world.

Standing outside 133 Gloucester Road, I imagined the small figure of Barrie and his larger-than-life dog embarking on their regular expedition northwards to Kensington Gardens and the Round Pond. One day in 1897 this was a stroll that would lead to a literary landmark.

It was around the Round Pond, with its crush of nurses with perambulators and their infant charges, that Barrie first encountered a five-year-old boy called George, his brother Jack and their baby brother Peter. On his regular strolls around Kensington Gardens, the boys fell in with Barrie who enthralled them with stirring tales of fairies, pirates, hangings and desert islands. Barrie was entranced by George. When, shortly afterwards, completely by chance, he found himself at a dinner seated next to the boys' mother, Sylvia Llewelyn Davies, the wife of Arthur, a young barrister, he was equally taken with her, describing her as 'the most beautiful creature I had ever seen'.

(Sylvia, incidentally, was the sister of actor Gerald du Maurier – it's astonishing how closely Britain's literary circles entwined on occasion.) In 1897, the Llewelyn Davies family, which grew to number five children – all boys, George, Jack, Peter, Michael and Nico – had moved to 31 Kensington Park Gardens in Notting Hill. And it was here that Barrie became an increasingly frequent visitor.

The Davies family was subtly remoulded in fiction by Barrie as the Darlings, but the house at 31 is clearly the one that Barrie describes as the home of the Darling family. The first time that I walked up Kensington Park Gardens, one of the most prosperous areas of West London with solidly built rows of four- and five-storey houses that sell for £8 million, I was astonished to discover that *Peter Pan*, a book that seems so much of a fantasy, actually has a basis in solid fact. Just a stone's throw from Portobello Road and Ladbroke Grove, here was the start of one of children's fiction's most amazing adventures. I stood once more outside Number 31 and, with a growing sense of awe, reflected that this was the place Barrie had in mind when he wrote his story. Was it there, at that upstairs window, that Peter Pan might have had his shadow bitten off by Nana the dog? Was it from this same window that Peter, Wendy, John and Michael departed on their flight to Neverland? Do you believe in fairies?

Within a few years of *Peter Pan*'s debut performance, the Davies family was struck by tragedy. Arthur, the father, died in 1907; Sylvia died three years later, leaving Barrie as the boys' official guardian. George, who had so captivated Barrie, was killed fighting in the First World War in 1915, and Michael was drowned a few years later in a boating accident whilst at university at Oxford. Peter Llewelyn Davies did grow up, unlike his literary namesake, but hated his constant link to the *Peter Pan* legend. In 1960, aged 63, he threw himself under a train.

But for now I was determined to forget the troubles that were to come and travel back to the turn of the century to take the walk that the Davies children, in the company of their nurse, must have taken regularly to Kensington Gardens. The Notting Hill/North Kensington area that I passed through is a solid, patrician part of London, fascinating for its grand houses, but rarely visited by tourists. When I reached Kensington Gardens I made for the top end of the Long Water, where the *Peter Pan* statue is to be found. Barrie himself commissioned and paid for this and instructed that it should be erected in secret on the night of April 30 1912. He was keen for children to think that it had turned up almost by magic. (While the children were no doubt excited, apparently Members of Parliament were less pleased. Questions were asked in the House: was it right for author to get such a huge plug for his works in a royal park?)

For his part, it seems that Barrie was a little disappointed with the statue, noting that 'it doesn't show the devil in Peter'. He had asked for it to be modelled on Michael Llewelyn Davies and had taken photographs of Michael appropriately attired; however, the sculptor, Sir George Frampton, used another model instead. The statue of Peter Pan shows a drippy youth more like *Just William*'s Violet Elizabeth than someone heroically prepared to tackle Captain Hook in armed combat.

To complete the *Peter Pan* trail I headed to Great Ormond Street Hospital, which is situated near Russell Square. After being approached by the hospital's board for a donation in 1929, Barrie decided to grant the hospital the benefits of *Peter Pan*'s copyright. This should have expired in 1987, 50 years after Barrie's death, but changes were made to the Copyright Act so that the hospital can benefit from *Peter Pan* in perpetuity. A condition of Barrie's gift to the hospital was that the actual amount of money generated should never be made public; the hospital will only say that it is the single most generous gift it has ever been given.

By special arrangement with the hospital's archivist you can visit the Peter Pan Gallery and look at the hospital's collection of *Peter Pan* memorabilia. In the gallery I was allowed to hold a letter in J M Barrie's own cramped, almost indecipherable handwriting in which he responds to the invitation to contribute to hospital funds. And, suddenly, *Peter Pan* ceased to be a remote work of fiction. Barrie's story, which began as something dreamed up to amuse some children on an afternoon's walk, had become a gift of good health to succeeding generations. The very best sort of fairy tale.

※

Sherlock Holmes? 'There are people out there who think he's a real person,' said Alex Werner, the lead curator of a Museum of London exhibition about the great detective staged in 2014. The exhibition, inspired by the success of the BBC's updated version of the Conan Doyle stories, starring Benedict Cumberbatch and Martin Freeman, allowed visitors to look at Sherlock Holmes in the context of late-Victorian London when the city was arguably not just capital of the UK, but – at the height of the British Empire – it was the centre of the world.

Museums rarely devote major exhibitions to fictional characters, but then, Sherlock Holmes, as Mr Werner pointed out, seems real. But what is the detective's allure that a museum devoted to him – situated at '221B Baker Street' – has been a roaring success since it opened in 1990?

When dreaming up a new tourist attraction, one imagines that there is one piece of long-standing advice which any aspiring entrepreneur should heed: nobody ever went broke underestimating the taste of the public; a corollary to this is Barnum's famous jibe: 'There's a sucker born every minute'.

Barnum knew that people wanted cheap entertainment – something fun and frivolous. Madame Tussauds has ploughed such a furrow and made a fortune. Just around the corner from Tussauds in Baker Street, there has long clearly been an opportunity for someone to exploit the Sherlock Holmes connection (and having a ready supply of pre- or post-Tussauds visitors on tap is not to be sneezed at).

In the Conan Doyle books, the great detective lived at 221B Baker Street – an invented address, as at the time he wrote the books the house numbers didn't go up this high. When the street was renumbered, the address fell into the ambit of the Abbey National Building Society, which occupied a big office block covering a string of 'odd' street numbers which included 221. The Abbey National took upon itself the task of answering letters sent to Sherlock Holmes at 221B Baker Street – so many letters, in fact, that they gave somebody the full-time job of dealing with the correspondence. (Who was sending letters to Sherlock Holmes, one wonders; what the hell were they writing to him about?)

This happy state of affairs for the Abbey National was threatened in 1990 when the new Sherlock Holmes museum took over a house at 239 Baker Street and decided to rename it 221B, a unilateral act of street-numbering independence that somehow won the support of Westminster Council (Lady Porter – leader of the council at the time – gave the museum her seal of approval by performing the opening ceremony). The Post Office then began delivering Sherlock Holmes' mail here and outraged the Abbey National; the matter went uncontested after 2005 when the Abbey National moved out of the handsome art deco building.

The Holmes museum consists, in truth, of very little: a four-storey building remodelled to resemble the house as it would have looked at the time of Holmes' sleuthing. Of course, when Holmes was supposedly living here, there wasn't, as there is now, a shop which takes up the whole of the ground floor selling deerstalkers, pipe racks and other assorted Holmesiana (but no seven per cent cocaine solution, I couldn't help noticing) – even the remarkably tolerant Mrs Hudson of the stories would surely have taken exception to this.

Upstairs, the rooms are furnished, we are assured, in authentic period style: here is Dr Watson's room, for example – there is the famous sitting room overlooking Baker Street. There are displays which reference episodes from the books and display cases with ho-hum information. It seems incredible that, at busy times, people queue more than two hours along Baker Street for the privilege of paying £10 to see a house near the fictional place where an invented detective is supposed to have lived. But perhaps I'm just a spoilsport.

The Sherlock Holmes Museum was monitored, exclusively it seemed to me, by student-age Scottish girls who stood at various points in the building, presumably to make sure that nobody wandered off with a deerstalker or a lifesized wax model of a murderer. In peak times, these minders (dressed as Victorian servants) have to try to manage the crowds who throng the narrow staircases connecting the tiny overfurnished rooms.

Who are these people ready to queue so long for so little? One of the minders told me that the Japanese are keen Holmes fans, it seems, followed by the Chinese, French and Spanish. Why do they come? 'I think most people really do believe that Sherlock Holmes was a real person – they think they're coming to see where he used to live.'

If you're looking for a Sherlock Holmes experience which comes free of charge, head down to Trafalgar Square and find the Sherlock Holmes pub in Northumberland Street. This is thought to have been the Northumberland Hotel which briefly appears in *The Hound of the Baskervilles*. The pub has an interesting assortment of Holmes memorabilia, a collection that was originally assembled for a display in Baker Street during the 1951 Festival of Britain. There is more here for Holmes fans than you can see in Baker Street.

I headed in an easterly direction again, via St Pancras, King's Cross and the British Library, beloved of researchers and writers alike, and arrived in the vicinity of Finsbury. One of the best little literary landmark places in London is here, the Islington Local History Centre in St John Street. Perhaps the most significant moment in the life of playwright Joe Orton was when, together with his lover Kenneth Halliwell, he was sent to prison for theft and malicious damage to more than 70 library books. Many of these books were borrowed from the lovely central Islington library in Holloway Road, which I knew well in the 1970s when I lived in Finsbury Park. Together, Orton and Halliwell 'doctored' books by adding new photos and often hilarious cover 'blurbs'. They claimed it was an act of protest about the fact that the library had so many 'rubbishy books'. In truth, the two men had too much time on their hands and enjoyed producing 'guerilla artwork' (the sort of thing that Terry Gilliam would do a few years later to great acclaim in *Monty Python*).

Islington Council was not impressed and prosecuted the couple, who were found guilty and were each sent to prison for six months. There was a suspicion that the severity of the sentence had more to with the fact that Orton and Halliwell were gay – which was against the law at the time. Halliwell found prison so humiliating he tried to commit suicide. For Orton, however, the experience was a liberating experience as far as his writing was concerned. After prison, he enjoyed a stellar rise as a playwright – it was a short blooming success, as five years after their release from prison, Orton was bludgeoned to death by Halliwell, who had been increasingly uneasy about his partner's success. After murdering Orton, Halliwell took his own life.

It is curious irony that, having once happily sent Orton to prison, Islington Council is now capitalising on the event at its local history centre. You can see some of the actual defaced books on display in the museum; you can ask a member of staff to see copies of all the defaced books at the centre. I spent a very jolly half-hour here.

※

J M Barrie was one of the main advocates who pressed for Thomas Hardy to be buried in Westminster Abbey's Poets' Corner after his death in 1928. The fact that a campaign had to be mounted for Hardy, one of the most highly regarded poets of the 20th century, indicates the slightly arbitrary selection process involved in achieving entry into this particular corner of the Kingdom of God (though, given that Hardy was an atheist, his likely interest in achieving such an entry must be considered slim, at best).

To get into Westminster Abbey to visit Poets' Corner involves an admission fee. I was slightly dumbfounded to discover that at the time I visited this was £20 – not much less than it costs to get into Madame Tussauds. Many British cathedrals have a 'recommended donation' in lieu of a straightforward admission charge; Salisbury Cathedral, for example, suggests £6.50. Nobody is suggesting any donation at Westminster Abbey: you pay or you don't get in. At the front entrance you can claim free entry on religious grounds but, frankly, I waited here for a little while and didn't observe anybody with the nerve to attempt this (besides, this would only give you very limited entry to the Abbey – not to Poets' Corner).

The man in front of me in the queue requested the discounted rate for over-60s. 'Identification!' snapped the ticket seller, as if she were an East German guard who had caught somebody loitering with intent near the Berlin Wall. Once inside the Abbey, I asked an official-looking person where to find Poets' Corner. The official looking person was not pleased:

'How did you get in here?' he demanded, *a propos* of nothing at all. I got in here, I said, by virtue of having forked out £20 – was there a problem?

'I thought you were in a group,' he replied mysteriously.

'I'm just me,' I said, adding: '…and I'm still looking for Poets' Corner…'

He continued to be unconvinced of my *bona fides.* 'Haven't you got the audio guide? You should have picked one up as you came in.'

'I didn't,' I said, 'because I really just wanted to see Poets' Corner.'

'Head through there and ask somebody in brown,' he snapped, still annoyed.

If Westminster Abbey wants to insist on people paying £20 for admission – and if I were them, I would seriously revisit this decision – then they need to be sure they're offering an experience which in some way exceeds visitors' expectations. There is certainly plenty of British history: here's Henry V's tomb, this is where Oliver Cromwell is buried – all stirring stuff for history lovers. Poets' Corner, however, is strangely eclectic: D H Lawrence gets a prominent mention but, try as I might, I couldn't spot the miniscule tribute to Shelley; Oscar Wilde – 'my favourite writer,' I heard one of the guides say – gets a bit of stained glass to himself. What would Wilde think about this? I imagine he's spinning in his tomb at Père Lachaise cemetery in Paris where he's buried. Charles Dickens, like Hardy, is buried here against his wishes. The family of impoverished playwright Ben Jonson couldn't afford a full grave, and so he was buried standing up, as it were, in order to save space; he was also accommodated in a less desirable part of the nave. His thigh bones twice came to light by accident in the 19th century – not quite the eternal repose he was probably expecting.

A lot of the people memorialised in Westminster Abbey aren't actually buried here – so in some ways this has became a Pantheon where the great and the good can be honoured. Except that most of the tombs and memorials that I looked at in other parts of the Abbey are for people I've never heard of. For centuries, it seems, the main requisite when it came to getting a tomb in Westminster Abbey was that you should be able to pay handsomely for the privilege – there is little equality in life, you could argue, so why should there be in death?

Looking at more recent additions to Poets' Corner – Dylan Thomas was inaugurated in 1982, for example – you can't help wondering who decides that they are worthy of the tribute? Is there a vote? Ted Hughes is here, but not Seamus Heaney; journalist David Frost has a memorial, but not George Orwell. Why? Getting into Poets' Corner has much to do with prevailing fashion and managerial tastes – much as it is at Madame Tussauds'. But with Tussauds, at least the out-of-fashion waxworks can be melted down and turned into someone else; in Poets' Corner, the floor has been cluttered up with names famous, infamous and extraordinarily obscure.

※

One writer who escaped the great Westminster body grab was Thomas Carlyle, whose wishes to be buried in his native Scotland were, ultimately, honoured – despite the offer of a place within the Abbey. Carlyle's House in Chelsea – his former home with his wife, Jane – sits in one of the sweetest parts of London.

These days, we see Chelsea through a Swinging London prism of dolly birds on the Kings Road and a *Blow-Up* world of louche photographers, pop stars and fashion. Yet, when the humble Carlyles came down to the Great Wen from Scotland in 1834, Chelsea was little more than a village near the Thames and was London a fast-growing dark mass on the horizon. Chelsea rents were cheap, so it was attractive to artists and writers: here potters potted, painters painted and writers wrote.

The Carlyles were a famous husband-and-wife partnership, with a reputation for not getting on (their house in Cheyne Row, wrote Virginia Woolf, was 'not so much a dwelling place as a battlefield'). She herself had high praise for the house, which has been open to the public since 1895, saying that an hour spent here 'will tell us more about them than we can learn from all the biographies'.[22]

Writer Samuel Butler made a famous wisecrack about the Carlyles, saying that it was 'very good of God to let Carlyle and Mrs Carlyle marry one another, and so make only two people miserable instead of four'.[23] Actually, while their marriage may have had some stormy moments, their extensive writings reveal a surprisingly strong bond of love and understanding.

We probably know more about the Carlyles than almost any other literary couple because Jane Carlyle, like her husband, was a tireless correspondent: you can read all of their wonderful letters online via the Carlyle's House National Trust website. Because the Carlyles became part of London's literary elite, they knew – and were good friends – with most of the stellar writers of the age.

This is Jane, for example, on a Christmas party in 1843, at which Charles Dickens did a turn as a conjuror 'for one whole hour...the best conjuror I ever saw (and I have paid to see several!)'. According to Jane, Dickens produced a plum pudding made out of raw flour and eggs 'boiled in a gentleman's hat' and turned a box full of bran into a box full of 'a live guinea pig!'

The special joy of Carlyle's House is that each of its rooms has retained not only their original look but also the spirit of the times when the Carlyles were here. The kitchen, for example, has a bed where the servant lived (much of Jane's correspondence is devoted to apparently never-ending servant problems). The garden – I could see a photo of Carlyle taking his ease here – is a delight, as is the top-floor attic study, which he had soundproofed when the cacophony of outside noise – particularly Italian organ grinders – began to get him down. Up in the attic I could also see one of the most famous charred manuscript fragments in literary history.

Carlyle was greatly in awe of philosopher John Stuart Mill, who had agreed to look at a handwritten copy of volume one of Carlyle's history of the French Revolution, which had taken five arduous months to produce. An ashen-faced Mill arrived on Carlyle's doorstep in March 1835 and had the awful task of revealing that the only copy of the book had been accidentally used by a servant to light a fire. All that Mill had to show were a few charred pages pulled from the blaze. (In recent times, theories have been advanced which suggest foul play: Mill was contemplating his own French Revolution tome so may not have been quite so disappointed to see Carlyle's literary endeavours going up in flames.) To Mill's credit, however, he was well-aware of the Carlyle's parlous financial state, so he readily offered compensation. 'Adversity is the diamond dust that heaven polishes its jewels with,' said Carlyle later.

Initially, Carlyle asked only for more paper so he could begin again, but was eventually persuaded to accept £100. Tackling volume one all over again immediately was too big a challenge; he wrote volumes two and three, before undertaking the miserable task of rewriting the lost manuscript. While it seems that Mill was less than impressed by Carlyle's book, he offered further compensation by praising it to the skies, an act which effectively guaranteed Carlyle's literary success. Dickens used Carlyle's history when he wrote *A Tale of Two Cities*.

Another fan of Carlyle's work was Oscar Wilde, who was just one of a long list of literary greats who visited the Sage of Chelsea at Cheyne Row. 'How great he was!' said Wilde, 'He made history a song for the first time in our language.'[24] When he was in Reading Gaol in 1896, Wilde wrote to the Home Secretary complaining about the prison library: among the works which he asked the library to acquire were Tennyson's poems, Keats' poems, Chaucer's poems, Christopher Marlowe's works, Ranke's *History of the Popes*, Dante's *Divine Comedy*, and Carlyle's *Sartor Resartus* and *Life of Frederick the Great*.

Walking around the Carlyle House, there were several information boards which almost apologetically made the point that Thomas Carlyle's work is largely unknown today. It shouldn't be – visit this excellent property and acquaint yourself with the writer, his world and his books.

By some strange chance, the only text of this book that my computer lost (my fault and not my iMac's) was this section on Carlyle – fortunately I was able to rewrite it from memory. Not so fortunate was T E Lawrence – Lawrence of Arabia – who left the manuscript of *Seven Pillars of Wisdom* in the cafe at Reading Station – when he arrived in Oxford he called the station, but the case, and the manuscript in it, had been taken (the published book is, apparently, an earlier inferior version).

Lost and accidentally destroyed manuscripts are a recurring theme in literature: Dylan Thomas lost the manuscript of *Under Milk Wood* no fewer than three times; the third time he lost it – no surprise perhaps – in a pub. Luckily, it was found by a friend.

※

If London had its own version of Parisian artists' colony Montmartre, it must be Hampstead and Highgate, which, until more recently, when it became the favourite destination of the mega-wealthy, was the louche bohemian hang-out of the capital. This corner of London has attracted everyone from artist Walter Sickert to Amy Winehouse via Dylan Thomas and W B Yeats. In the seventies, I worked on electoral registration for Hampstead and found myself knocking on doors answered by well-known faces like Alan Ayckbourn, Bill Oddie, Terry Gilliam and Melvyn Bragg.

Another famous resident here was Keats, whose old home in Hampstead is one of the few museums in London to be devoted to a poet.

The reason why I like the poetry of John Keats so much is probably because I never had to study it at either school or university. I'd studied the Romantic Poets, though, and so knew in general terms about Keats' short tragic life – dead of TB at the age of 25, before which time he had managed to train as an apothecary and surgeon, as well as finding a degree of celebrity as a poet. By the time Keats was my age now, he'd been dead 35 years.

One year, we were required to take our daughter to the Hay-on-Wye Literary Festival to see Toni Morrison, whose book she was studying at school. To have something to listen to during the long drive home, from one of the Hay bookstalls I bought a CD of poetry performed by Simon Russell Beale and Anton Lesser. This included several Keats poems, including 'Ode to a Nightingale' and 'Ode to a Grecian Urn' – these poems resonated in a way which others hadn't. Most affecting was a subsequent visit to the Keats–Shelley Memorial House on Rome's Spanish Steps, where Keats died in 1821 – his bedroom is kept as it was when he died. In Rome's protestant cemetery – effectively a large refuge for feral cats – you can see where Keats is buried, with the inscription on his tomb 'Here lies One Whose Name was Writ in Water'.

Last summer I saw that, one evening in June, Simon Russell Beale and Dame Eileen Atkins would be performing Keats poetry at a special event at Keats House as part of the annual Keats festival. In the event, Eileen Atkins wasn't able to attend; she was replaced by Dame Janet Suzman (a reasonable substitute in the circumstances). It was a magical evening, listening to poems such as 'Ode to a Nightingale' in the very place where Keats had heard the nightingale in 1819 and wrote about it:

> *My heart aches, and a drowsy numbness pains*
> *My sense, as though of hemlock I had drunk...*

My one regret was that I wasn't able to get to the London house early enough that day to visit the Keats Museum itself. By the time that I did, the nights were drawing in: rainy and dark. From the outside the museum seemed warm and welcoming – this was misleading. Once inside, the house was full of cacophonous sound: it was 'Family Day: Witches and Wizards', which, for some reason, involved a small group of musicians playing snatches from *Peter and the Wolf*. There wasn't much of a welcome from the person at the ticket desk.

'No discount for journalists,' she announced, rather pleased, after studying some literature behind the desk.

'Can I take a photograph of the shop?' I asked.

'No', she said, 'No photographs anywhere.'

Actually all the places I'd visited up to this point, were happy with photographs, though many asked that flashes not be used (this is, indeed, the position that the Keats House website takes as well, though its staff appear to disagree). For some reason, Keats House was at the forefront of the Writers' Museum Awkward Squad.

There were further disappointments. It would have taken the City of London Corporation, the managers of the property, just a brief excursion to discover what other similar museums in the

UK were doing to make them more interesting and accessible. Either the Corporation couldn't be bothered or didn't care – either way, the house was sadly lacklustre, offering no significant explanation of either the life of Keats or the context and history to his poetry. Given that it was in this very house where he wrote his greatest work, and where he conducted his courtship of Fanny Brawne, they had extraordinary material to work with. Sadly, it seems, the only effort seems to be in running Family Days and other events covering subjects wholly irrelevant to the life and works of Keats. The Keats Museum could be a Ferrari of literary attractions; instead, it had the feel of an old Ford Escort misfiring and underperforming.

※

Just around the corner from Keats House in Willow Road is a place, now a National Trust property, that had an unlikely impact on modern fiction. Shortly before the Second World War, Hungarian-born architect Erno Goldfinger acquired a terrace of run-down workers cottages in Hampstead's Willow Road, in a spot directly facing the Heath. A plan to demolish the cottages and build a block of flats – Goldfinger was a great believer in tower blocks (his most famous creation was Trellick Tower in West London) – was rejected by the council. He subsequently reapplied for permission to build a small terrace of ultra-modern houses, a scheme which, unsurprisingly perhaps, became the focus of a local protest campaign.

One of those who supported the protest group was young journalist called Ian Fleming. It is easy to see why Fleming was keen to preserve Hampstead's special ambience (more recently, the community famously fought a 12-year battle to keep McDonalds out of the high street). The area has been a favourite haunt of writers including Dickens, William Blake, Gerard Manley Hopkins, Auden, Orwell, Waugh, Eliot, Lawrence,

R L Stevenson, H G Wells, Goldsmith, Galsworthy, Priestley, A A Milne, Amis, Katherine Mansfield, Aldous Huxley, Agatha Christie, Stella Gibbons and Margaret Drabble. It's a place of a fine architecture, good pubs, excellent restaurants – and with the Heath, the best views and walks in London.

Such was Fleming's dislike for the Hungarian architect, that when he wrote a novel about a criminal mastermind's plan to steal the US Government's gold reserves at Fort Knox for the Soviet Union, giving him the name 'Goldfinger' was not only appropriate, but it also offered the perfect revenge for 'the spoiling' of Willow Road. Goldfinger in real life was not amused; he threatened to sue the publisher, though in the event settled out of court in return for a prominent warning in the book that 'all characters are fictitious'. As if anybody might have thought that Goldfinger the architect was a part-time criminal Mr Big.

The comedian Peter Cook once lived at 17 Church Row, which had also been the residence of H G Wells. The house had been bought at the beginning of Cook's climb to stratospheric success – this is where he did much of his writing with Dudley Moore and where he entertained the likes of John Lennon (it is claimed that Lennon wrote 'Lucy in the Sky with Diamonds' for Cook's first wife, Wendy). Two of Cook's other collaborators from *Beyond the Fringe* – Jonathan Miller and Alan Bennett – lived practically opposite each other for many years in Gloucester Crescent near Camden Town. It was in Alan Bennett's garden that Miss Mary Shepherd, *The Lady In The Van,* star of book, stage and screen, arrived with her van and stayed for 15 years. As I was standing looking at the spot where *The Lady in the Van* parked her van, a man came out of the house behind me and shuffled across the road. It was Dr Jonathan Miller: a moment of Zen.

7

Stoke Poges to Stratford

In which our literary traveller leaves London, rifles through Eton, enjoys a giant peach of a children's museum, Pepys at Cambridge and learns how to be or not to be a Shakespearean tourist.

18TH-CENTURY writer Thomas Gray enjoyed his time at Eton College so much, that he wrote a poem about it: 'Ode on a Distant Prospect of Eton College', which famously ends with the observation 'where ignorance is bliss, 'Tis folly to be wise'. The message is that grown-up life is generally pretty ghastly so it's best that youngsters remain in blissful ignorance of this awful fact.

Except that, for many who have passed through its hallowed halls of learning, Eton was definitely no paradise. Famous ex-alumnus George Orwell looked back on his schooldays with a shudder; in one of his essays he reflects on when he was a pupil and had to inhale the stench of:

> sweaty stockings, dirty towels, faecal smells blowing along corridors, forks with old food between the prongs, neck-of-mutton stew, and the banging doors

of the lavatories and the echoing chamber-pots in the dormitories.[25]

The best days of your life, eh?

While Eton has been the *alma mater* of several prime ministers, it has also educated many leading writers which, in addition to Orwell and Thomas Gray, include Shelley, Aldous Huxley, Ian Fleming, Henry Fielding and Cyril Connolly. Eton College runs public tours if you would like to see what £12,000 per term buys you in public school education (potential entrants are no longer registered at birth, you might be relieved to hear).

It was in a place very close to Eton that Gray was inspired to write his most famous verse. The opening lines of Thomas Gray's 'Elegy in a country churchyard' summon up the very essence of rural life:

> *The curfew tolls the knell of parting day,*
> *The lowing herd wind slowly o'er the lea,*
> *The ploughman homeward plods his weary way,*
> *And leaves the world to darkness and to me...*

It is thought that the poem, published in 1751, was inspired by a visit to the churchyard of St Giles Church in Stoke Poges. When Gray began the poem during a visit to his aunt, just after his friend Richard West had died, Stoke Poges really was, as Gray described in his Elegy, 'Far from the madding crowd's ignoble strife' – a line later borrowed by Thomas Hardy for the title of his novel (another line, 'The paths of glory lead but to the grave', was used for Stanley Kubrick's First World War film *Paths of Glory*). The church happily remains in a rural oasis, but Stoke Poges, three miles from Eton, is really now just a London suburb, with the ever-present sound of aircraft taking off and landing nearby at Heathrow. In the field next to the church is a Thomas

Gray monument built by James Wyatt in 1799, following instructions from the then-owner of Stoke Park, John Penn, grandson of William Penn, the founder of Pennsylvania. The monument is a large stone pedestal topped by a stone sarcophagus that has panels which display verses from Gray's 'Elegy'.

※

It was a 45-minute drive from Eton to Great Missenden through Berkshire/Buckinghamshire border country. Along the way, I passed a stretch of the Thames near Cookham believed to have helped inspire Kenneth Grahame to write *The Wind in the Willows*. Further north, meanwhile, lay the wooded hills that provided the setting for novels by Roald Dahl such as *Danny the Champion of the World* and *Fantastic Mr Fox*.

A 2008 survey for the Costa Book Awards claimed that the best-loved writer in the UK was Enid Blyton, followed by Roald Dahl – both were placed ahead of Shakespeare, Jane Austen and Charles Dickens. How much weight I place on this, I'm not sure; these type of articles are two-a-penny these days; such is the frequency of 'surveys' carried out every day by some hopeful PR company keen to grab a few column inches of publicity for their client. The poll might easily have been undertaken among Man Utd fans on behalf of Rawlplugs and would be worth all that this would suggest as sober literary criticism.

It's debatable about exactly where they stand in national popularity, but it's undeniable that popular writers such as Blyton and Dahl deserve their museums as much as the likes of Shakespeare and Jane Austen. I'm not sure whether anyone would contemplate an Enid Blyton museum but, since 2005, Roald Dahl has had his own museum in Great Missenden, the charming Buckinghamshire town where he lived for much of his life. The town also provided the settings for many of his books, which he wrote in the writing hut in the garden of his house; the hut has been carefully transported to the museum. His daily writing process is explained – on video – by the writer himself.

The museum, however, poses more questions about the writer and his life than it is prepared to answer.

When I was a child, on my daily Number 49 bus ride to school we had a Red and White bus conductor, whose uniform was covered in 'Golly' golliwog badges. We schoolchildren considered this odd, simply because it seemed strange that a grown woman had chosen to cover herself in bits of metal usually collected by eight year olds.

'Golly', introduced in the 1920s, was the symbol of Robertson's marmalade – children collected the marmalade pot tokens in order to obtain the Golly badges. Golliwogs were not frowned upon at that time for what they were – nobody had been worried that the Red and White Bus Company was employing racists. People in our part of the world had no idea that golliwogs were a mocking caricature of black people, just as it never really occurred to me that it was very wrong for the popular sixties TV programme *The Black and White Minstrel Show* to feature white people pretending to be black people singing songs about riverboats on the Mississippi. (What seemed odd to me about this BBC programme was that, while the men all wore blackface makeup, the women, if memory serves right, were white and danced in what seemed to be one-piece bathing costumes, top hats and high heels.)

Despite the fact that there were no black people where I lived in the Wye Valley, I should really have been more racially aware; there were lots of black singers, for example, on the radio and a growing number of black actors, particularly in US TV and cinema. South Africa's apartheid policy was in the news, as were the racist reasons that Rhodesia had declared unilateral independence. Yet nobody thought it reprehensible, for example, that at that time Laurence Olivier had 'blacked up' to play Othello.

But you could argue that writers, especially children's writers, had a particular duty to avoid anything that hinted at racism. Blyton, it has to be said, was well past the stage of hinting. One imagines that when Enid Blyton featured a trio of golliwogs (Golly, Woggy, and Nigger) from Golly Town – and when she wrote a story which involved a golliwog effectively carjacking Noddy – she was old enough and wise enough to know she was doing a great wrong.

Yet it took until 1978 for the BBC to junk its Minstrel show, while Robertsons clung on to its offensive symbol until 2001. In recent years, Blyton has been subject to a huge re-editing process designed to make her books – including the Famous Five and Secret Seven – fit for the 21st century; to some resistance, it must be said, as this has predominantly included modernising the language. Nobody would contemplate re-editing *The Railway Children*, complained one high profile Blyton fan; the simple answer to this is that Edith Nesbit wasn't a bigot.

I have never been terribly fond of Roald Dahl and his works, not just because he too has long been accused of racism – and misogyny – but because I always found his writing annoyingly stilted and unnecessarily unpleasant and occasionally vicious.

People who write largely for children tend not to have a good record on the level-headed and likeability front. Even his most enthusiastic fans would have to admit that Hans Christian Andersen wasn't somebody you would care to spend much time with; as we have already seen, when he imposed himself on Dickens, a few days after his huge family moved into Gad's Hill, the Danish author succeeded in driving Dickens round the bend. *The Wind in the Willows* author Kenneth Grahame was an unhappy man; *Peter Pan* creator J M Barrie had his demons; *Alice in Wonderland* author Lewis Carroll's obsession with young girls has inevitably been the subject of some discussion. However, for some writers – to reverse the Shakespeare line – the evil lies interred with heir bones, while the good lives after them. Poet Ted Hughes, for example, survived what can at best be described as a calamitous private life to emerge fully rehabilitated with a memorial in Westminster Abbey's Poets' Corner.

For his part, Roald Dahl is portrayed in The Roald Dahl Museum and Story Centre in Great Missenden as a lovable old man full of jolly tales and wonderful wheezes. Dahl and his wife, actress Patricia Neal, suffered some terrible luck – their daughter Olivia died of measles, their baby son Theo was hit in his pram by a New York taxi and suffered appalling brain damage, and Patricia, aged just 39, suffered three debilitating strokes.

Whether Dahl's writing became as vicious as it did because of his troubles, it is impossible to say. According to Jeremy Treglown's 1994 unauthorised biography, as he grew older, visits to literary events made Dahl increasingly cantankerous, and interviewers were not permitted to disagree with his views. He also seems to have grown envious of the success of other writers in London's literary circles, such as Salman Rushdie, and gone out of his way to pick fights – once telling the Indian-born author how much he admired Enoch Powell and his views on immigration, and writing to *The Times* when Rushdie was receiving death threats to argue that writers should censor themselves – 'an odd line to be taken by the inventor of the Oompa-Loompas.'[26]

As far as the museum is concerned, it would not be a disservice to his memory to recollect some of the less happy episodes of his chequered career – the times when his behaviour was less than exemplary. *Charlie and the Chocolate Factory,* for example, came in for accusations of casual racism involving the Oompa-Loompas who, in the first edition of the book, were 3,000 black pygmies brought by Mr Willy Wonka from what used to be referred to in unenlightened times as 'darkest Africa': after strong protests the Oompa-Loompas were hastily revised, becoming hippie-ish dwarves with long brown hair and 'rosy-white' skin (the 1971 film adaptation, *Willy Wonka and the Chocolate Factory*, got around this altogether by painting its Oompa-Loompas orange). But neither this nor any of the other controversy which was stirred up by other Dahl works, such as charges of misogyny in *The Witches* or *Matilda* (positive portrayals of women in Dahl are, it must be said, few and far between), is touched on in the Roald Dahl Museum.

This is a shame, because the Dahl museum is actually presented in a very intelligent, straightforward manner – one of the most effective of its sort that I visited in the course of my travels. As a day out for children who like Roald Dahl, it is unbeatable. There are few attractions of this sort in the UK so well geared up to appeal to children and which seek to stimulate their imaginations. In every area of the museum, from the Twits cafe to the shop, and in each of the relatively small but information-packed rooms, everything was done with great wit and huge intelligence (everything, that is, except to offer some sort of critical counterpoint to the sunny view of Dahl). Despite my misgivings, I regret the fact that the museum doesn't seem terribly well visited – there are fewer online reviews available, for example, than you might expect for a museum devoted to such a popular best-selling writer, and a place which has had so much money spent on it. The reasons that attendance is disappointing probably lie in the fact that Great Missenden is relatively remote, car parking is some way removed from the museum and the admission price is quite expensive. Anyone, however, thinking of setting up a writer's museum would do well to come to Great Missenden to see what can be achieved.

Airbrushing out the awkward bits, though, should never be an option in any place of learning. Every writer's life probably has parts that they wish they could conveniently airbrush out: generally speaking, they're a conceited bunch who often do what they have to in order to get published and stay at the top. In this they're no different from any other branch of the entertainment business. We expect more from writers, however; the best writers can touch our soul and we would prefer that the people who have access to our deepest emotions also have the highest moral credentials.

Apart from the museum, there was much else for the Dahl enthusiast to enjoy in Great Missenden. It was the town's library, built in 1970, that Dahl imagined Matilda visiting while her mum went off to Aylesbury to play bingo. In the High Street almost opposite the museum, I looked out for the ancient petrol pumps which inspired the description of the garage in *Danny the Champion of the World*. Crown House at 70 High Street inspired Sophie's 'norphanage' in *The BFG*. Finally, I headed for the Church of St Peter and St Paul, and followed the BFG footprints from the memorial bench in the graveyard to visit Roald Dahl's grave.

※

Roald Dahl never went to university, despite doing relatively well at his public school, Repton – he went straight from school to a job.

A university education is by no means a stepping stone to success as a writer. Sir Tom Stoppard, for example, chose a job on the Bristol-based Western Daily Press in preference to university, though he says he later regretted the decision. Much of his 2006 play *Rock'n'Roll* is set at Cambridge University, involving one of Cambridge's most famous sons, Pink Floyd member Syd Barrett (no relation to me). The play looks at the effect of rock music in the Cold War, particularly in what was then Czechoslovakia, the country of Stoppard's birth.

You don't have to have been a Cambridge graduate, then, to be a great writer – though, in fact, an army of great writers were Cambridge graduates. When it comes to poets, the University of Cambridge can boast the big names: the roster includes Marlowe, Spenser, Milton, Wordsworth, Coleridge, Byron and Tennyson – other writers connected to the university include Robert Herrick, Laurence Sterne, E M Forster, Rupert Brooke, Charles Kingsley, Thomas Gray, Francis Bacon (often cited as the 'real' author of Shakespeare's plays), George Herbert, W M Thackeray and A E Housman. A more recent vintage of graduates includes Sylvia Plath, A S Byatt, Zadie Smith, Douglas Adams, Nick Hornby, Clive James, P D James, Ronald Searle and Tom Sharpe. Tom Sharpe was student at Pembroke College and, after graduating, lectured at the less eminent Cambridge College of Arts and Technology, from where he developed the story of Wilt, a man who has the wholly unrewarding task of teaching English literature to indifferent apprentice plasterers, joiners and butchers.

Perhaps the most intriguing name on the list of Cambridge authors, though, is Samuel Pepys.

I started keeping my first diary when I was ten years old. I had a Letts School-Boy's Diary, which I bought at what I seem to recall was the Daily Mail Boys' and Girls' Exhibition in Olympia – Letts put my monogrammed initials on the front cover of the diary as a special treat for buying the diary at the exhibition. I particularly remember the occasion because it was here that I had my photograph taken with Tony Hart when he signed his autograph and drew a picture of Bengo the Boxer Puppy. And it was here that I first saw a demonstration of colour television. Where we lived in the Wye Valley we could hardly get a black and white signal or any sort of ITV signal – the idea of colour or even multi-channel reception seemed preposterous.

I kept up the diary, but I keenly felt the lack of anything significant to write about. Most of my entries were of the nature: 'Went to school. Came home.' On one awful day I dropped the diary on the bus and an idiot of a boy sitting behind me read everything out to everyone's great amusement. A regular weekend entry was that my grandmother and grandfather 'came out' – that is, they came out to see us.

'They came out,' chortled the bully, 'What – were they in East Berlin?' Cue general mirth. I felt less inclined to keep a diary after this, but maintained a profound admiration for anybody who had the rigour to keep a diary up.

Samuel Pepys was 26 when he began his diary in 1660, a habit which he kept until 1669, when he abandoned the project for fear that the very act of writing it would permanently damage his eyesight. He lived for another 33 years with this anxiety about his eyes – though, despite some impaired vision, his sight never failed completely, so his anxiety may have been misplaced. When you see his original diaries in the wonderful Pepys Library at Cambridge's Magdalene College, however, and the tiny writing which he did nightly in very poor light, you can see why he was worried.

We should, nonetheless, be grateful that, even for just a relatively short time, he was able to offer such a vivid view of life in London during one of its most extraordinary decades. The year he began his diary marked the restoration of the monarchy with the return of King Charles II; later, Pepys would record the Great Plague of 1665 and, in the following year, the Great Fire of London.

But the real appeal of Pepys' diaries lies in the exhaustive detail of his everyday life – for example, his ardent desire for extra-marital sex (often described in cod Spanish, presumably in case his shorthand wasn't obscure enough to fool his poor long-suffering wife). As things turned out, he needn't have worried about his wife discovering his infidelities via his diary because she actually caught him in the act in their own bedroom (an event which Pepys then duly recounted in his diary) – a seismic shock from which the Pepys household seems to have never fully recovered.

One of the great thrills of visiting the wonderful Pepys Library, magnificently run by Dr Jane Hughes, a Fellow at Magdalene College, was the insight I got into Pepys' extraordinary life; it offered Pepys fans such as myself a chance to 'meet' my idol. The Pepys Library was established in Cambridge in 1724 after the death of Pepys' unmarried heir John Jackson. It would be another hundred years before his shorthand diaries were transcribed into English and selectively published (for the next hundred years, it was firmly believed that the more salacious sections of the diaries could never be published – the full version finally appeared in nine volumes from 1970–83). It seems certain that Pepys fully expected his diaries to be published because he took the trouble and expense to have them carefully bound, as well as including them in the library collection that he bequeathed to Magdalene College. He also wrote them, not in some hard-to-fathom cipher, as some people think, but in a standard form of shorthand. The Reverend John Smith laboured for three years struggling to work out Pepys' shorthand system; it was only later that it was discovered that, not only was there a published key to this Shelton shorthand system, but it was actually stored in Pepys' library, a few shelves above the bound diary volumes.

The library, housed in the New Building (known as the Pepys Building), accommodates the Pepys Library almost exactly as the diarist kept it during his lifetime. The large collection of books, which numbered more than 3,000 volumes of books, manuscripts and prints, together make up one of the most important 17th-century private libraries still in existence. In addition to the Pepys diaries manuscript, the library contains very early printed works by William Caxton, Wynkyn de Worde and Richard Pynson. In addition, it has Sir Francis Drake's personal nautical pocket almanac and over 1,800 printed ballads. The books are contained in the twelve oak bookcases – or 'presses' – that Pepys had specially built for them; according to the Fellow I spoke to, they are believed to be the first glass-fronted bookcases ever made. In his diaries, Pepys records that before the bookcases the volumes were 'lying one upon another on my chairs' – which meant that he had lost the use of his chairs.

The opening hours of the museum are a little eccentric – visits are generally allowed in the afternoons, but you should check well ahead if you are planning to take a look. If you know the diaries, a trip here will be like receiving a personal invitation from Pepys himself; if you don't know the diaries, a visit will be the perfect opportunity to find out more. And Pepys is being kept alive in a modern idiom: the Pepys blog posts a diary entry daily. It began in 2002, finished in mid-2012, and in 2013 began cycling through them again. Pepys also now has a Twitter account, meaning that, even from beyond the grave, his social media credentials are better than mine.

One of the great outings in Cambridge is to take a stroll or a punt along the Cam to Grantchester. Certain I would end up in the river if I tried punting, I opted for a stroll.

'Grantchester Meadows' was a track that Cambridge's Roger Waters included on the double LP *Ummagumma* – thought to be Cambridge slang for having sex, Grantchester Meadows was close to where fellow band-member David Gilmour lived at the time. Grantchester itself, however, is forever associated with a 1912 poem, 'The Old Vicarage, Grantchester', by Rupert Brooke which concludes:

> *...oh! yet*
> *Stands the Church clock at ten to three?*
> *And is there honey still for tea?*

When Rupert Brooke wrote this poem two years before the outbreak of the First World War, the hands of the Grantchester church clock were actually stuck at 3.30pm: not much use to him as a rhyme when in the next line he was serving up honey for tea. When the poem became famous during the Great War, chiming – as it were – with the homesickness of British forces for life at home, those responsible for the church clock are said to have shifted its hands to ten to three: life imitating art?

Time in other ways, however, hasn't been quite so kind to Brooke and Grantchester. During the First World War, the new breed of war poets typified by Siegfried Sassoon and Wilfred Owen made Brooke's cheery homilies to sacrifice seem rather naïve and slightly gullible. There was also trouble when the Government made it clear that they wanted Brooke's name on the local memorial, even though he wasn't actually from Grantchester, and even though he hadn't died in the battle at Gallipoli to which he had been sailing when he died from an infected mosquito bite that he'd suffered on the sea voyage.

An hour's drive north from Grantchester to the town of March led me through the flat Fenlands. This largely featureless reclaimed land – a touch of Holland – seems to have instilled a great sense of religious feeling in its inhabitants. This area became known as the English 'Holy Land' because of the opulence of the churches and cathedrals of Peterborough, Ely, Ramsey, Crowland and Thorney.

Even some of the lesser churches, such as St Wendreda's in the Cambridgeshire town of March, are awe-inspiring. St Wendreda's features in Dorothy L Sayers' 1934 novel *The Nine Tailors*. This tale of church bell-ringing and murder, which requires the detective skills of Lord Peter Wimsey, has the fictional setting of Fenchurch St Paul. The church in the novel, with its amazing roof, however, is clearly modelled on St

Wendreda's. Sayers writes:

> Incredibly aloof, flinging back the light in a dusky
> shimmer of bright hair and gilded outspread wings,
> soared the ranked angels, cherubin and seraphim, choir
> over choir from corbel and hammer-beam floating
> fade to face uplifted.[27]

Dorothy L Sayers knew both this church and her Bible well –
Wimsey's reaction upon seeing this sight is to quote from the
Book of Psalms – because she was the daughter of a vicar and
was brought up nearby, in Bluntisham. If you're visiting March
and wish to see the famous angels, the key is available from the
local pub from 12 o'clock onwards.

※

Britain's two great academic cities, Cambridge and Oxford, are
80 miles apart on a slow road that passes through Bedford and
Milton Keynes; a journey that I might have expected to take
little more than an hour by motorway ended up lasting more
than two hours (much of this spent negotiating what seem to
be about 300 roundabouts, which mark the periphery of
Milton Keynes).

Before Dorothy L Sayers' family moved east, they had lived
in Oxford. The family was living at the Head Master's House,
Christ Church Cathedral, Oxford when Sayers was born; her
father was employed in the Choir School as chaplain and
headmaster. Sayers subsequently studied at Oxford's Somerville
College; she graduated with honours but, at the time she
graduated, women could not be awarded a degree.

After graduating, one of her first jobs was working at the
famous Blackwell bookshop, where she was an assistant to Basil
Blackwell – the office where Sayers worked has been preserved

to look as it did when Blackwell died in 1984 (although it looks as though he made few alterations to the way it was in the early 20th century, when she was employed there).

A visit to the extraordinary bookshop was one of the many fascinating stops that I made on Blackwell's excellent literary walking tour of the city, which offered a fascinating glimpse at many hidden sights. Blackwell bookshop is an Aladdin's cave of treasures: I made sure to see the extraordinary basement Norrington room, a vast cavern of books. The tour took me past the places connected with everyone from C S Lewis and Lewis Carroll to Evelyn Waugh and T E Lawrence. Hertford College has the famous Bridge of Sighs linking two college buildings: I peeked inside the gateway to the college and spied the ground floor rooms that Waugh had stayed in – these were Charles Ryder's in *Brideshead Revisited*, where Sebastian Flyte is sick through Charles' open window.

Alice in Wonderland fans can also follow the route taken in 1862, when mathematics lecturer Charles Lutwidge Dodgson (who wrote as Lewis Carroll) embarked on a summer boat trip to Godstow with ten-year old Alice Liddell and her two sisters. On the boat trip up the Isis, Carroll entertained the girls with stories of Alice and her search for adventures. He later wrote up the stories and they became *Alice's Adventures in Wonderland*. Inside the Great Hall at Christ Church – used in the filming of *Harry Potter* – is a window dedicated to Lewis Carroll and his stories, with a portrait of Alice Liddell.

One of the most interesting literary stories about Oxford concerns *Lord of the Rings* and *The Hobbit* author J R R Tolkien. At the beginning of his career in 1919 and 1920, he was employed by the *Oxford English Dictionary*. He subsequently claimed that during this period he 'learned more in those two years than in any other equal period of my life'.[28] Tolkien's job was primarily to work on words near the beginning of the letter W: from 'waggle' to, appropriately enough perhaps, 'warlock'.

(It's also interesting to note that as a student, in 1911, Tolkien attended Oxford's Exeter College. He was followed there more than 50 years later by another future fantasy writer, Philip Pullman, who would go on to immortalise Exeter College as the fictitious Jordan College in the alternative Oxford of his 'His Dark Materials' trilogy – though, in Pullman's world, Jordan College is the oldest, largest and richest. He later wrote in the *Guardian* that 'the story is a fantasy; but perhaps a great deal of Oxford is imaginary anyway. In Oxford, likelihood evaporates.'[29] As I walked beneath those dreaming spires, whence so much of the fantastical has sprung, this seemed a plausible explanation indeed.)

The Blackwell tour also features one of the most interesting Shakespeare sites not in Stratford. Situated on Cornmarket Street, right in the heart of Oxford, above a shop and bookmaker's, lies one of Oxford's more secret historical treasures, the Painted Rooms – the remains of the 14th-century Crown Tavern with remarkable Elizabethan wall paintings. It is claimed that Shakespeare was acquainted with the vintners John and Jane Davenant, and he is thought to have stayed as their guest when he was travelling between London and Stratford-upon-Avon. According to some sources, Jane is the only person who was romantically linked to Shakespeare other than his wife Anne Hathaway. The Davenant's son, also William, who was Shakespeare's godson, became the first poet laureate; apparently, he was wont to let it be known that he was the son and not just godson to the Bard. This may be nothing more than hearsay, but what is true is that these fascinating Painted Rooms, the place 'where Shakespeare slept', remain hidden and usually inaccessible to the public.

※

It has been estimated that it would have taken Shakespeare around 13 hours to walk the 50 miles from Oxford to Stratford-upon-Avon: if this is true he was an extremely rapid walker in what were almost certainly testing walking conditions! Not many walk between London and Stratford these days – most seem to travel in groups in a continuous procession of tourist coaches. This has been a well-travelled literary pilgrimage route for more than 200 years.

Even as long ago as the 1930s, writers of a humorous bent could find much to laugh at in this mad tourist scramble. Richmal Crompton, author of the peerless *Just William* books, probably knew that bringing her hero into any sort of encounter with Shakespeare was likely to result in bedlam. In the short story 'William and the Lost Tourist', the guileless American tourist Sadie Burford, with William's encouragement, manages to mistake young William's village for the town of Shakespeare's birth. The ever-helpful William obliges by showing Sadie the thatched house of deaf old Mrs Maloney, claiming it to be Anne Hathaway's cottage.

In this parable of modern tourism, Miss Burford returns to her motor car where her father is waiting. 'Seen it?' asks her father laconically, 'Got it ticked off?'[30] They return home satisfied that they have properly 'done' England. And in 'William Holds the Stage', our hero locks horns at school with the appalling Mr Wellbecker (provider of the ill-fated Wellbecker Shakespeare Acting Shield). Verbal chaos ensues when Mr Wellbecker attempts to explain to William his theory that the works of Shakespeare were actually written by Bacon.

Is it possible to learn anything more substantial about Shakespeare by visiting Stratford-upon-Avon? Even in Richmal Crompton's day it seems that a trip to Anne Hathaway's Cottage had already become the ultimate tourist cliché.

Indeed, there is much that is crass about Stratford's relentless Shakespeare industry. Across the road from where I parked the car stood Iago Jewellers ('The Moor The Merrier!') (I made up that last bit – but the 'Iago Jewellers' is true). Iago was the villain in *Othello* – why would you name a jeweller after him? Perhaps the owner really is called 'Iago' and lives in Stratford-upon-Avon – what would be the chances of this?

In the Shakespeare Birthplace Trust souvenir shop, there is no sign of a 'Desdemona' working on the till, but there is plenty of tourist tat on the shelves. Postcards feature a white mouse dressed up in Elizabethan costume: it's unclear whether the mouse is pretending to be Shakespeare or Elizabeth I? It could be either. Why a mouse? Why a Shakespeare Birthplace Duck? I've no idea, but you can have one for £4.99. Too cheap? How about a William Shakespeare Anniversary fountain pen for £1,950: 'To celebrate the 450th anniversary of the poet's birth, the Shakespeare Birthplace Trust has commissioned an exclusive run of 450 beautifully crafted fountain pens...' And why not – how else would you celebrate such an important landmark but with a ridiculously expensive writing instrument? But among the Shakespeare Birthplace Advent Calendars and Shakespeare's First Folio tea towels ('100% cotton'), the shop offers lots of serious academic and historical books on Shakespeare.

Even the legendary American showman P T Barnum recognised the pulling power of Shakespeare. His plan to buy Shakespeare's birthplace, and to ship it to America stone by stone, persuaded Dickens and other writers to raise the £3,000 necessary to preserve the house for the nation.

⋙

It is said that, when John Lennon was told that a poll had named Ringo Starr 'The Best Drummer in the World', John wasn't impressed: 'Best in the world? Ringo's not even the best drummer in The Beatles.'

This remark occurred to me when I went to pay homage at the house where William Shakespeare was born – though, of course, like most things regarding Shakespeare, this comes with a 'probably' attached.

It's not hard to suspend disbelief, however: somebody had to have written the plays we attribute to Shakespeare, after all, and it may just as well be Shakespeare. The man, is after all, buried in Stratford's Holy Trinity Church (which has the nerve to charge visitors up to £2 a go for the privilege of looking at his grave – ecclesiastical daylight robbery).

Shakespeare's Birthplace, you might have thought, is arguably the most significant literary shrine anywhere – it must, in numerical terms at least, be one of the world's top tourist attractions. Not so. In terms of annual visitor numbers, Shakespeare's Birthplace attracts around 400,000 people, leaving it comfortably outside the Top 50 list of major UK sights compiled by the Association of Leading Visitor Attractions. According to one review website's ratings for Stratford, the Birthplace is ranked in 13th place, trailing behind the likes of the MAD Museum – an exhibition of kinetic art – and the Stratford-upon-Avon Canal.

Whether this tells us more about Shakespeare's Birthplace or the accuracy of online ranking algorithms remains to be seen – but, to take them as rote, Shakespeare's Birthplace would be not only not the most significant literary shrine in the world – it would not even be in the top ten tourist attractions in Stratford. Cost may have something to do with this: the most expensive pass, covering the five Stratford houses connected with Shakespeare, costs over £60 for a family – the cheapest family pass costs over £40. The real problem must be, however, that when people are looking for an outing, anything connected with Shakespeare must summon up too many unhappy memories of schoolwork to warrant blowing £50.

Outside the Birthplace House, I overheard an American mother hoping to convince her teenage daughter that they ought to 'do something Shakespeare-y', but her daughter doggedly refused to look up from her phone.

'You want to see a play, hon? You like the theatre, doncha?'

'What play?'

'Does it make a difference?'

'Not really,' said the girl: 'The plays are all *boring*.'

'Shall we go in here and see where he was born? It'll be fun – there are people in, like, costumes.'

'Jeez, no, ma – I told you already. I'm dying of boredom just standing here.'

'OK, hon – so really? That's a no?'

The problem that the Shakespeare Birthplace Trust faces is that the greatest writer of English literature is widely perceived to be boring. Had the daughter been persuaded to enter the Birthplace Trust, however, she would have discovered that strenuous efforts have been made to make the Bard more accessible. For example, the opening video presentation includes a fun clip with Homer Simpson as Macbeth:

> *To-morrow, and to-morrow, and to-morrow,*
> *Creeps in this petty pace from day to day,*
> *To the last syllable of recorded time;*
> *And all our yesterdays have lighted fools*
> *The way to dusty death.*

It's from an episode called 'Four Great Women and a Manicure', in which Homer is cast as a tree in a Springfield amateur production of *Macbeth*; Marge encourages Homer to murder Sideshow Mel so that he can take the leading role. The humour in this depends on a working knowledge of *Macbeth*'s plot – the makers of *The Simpsons* have a bit of a thing for Shakespeare, it seems.

If the Birthplace Trust has deftly managed to refine its presentation style in order to maximise appeal, it would only be fair to point out that it has had plenty of time to get its act together. Tourists have been coming to Stratford to pay homage to the Bard for around 250 years. Today, Stratford estimates that it welcomes more than five million visitors every year, generating nearly half a billion pounds in revenue. But there is still much to be done to make more people aware of who Shakespeare was and why it's worth visiting Startford to learn more about him. Out of 1,000 children aged 6–12 who were questioned, according to 2012 market research, nearly a third did not even know who the country's most famous playwright was. Of the 2,000 adults questioned in the study, 27% said they had never read a play by Shakespeare (which would suggest, alarmingly, that 27% of adults somehow never attended school...); around one in eight were unaware that he was a British playwright, and nearly half were unable to complete the world famous line: 'O Romeo, Romeo...' from *Romeo and Juliet*. In the 18–24 age range, 5% claimed to think that Shakespeare's most famous play was *Cinderella*, while 2% from the same age group thought the Bard was a fictional character.[31] There are lies, damned lies and consumer surveys, but you feel there is more than element of truth to this.

There are experts who believe that a visit to Stratford is the nearest thing to a pilgrimage that the secular world can enjoy in the 21st century – that it's a pilgrimage that every school in the UK should be organising for their pupils. Certainly, there is much to see, and a lot to learn, not just about Shakespeare, but also about British history. At Shakespeare's Birthplace – the house where the bard was born – visitors can explore the workshop of his father, the glove maker; there's even chance to make your own glove puppet inspired by some of Shakespeare's most famous characters. Also in Stratford are Hall's Croft, the home of Shakespeare's daughter Susanna; Anne Hathaway's Cottage ('air-brushed English rural charm,' complained one expert); Harvard House, one of Stratford-upon-Avon's most striking Elizabethan townhouses; and Mary Arden's Farm, the home of Shakespeare's mother.

Sir Walter Scott, a big Shakespeare fan, famously visited the room in the Birthplace House where Shakespeare was said to have been born. This was like The Beatles visiting Elvis Presley's Graceland. In his mind, Scott saw this visit as a coming together of two mighty literary beasts: the 'Wizard of the North' meets the Bard of Avon. How to mark this momentous event? Simple – like such distinguished graffiti artists before and after him as Charles Dickens, Mark Twain and Alfred, Lord Tennyson, Scott got out his penknife and carved his name on the room's windowsill.

8

Swansea to Shrewsbury

In which our literature lover bobs into Dylan country, discovers the Welsh valley village relocated to Malibu, reveals his own small place in literary tourism and goes walkabout with a Shropshire lad.

WALES is famously 'The Land of Song' rather than the 'The Land of Literature'. Its history is one of rousing nonconformist hymns and stirring male voice choirs; the list of musical greats is a long one: Tom Jones, Shirley Bassey, Bryn Terfel, The Stereophonics and, er, Shakin' Stevens...

In the field of writing, the Pantheon isn't exactly overcrowded: there's Dylan Thomas, Roald Dahl (he grew up in Cardiff), Kingsley Amis (who spent some time in Swansea), Ken Follett, Leslie Thomas, metaphysical poet George Herbert and the writers of *The Mabinogion*, the earliest prose literature of Britain.

If it's a relatively small list, though, one name at least is Very Big. Dylan Thomas, named by his parents after Dylan ail Don, a character in *The Mabinogion*, a writer whose fame has managed to increase every decade since his untimely death in 1953. His output was modest: some poems, some prose works and possibly the most famous radio play in broadcasting history: *Under Milk Wood*.

A prophet is not without honour, however, except in his own principality. When I was growing up in Wales in the 1960s, anyone who talked about 'Dylan' would naturally have been assumed to be talking about US singer Bob Dylan. Bob Dylan – born Robert Zimmerman – had been a fan of Dylan Thomas; when launching himself on a career in the folk music clubs of New York, Zimmerman decided to adopt the poet's first name as his surname; in America, he said: 'You call yourself what you want to call yourself. This is the land of the free.'

To those of us in 'the land of our fathers' this homage came as a big surprise. Dylan Thomas may have had a cult following in Bob Dylan's hometown Hibbing, Minnesota, but he wasn't particularly highly rated in my part of Wales. Sometime Welsh resident, poet Robert Graves, crisply summed up the tide of feeling of many locals when he described Dylan in his Oxford poetry lectures as 'a demagogic Welsh masturbator who failed to pay his bills'.[32] (Given that Robert Graves' own personal life may fairly be characterised as 'complicated', you might consider it a little rich for him to aim stones from his not-unblemished glasshouse – but such is literary life, it seems.)

This is probably hard for a modern generation to believe but, long before Cardiff became a hen party capital, Wales prized temperance, chastity and polite behaviour. Dylan was a very well brought up boy from a hardworking lower middle-class family; he seemed to consider it a smart career move as an aspiring man of literature to present himself as a roistering boy with a glass of whiskey in one hand and a smouldering cigarette in the other – not to mention a relaxed attitude to marital fidelity. It remains a subject of debate as to how much of the 'wild poet' thing was a carefully crafted image and how much was really him. But if Wales didn't like the way that Dylan Thomas turned out, Dylan Thomas for his part didn't seem to nurture much affection for Wales. 'Land of my fathers?' he wrote into the adapted screenplay for the 1948 British melodrama *The Three Weird Sisters*, 'My fathers can keep it!'

This wasn't quite true either; apart from brief sojourns in London and lucrative performance trips to the US, Dylan Thomas always returned to Wales, which was both his home and his main source of inspiration until his death in New York City in 1953, at the age of 39. In the 1960s, however, when Welsh Nationalism was gaining ground, Thomas – emphatically not a Welsh speaker – was not someone who was considered an appropriate literary figurehead for Plaid Cymru; for the newly minted Nationalists of the sixties, the Welsh language was everything. Dylan Thomas could have been their Poet of Wales, in the way that Robbie Burns was an inspiration for the Scottish National Party, or just as Yeats became a poster boy for Irish nationalists. Thomas, it seemed, had indeed become a prophet without honour in his own country. (I suspect that Thomas would probably have been delighted by this: Robert Pocock, who knew Thomas during his BBC years, has written 'I only once heard Dylan express an opinion on Welsh Nationalism. He used three words. Two of them were "Welsh Nationalism".')[33]

But, as he was the only significant Welsh literary figure widely known around the world, Wales had to learn to love Dylan Thomas. Richard Burton, another Welsh bad boy, but one who never fell from grace, had always been a tireless advocate; his part in the original BBC radio production of *Under Milk Wood* helped it to become one of the landmark performances in British arts in the second half of the 20th century. In 1982, Thomas was granted a place in Westminster Abbey's Poets' Corner – he lies somewhat uncomfortably between Lord Byron and George Eliot with a memorial that he himself would probably have found ridiculous. It probably took another 30 years until Wales found itself able fully to embrace its most famous poet with an energetic range of events arranged to mark the centenary of his birth in 2014.

Actually, it seems that the event to some extent only served to re-open old wounds and long-held grievances that had festered over the years. You didn't need to dig far below the surface to find the fault lines – on a trip to Swansea as the centenary festivities were moving into top gear, I met a lady in a pub near the newly relaunched Dylan Thomas Centre, the beneficiary of a £1 million grant from the National Lottery.

The lady in the pub hadn't yet had a chance to see the re-configured exhibition, but already she was annoyed: 'They've cut Swansea out of the story. I've heard that, according to the exhibition, he lived in Laugharne and then he went to New York and died – nothing about Swansea. It's a disgrace.'

But Swansea has another, much more interesting, attraction that puts the city at the top of the list of any Dylan Thomas trip to Wales.

To begin at the beginning, to borrow a line from Dylan Thomas, I needed to head for his Swansea birthplace, 5 Cwmdonkin Drive – an attractive, solidly built semi-detached house with a glorious view over Swansea's Mumbles coast. Here you can enjoy the ultimate Dylan Thomas experience: the chance to sleep in the poet's childhood bedroom. Thomas' bedroom, like the rest of the house, has been restored to look just as it did back in the 1930s. Step into the tiny room and you are enveloped in a jumble of books, confronted with an ashtray brimming with Woodbine fag ends and a mess of scrunched-up paper full of lines of hurriedly written poetry.

My friend Malcolm was keen to have the Dylan bedroom experience; I was less enthusiastic. Certainly, the property's owner, Geoff Haden, had performed miracles in restoring the house to its Thomas-era state. I confess, however, I found it a bit scary – like one of those haunted houses where you pay to walk around in the dark and somebody jumps out on you dressed as the killer from *Psycho*. I have a fragile sleep pattern, and find it difficult to nod off even if I'm in the lap of luxury of the Presidential suite at the Beverly Wilshire; trying to bed down for the night in a place that that was more a museum than a hotel was above and beyond the call of duty. As darkness fell, I made my excuses and fled to the Swansea Premier Inn (good value at £45 for the night) and left Malcolm to commune with the spirit of Dylan Thomas.

I returned next morning, worried that a ghostly encounter might have turned his hair white. As it turned out, Malcolm did not go gentle into that good night either: the smell of old Woodbines and the authentic whiff of thirties dust had triggered his occasional asthma. Dylan had suffered for his art; now it seemed it was Malcolm's turn. He rallied a little after breakfast in the Thomas kitchen; I recited a few lines from *Under Milk Wood*, and we left.

It's hard to think of him as a sports person, but one of Thomas' favourite Swansea locations was the St Helen's cricket ground, where the poet joyfully met up with his close friend, cricket commentator John Arlott – 'the voice of summer' - and where the two unlikely chums whiled away many summer afternoons watching Glamorgan.

Before leaving Mumbles, there was time to enjoy Cwmdonkin Park and to take a short stroll to 24 The Grove, home of Kingsley Amis in the 1950s at the time he was finishing *Lucky Jim*. You probably won't be surprised to learn that Amis was an implacable foe of Thomas' work, which he parodies in his novel *That Uncertain Feeling*. It's a shame that Thomas and Amis never came face to face in Cwmdonkin Park – that's a literary death match you could have sold tickets for.

It was an 80-minute drive from Swansea to the Boathouse at Laugharne, the house that has become most firmly associated with Dylan Thomas – this is where he lived when he worked in his famous writing shed for the last four years of his life. It must have been freezing in here for much of the year, but he had the compensation of peace, quiet and one of the loveliest views in Wales.

From the Boathouse, I stood on the terrace and gazed towards the Gower, an area full of happy youthful memories for Dylan. It's not just poetry lovers who come here; Laugharne attracts wildlife lovers as it boasts a native population of birds that includes lapwings, herons, egrets and oystercatchers – you can also sometimes see otters and seals. I spotted only a phalanx of boisterous French sixth form boys and girls, who had found a sheltered oasis in the woods to smoke, drink cans of beer, snog and swear ('*Maurice – putain!*'). Dylan would have been delighted.

If Dylan Thomas put Laugharne on the map, then Laugharne is helping to keep him there. There are few literary landmark pleasures to compare with sitting out on the Boathouse terrace on a sunny day with a mug of strong tea (they sell replica Dylan Thomas mugs in the shop – I now have my morning coffee in one) and a slice of *bara brith* currant loaf. The Boathouse is a friendly, efficiently managed place with plenty to see and enjoy, and intelligent presentations about Thomas' life and poetry. Not too much effort has been spent restoring the place to how it must have looked. There is a furnished front parlour; more interesting is the upstairs exhibition area with a film telling the story of Thomas' life in Laugharne. Spare time, too, to visit the famous Writing Shed.

Also impressive was Brown's Hotel, where Dylan would have been found propping up the bar while he was in residence at the Boathouse. I doubt whether Dylan would recognise the old bar these days, as Brown's has been spruced up to pristine boutique hotel status.

Before leaving, I went to pay my respects at Thomas' grave. After Dylan died in New York at the age of 39, his body was brought back to Laugharne, where he was buried in the cemetery of St Martin's. When his wife Caitlin died 41 years later she was buried with Dylan as she had requested. The French kids were here now.

'Where is Dee-lan, please – you know, sir?' I pointed the way. 'Thank you, sir! Thank you very much.'

They giggled, but they had put out their cigarettes; this was their mark of respect.

There is a dispute about which Welsh place was the inspiration for *Under Milk Wood*: the two contenders, both areas where he lived, are Laugharne and New Quay.

In September 1944, Dylan Thomas and his wife Caitlin moved to New Quay, taking a bungalow called Majoda – Thomas referred to it unpoetically as the 'shack at the end of a cliff'. His stay, as far as poetry was concerned, was fruitful. While at the house he wrote several poems, including 'Fern Hill', which he began at Majoda and completed the following summer. He was also inspired to write the radio piece *Quite Early One Morning*, an early prototype of his later play *Under Milk Wood*. The Welsh writer's life at their clifftop home at New Quay wasn't quite *Under Milk Wood* – the New Quay adventure turned into something more 'Dai Hard' when the Thomas' home, which overlooked Cardigan Bay, came under attack from an angry husband with a machine gun. One night in March 1945, William Killick, who had recently returned from active service in the Second World War, was sufficiently exercised by reports of his wife's infidelity with Dylan Thomas to set about wreaking revenge. After the pubs had closed (not an especially late hour in Wales at this time!), Thomas returned to the bungalow for a drinking session with his chums. William Killick approached the bungalow window and loosed off a clip from his Sten gun. He then fired off another for good measure before shouting a threat to toss in a hand grenade. History's other great versifying lothario, Lord Byron, must have gazed from the heavens open mouthed in admiration.

※

The song 'We'll keep a welcome' is one of those that you might imagine is as old as the welcoming hillsides themselves. In fact, it wasn't written until the Second World War, the lyrics composed by Mai Jones, a stationmaster's daughter from Newport. But by the 1950s it was already clear that the best days of the Welsh Valleys were fast running out. The glorious picture of hard-pressed mining communities striding purposely to a sun-filled future with a rousing song in their hearts was already beginning to look like a faded dream. But then *How Green Was My Valley* – from which this 'marching to work singing' image was a *leitmotif* – was only ever really a fantasy.

If you were wondering where Yoda from *Star Wars* learned to speak English, it was probably in the mining valleys of South Wales. Here, according to *How Green Was My Valley* at least, most people had an annoying habit of back-talking. 'Oh, there is sorry I am', 'a girl from the pits she was', 'watching the mountain, I was'. If the dialogue sounds odd, the whole of the book has a bit of an otherworldly feel to it.

The 1939 novel, written by Richard Llewellyn, is set at the end of the 19th century; we follow the story of the Morgans, an upstanding South Wales valleys mining family. Events unfold through the eyes of the youngest son, Huw. There are mining accidents, male voice choirs and various misadventures before Huw grows up, having acquired sufficient education to abandon the now despoiled valley. When I look at it now – book or film – rather than seeming like a work of great artistic merit it conjures up the contrived world of a 1980s industrial heritage theme park; those Thatcher-era attractions that famously used to pay unemployed miners to act the part of their Victorian ancestors ('Mining you're looking for, is it?'). In Llewellyn's book, you discover Welsh colliery village life, not as it actually was in the 19th century, but how it might look if you shot it through a soft-focus lens. Included are mostly nice bits: the rousing male voice choirs and the warm family life; but omitted are the grinding poverty, the rickets and the ringworm.

My first encounter with *How Green Was My Valley* was not with the book, but with the 1941 film adaptation; I have to say that I was a fan. In truth, however, while the book is a bit of a travesty of Welsh life, the film magnifies this false rose-coloured view and blows it up it into wide screen Cinemascope. It is said that the director John Ford, better known perhaps for his John Wayne westerns, had intended to film *How Green Was My Valley* as a four-hour epic, shot on location in the Welsh valleys. His plan was stymied by the outbreak of war and the threat of U-boats to transatlantic travel. Would he really have filmed it in South Wales, though? One thinks probably not: Hollywood has never really been in the business of telling it like it is, or – in the case of historical epics – like it was.

So Ford built an 'authentic' Welsh mining village on a hillside on the Fox Ranch near the Californian seaside resort of Malibu – I have pencilled in a bucket list trip to see what might still remain of this Hobbit town in what is now Malibu State Park. Ford filled up the cast with a hefty contingent of actors with Irish ancestry, such as Maureen O'Hara and Barry Fitzgerald – 'Isn't Wales in Ireland?', a Los Angeles car hire employee once asked me.

To John Ford's credit, however, the Welsh choral singing in *How Green Was My Valley* is impressive – it was by a choir of Los Angeles-based Celts – and there is no effort to shy away from the 'what about the workers?' storyline that probably sounded distinctly Marxist to the studio bosses. In a year when it was competing for Oscars with the now-highly regarded likes of *Citizen Kane* and *The Maltese Falcon, How Green Was My Valley* managed to sweep all before it at the 1941 Academy Awards, bagging five Oscars including Best Picture and Best Director. Showbiz, that is, boyo.

Had John Ford actually arrived in South Wales with his film crew, it would have been interesting to know where they would have set up their camera, as the book has no clearly identifiable location. The author, Richard Llewellyn, claimed that he had written his book based on his memories of Wales as a child and the stories he had heard in Gilfach Goch when he stayed with his grandfather. Probably nonsense, this is.

Welsh literature throws up an interesting dichotomy. Its most famous writer, Dylan Thomas, was a Welshman who for much of his life seems not to have been terribly enamoured with Wales. Interestingly, two of its better known writers – Richard Llewellyn and Alexander Cordell, author of *Rape of the Fair Country* – were both Englishmen and both highly keen to embrace Wales. Richard Llewellyn was so keen to buff up his Welshness that he re-edited his biography. His full name was actually Richard David Vivian Llewellyn Lloyd, though he seems to have been known as Vivian Lloyd. He claimed to be a son of the colliery cottage, yet he was really from Hendon in North London, the son of a publican – Lloyd's first job was washing up in Claridges. He acquired his knowledge of Gilfach Goch mining not from his grandfather, but from William Griffiths and his three brothers, who became famous in Welsh literary circles for running Griffs, a Welsh bookshop in London's Cecil Court. The Griffiths had a fund of stories about their coal-mining father and their childhood in Gilfach Goch. It was only after the book became a bestseller that Lloyd bought a farm in Pembrokeshire and set about cultivating his Welshness.

Given that literature is about writers telling tales, it should probably not be so surprising that authors are prone to occasional flights of fancy when it comes to setting out their own life story. If art is a kind of lying, it has been observed, then lying can also be a bit of a work of art. One of the most impressive reinventions was accomplished by Archibald Stansfeld Belaney, who was born near Hastings in 1888 and proved to be a studious youth when he attended Hastings Grammar School; incredibly, in later life, after moving to North America, Belaney reinvented himself as a Canadian Native American called Grey Owl. In 1931 Grey Owl wrote a book, *The Men of the Last Frontier*, which was very favourably reviewed and was one of the first works to draw people's attention to the growing dangers threatening wildlife and their natural habitats. It was also partly a memoir, which talked about a Scottish father and Apache Indian mother, but somehow failed to mention Grey Owl's upbringing in Hastings and his excellent academic record at grammar school – you can't help thinking that this would have made it a much better book. After Belaney's death in 1938, his true identity was revealed; erstwhile supporters claimed that Grey Owl's lack of candour about his real origins had damaged the value of his valuable conservation efforts.

Does Llewellyn's subterfuge about his background matter? The late Christopher Hitchens, a journalist of the left, cites *How Green Was My Valley* as one of the key books he read growing up which helped to shape his views about politics, literature and coming-of-age sex (Huw's coupling with Ceinwen in chapter 30, with its hammers that strike 'white hot steel', takes the book throbbingly towards D H Lawrence country). Despite its apparent inauthenticity, *How Green Was My Valley* manages to contain a number of key truths about life in the Welsh valleys: the importance of family, the place of the church, the value of hard work and the possibilities of escaping from life underground through academic study. Not exactly a Marxist tract, it is, however, positive and uplifting.

Rape of the Fair Country by Alexander Cordell is a less sugary account of the events which led to the Chartist uprising in Newport: the first serious workers' uprising in the UK. It was a movement which, among other things, demanded universal suffrage, raising fears among the upper classes that Britain was on the brink of the sort of revolution which was then raging through Europe. I went to school on Stow Hill in Newport, a couple of hundred yards from the Westgate Hotel, where I remember seeing the bullet holes in the door frame – it was here that the Riot Act was read and where the militia subsequently fired on the Chartist demonstrators. Walking past the Westgate, I noticed sadly that the famous doorway was boarded up – temporarily, I hope.

I grew up in South Wales in the sixties, when the coal mines were slowly coming to the end of the road (a process rapidly speeded up by events before and after the Miners' Strike in 1984). On my drive along the Heads of the Valley road from the Rhondda country of *How Green Was My Valley* to Abergavenny, I dipped in and out of some of the towns which, during the 19th century, were spun upwards by Dame Fortune, but have now been plunged downwards once more. This was once the region that fired the Industrial Revolution; now, at a cursory glance, all you can see is decay. But, happily, there was still enough here to remind me of a more glorious past. While the collieries have mostly vanished and the iron works have disappeared, I enjoyed searching out reminders of a more progressive time in our national life. I took a detour to Blackwood, where much of the planning of the Chartist uprising took place in the Coach and Horses pub. There is much dilapidation in the area; this is a world disfigured by high unemployment, particularly among school leavers. There is a danger that the proud valley heritage celebrated by Richard Llewellyn and Alexander Cordell has been buried with the slag heaps. And yet, in Blackwood for example, it is hard to miss the revived Miners' Institute, which was built from a deduction taken from miners' wages in the 1920s. It began as a snooker hall, but shortly afterwards additional floors were built to house a reading room, library, stage, auditorium, dance floor and rehearsal rooms for local societies. In other mining towns, the Miners' Institutes have been allowed to fall into complete dereliction; here in Blackwood, after an expensive refurbishment, it has once again taken its place at the heart of the community – in recent times, for example, staging a concert by local band The Manic Street Preachers.

※

At the end of the 19th century, coalmining and steelmaking in the Welsh Valleys were generating more wealth than any other place on earth (for proof of this, take a look at the Victorian baroque fantasy of Cardiff Castle). Yet some 50 miles from the Rhondda Valley – across the Brecon Beacons in the sweet countryside west of Hereford – rural life proceeded much as it had done for centuries.

The area that lies to the southwest of Hereford, and to the southeast of Hay-on-Wye, is the appropriately named Golden Valley, a favourite of C S Lewis and prominently featured in the 1993 movie *Shadowlands*. Hay-on-Wye now has a national profile thanks to the star names attracted to its annual literary festival, including two former US Presidents, Jimmy Carter and Bill Clinton (Clinton described the festival as 'The Woodstock of the Mind'). The event grew out of the fact that in the sixties Hay began to become a major centre of secondhand books; even the town's cinema and fire station were transformed into vast bookshops. The book business, however, is no longer what it was – when I passed through Hay, there were noticeably fewer bookshops and more general antique shops and upmarket clothes stores. If the Reverend Francis Kilvert were to return today, he would be amazed at its transformation.

Born in Wiltshire in 1840 and educated in Bath, Francis Kilvert studied at Wadham College, Oxford, and took a fourth class degree – I didn't know that fourth class was an option – before being ordained and becoming a curate in Radnorshire. He was finally appointed vicar of Bredwardine at the end of 1877. He kept a diary from the start of 1870 until his death in 1879. His journals, however, remained unknown until a selection from his diaries was published in 1938. Hay, like the rest of the area in his time, was a town where very little seems to have happened, and Kilvert described this quiet life in loving, very amusing, detail.

In 1974, I bought an ancient mahogany Bluthner Baby Grand Piano at an auction for £30. You might think that, since antique Bluther pianos currently sell for several thousand pounds, this was a sound investment. Actually, it was a terrible buy: the piano had woodworm or dry rot or both. What attracted me was that the auction took place in the vicarage of Bredwardine in Herefordshire, which had once been the home of the Reverend Kilvert. Sad to relate, my lovely piano slowly disintegrated in my father's shed, but I've never lost my affection for Kilvert and his writing.

After their publication, almost 60 years after his death, *Kilvert's Diaries* became a huge success, reckoned to be as important as the novels of Thomas Hardy in describing the rapidly disappearing traditional rural life of 19th-century England and Wales. What nobody expected was that a Victorian clergyman, who one would have expected to be a very tight-laced man in a very repressed society, was in fact so open, honest and often very funny in his writing. The diaries were, actually, too frank and too revealing for his wife and family, who between them destroyed much of what he had written, saying that in various ways it was too personal.

What remains, however, is magnificent: his descriptions, for example, of the Wye Valley and the Welsh border have been hailed as classics of landscape writing. They are also, at times, introspective. On Tuesday 3 November 1874, for example, he wrote.

> Why do I keep this voluminous journal? I can hardly tell. Partly because life appears to me such a curious and wonderful thing that it almost seems a pity that such a humble and uneventful life such as mine should pass altogether away without some such record as this, and partly too because I think the record may amuse and interest some who come after me.[35]

On 16 March 1870, prompted by the sound of a bird singing unseen, Kilvert had written that the words of a good man might live long after he was silent and out of sight, and he quoted: 'He being dead yet speaketh'. Those five words were carved above his grave in the lovely churchyard at Bredwardine, and, for the modern reader, reflect his justified hope that his diary would be read after his death. I wish I still had the piano.

Kilvert strikes a particular chord with me because I am from the Wye Valley, which has a rich literary history – and a long-distinguished tradition of literary tourism. It's only as I began writing this book that I started to remember that I've played my own, albeit small, part in literary tourism. I wrote a piece about the Wye Valley in about 1987 and rounded up the usual literary suspects: Wordsworth, Coleridge etc. A few days after the article appeared, I had a letter from a reader wondering why I hadn't included Flora Klickmann in the piece.

Flora who?

Flora Klickmann, it transpired, was a former editor of the *Girls' Own Paper,* who produced a string of best-selling books about her lightly fictionalised life in the Wye Valley in a cottage a couple of miles from Tintern. The series of books began during the First World War with *The Flower Patch Among the Hills* – judging by the number of secondhand copies available on various internet sites, it must have sold in its hundreds of thousands. She died just two years before our family moved to Tintern: surprised that I hadn't heard of her, I read her books and thought they needed to be brought before a modern audience. With the encouragement of Monmouthshire County Council, I arranged a small exhibition of her life and work at a former signal box in Tintern station. The Wye Valley railway line was a victim of the Beeching Axe, but now Tintern station has become a very popular tourist attraction. Surprisingly, a lot of people visited the Klickmann exhibition, and I think it served to revive interest in her work (the secondhand bookshop in Tintern now has shelves full of her books, which I heartily recommend).

My principal memories of the exhibition, however, are the largely misspelt obscene comments and crude vulgar drawings left by children – I presumed they were children – in the visitors' book. The people who ran the station had to keep ripping out the sullied pages; in the end, the book became a sad, thin dishevelled tome which I still have somewhere. It taught me a valuable lesson: build it and they will come, but often you'll wish that many of those who come had stayed at home.

It would be interesting to know if Flora Klickmann ever happened to meet that other great late Victorian chronicler of the borderlands, A E Housman:

> *Into my heart on air that kills*
> *From yon far country blows:*
> *What are those blue remembered hills,*

What spires, what farms are those?
That is the land of lost content,
I see it shining plain,
The happy highways where I went
And cannot come again.
XL 'A Shropshire Lad' by A E Housman[36]

Curiously, many people discovered this poignant Housman verse when it was used over the closing shots of Nicolas Roeg's 1971 movie *Walkabout,* which tells the story of Jenny Agutter's character who gets lost in the Australian Outback with her little brother and a young Aborigine on his ritual 'walkabout'. Dennis Potter, meanwhile, used 'blue remembered hills' as the title of his 1979 Play For Today wartime drama starring, among others, Colin Welland and Helen Mirren, adult actors playing children in Potter's Forest of Dean. It was one of his most affecting dramas.

Like Potter – and like me – Housman was from the borderlands: born and brought up in Bromsgrove, Worcestershire, but with the 'blue remembered hills' of Wales always looming to the west. There seems to be good reason to suppose that he probably never visited Shropshire until he was an adult. It has been suggested that he wrote the cycle of 63 poems that make up *A Shropshire Lad* with a local tourist guidebook on his desk. Inspector Poirot would have quickly exposed Housman's embarrassing lack of precise knowledge of the area. 'The vane on Hughley steeple veers bright, a far-known sign,' wrote Housman: yet Hughley has no steeple (apparently he had another village in mind but 'Hughley' worked better in the verse).

The poet was unrepentant: 'I did not apprehend that the faithful would be making pilgrimages to these holy places,' wrote Housman when his brother Laurence tackled him over the error.[37] And, indeed, Housman has nothing to be embarrassed about. It seems certain that Shakespeare never visited *Romeo and Juliet's* Verona nor any of the other foreign places he describes in his plays: in *The Winter's Tale*, for example, he gives landlocked Bohemia a coastline! To Housman 'Shropshire' is a place of the imagination – beautiful yet troubled.

You don't have to be a Freudian psychiatrist to speculate that the troubled Shropshire of Housman's imagination reflected his own angst. His homosexual passion for an Oxford college roommate was rebuffed, almost wholly derailing his academic career. But he persevered, to become one of Britain's most important classical scholars, eventually taking the Kennedy Professorship of Latin at Trinity College, Cambridge in 1911, 30 years after failing his Oxford finals. The publication of *A Shropshire Lad* in 1896, a project which Housman had to finance himself as no publisher would take it on, surprised his student and university colleagues with its raw emotion and sublime poetry. A work of shuddering nostalgia, *A Shropshire Lad* is such a perfect book for a desert island, I'm amazed that only one person seems to have chosen it on the BBC's *Desert Island Discs*.

Housman's ashes are buried outside St Laurence's Church in Ludlow. They were buried under the north wall, mingled with soil and mould gathered from under the trees of his childhood homes Perry Hall and the Clock House, Fockbury. The inscription on the tomb are lines Housman wrote for his mother:

> *Good-night; ensured release,*
> *Imperishable peace,*
> *Have these for yours*

On Mondays, the St Laurence church bells still chime their special tune for market-goers, as Housman writes in 'The Recruit':

> *Or come you home of Monday*
> *When Ludlow market hums*
> *And Ludlow chimes are playing*
> *'The conquering hero comes'*

The Ludlow branch of the Housman Society has developed the 'Housman Trail,' a 40-mile route connecting places that are mentioned in *A Shropshire Lad,* from Bewdley and Bredin to Utoxeter and Wrekin. Ludlow is probably the perfect English market town with a thriving gastronomical scene.

Of all the places that I visited, this is the literary location that probably made the most positive impression. In truth it's a bit 'Chelsea in the countryside', but still charming nevertheless. I had lunch in a lovely tea room across the road from St Laurence's Church with Housman's poems propped up behind my bowl of carrot and coriander soup and toasted the master poet with a glass of local English Three Choirs Bacchus wine. If you love Housman and like fine dining, this is a place where you could happily spend a fortnight.

✺

About half an hour's drive west from Ludlow via Craven Arms is the village of Clun (according to Housman one of 'the quietest places/ Under the sun'). The town is famous for its packhorse bridge, across which sheep were driven on a journey that took them to markets in England. I took a short detour to nearby Clunton, which was the final home of *Look Back In Anger* author John Osborne, who was buried at St George's Church: his tombstone carries the inscription 'Playwright, actor and friend' – although he'd actually managed to fall out with quite a lot of his friends towards the end of his life. After his death, Osborne's house was acquired by the Arvon Foundation, which runs an annual programme of residential courses and retreats 'offering people time and space to write'. In Clunton, I found a safe place to park, dialled up Elgar's 'Enigma Variations' on Spotify and ate a Welsh cake while drinking in a view of the sweetest countryside as Nimrod swirled around me. I nurture a hope that heaven might be a bit like this.

Whenever he travelled up to London, John Osborne was pleased to take advantage of the rail service from his nearest station, Craven Arms, which offered a connection to London via Shrewsbury. Actually, the perfect way to arrive in Shropshire is by train. Travel up from Abergavenny via Hereford and Leominster (a train route which somehow survived the Beeching axe): this is one of my top five train rides in Britain.

I checked the timetable in the station: it takes 30 minutes by train from Craven Arms to Shrewsbury, travelling through gently rolling Shropshire Hills to the upper reaches of the Severn Valley. Ellis Peters, whose real name was Edith Pargeter, is probably Shropshire's best-known author of recent times. She wrote the *Cadfael* mysteries about medieval herbalist and part-time detective Brother Cadfael of Shrewsbury Abbey. Fittingly, Peters – who died in 1995 – has a memorial in the Abbey.

Shrewsbury School, meanwhile, is the Alma Mater of *Private Eye*: it was at the school that the magazine's founder, Richard Ingrams, first met contributors and fellow Old Salopians Willie Rushton, Christopher Booker and Paul Foot. But the town's principal literary claim to fame is as the home of First World War poet Wilfred Owen. On Monday 11 November 1918 – the day of the week that, in Ludlow, St Laurence's chimes would have been playing 'The conquering hero' – the bells all across the country were ringing out to celebrate the declaration of the Armistice and the end of the First World War. This was the day of peace on which Sarah Owen received the telegram which informed her that her son – Lieutenant Wilfred Owen – had been killed in action seven days earlier.

One of the foremost poets of the First World War, the author of 'Dulce et Decorum Est' and 'Anthem for Doomed Youth', Wilfred Owen was born near Oswestry in Shropshire on 18 March 1893. Through Owen's father's job, the family went north to live in Birkenhead before moving back to Shropshire, where Owen attended Shrewsbury Technical School. He decided to enlist in the Army in 1915; in 1917 he was sent to Craiglockhart Hospital in Scotland suffering from shellshock. During his recovery, he encountered poet Siegfried Sassoon, who had a profound influence on Owen's development as a poet.

Owen decided to return to the front line, and was subsequently killed in action in the closing stages of the war. He had been instructed to lead an attack across the Sambre-Oise canal near Ors in northern France; he died, and received a posthumous Military Cross for his leadership. I've been to Ors and seen both the place on the canal where he died and his grave in a special section of the municipal cemetery. A cottage in the woods, in whose smoky cellar he spent his last night writing a poignant letter to his mother before the attack, was recently converted into an excellent Owen memorial. The last house where Owen lived in Shrewsbury, meanwhile, 69 Monksmoor Road, was granted listed status by the Government in 2014 as part of the centennial commemorations of the outbreak of the First World War.

Owen is another of those writers, like Dylan Thomas, whose reputation has continued to grow in each decade. Barely known in the years after his death, his popularity grew during the Second World War, when his perceptions about war and the brutality of conflict found a new, sympathetic audience. Owen gained worldwide recognition when Benjamin Britten chose nine of Owen's poems for his *War Requiem,* commissioned for the 1962 reconsecration of the new Coventry Cathedral – an event followed shortly afterwards by the 50th anniversary of the outbreak of the First World War, which refocused attention on the War Poets.

A sculpture, commissioned to celebrate Owen's life and works and unveiled outside Shrewsbury Abbey on the centenary of his birth in 1993, is inscribed with the lines 'I am the enemy you killed, my friend', from Owen's 1918 poem 'Strange Meeting'. Its name, *Symmetry,* feels apt enough.

9

Eastwood to Whitby

In which our travelling bookworm finds a writer who disliked Eastwood (and an Eastwood who disliked him), goes North and South (and West and East), has a spot of Larkin about in Hull and has a bite to eat in Vampire country.

IF there are 'much loved' literary figures in the UK – Sir John Betjeman, for example – we must accept there are also 'much unloved' characters. One of the least-loved British writers – certainly during his lifetime – was Nottinghamshire-born D H Lawrence. He hardly endeared himself to the people of Nottingham by calling it 'this dismal place'. Asked if he would like to live again in Eastwood, his home village, he replied: 'I hate the damn place'.

That would be a 'no' then? Well, not entirely – describing his home in later life, Lawrence did also refer to it as 'the country of my heart', so it can't have been all unhappy memories. But if he didn't like the people of his home town, he was also well aware that the people of Nottinghamshire weren't that keen on him. Even as a boy in Eastwood – clever, bookish, with a preference for the company of girls, suffering prolonged bouts of ill health and cosseted by an anxious mother – he seems to have been ostracised by his peers. 'Dicky Dicky Denches plays with the wenches,' they jeered at him in the school playground.[38]

It may be the case that, when Lawrence began to make a name for himself as a writer and showed no desire to honour the place of his birth, there was some suggestion of locals getting their retaliation in first. The thrust of it seemed to be, largely, 'he and his mother were always too big for their boots anyway – we never liked them'. In fairness, though, Lawrence seems not to have been the easiest of people to like – although peers recall that he found it easy to make friends, he also seems to have found it difficult to maintain those friendships. His choice to use locals (right down to their names) in his books may not have helped matters, admittedly.

And he had an uncanny knack for getting himself into impossible situations. When he moved to Cornwall during the First World War, he ought to have realised that having a German wife – who was, to boot, a distant relation of fighter ace Manfred von Richthofen, the 'Red Baron' – could potentially be the cause of friction with his neighbours. Indeed, locals began to get the idea that, in the course of their regular coastal walks, Lawrence and his wife were signalling messages to German U-boats – the couple were eventually told to leave Cornwall. Soon Lawrence left the UK altogether and began a 'savage pilgrimage' which took the couple to Australia, Italy, Ceylon, the United States, Mexico and the South of France, where he died in 1930 aged 44.

Perhaps the most significant episode of Lawrence's life occurred 30 years after his death, when his novel *Lady Chatterley's Lover* was published in an unexpurgated version by Penguin, which led to the publisher being brought to court charged with obscenity. Penguin was subsequently found not guilty; a defining moment which many say helped propel the UK towards the Swinging Sixties (Larkin referenced the

Chatterley ban in his famous poem 'Annus Mirabilis'). But having their most famous son linked to what was widely referred to as 'pornography' did nothing to endear Lawrence's name to his native Eastwood.

A simple matter of economics, however, meant that Nottinghamshire could not ignore him. In Lawrence's time, there had been 10 pits in and around Eastwood; the last one in the area closed in 1985 in the wake of the Miners' Strike. At a cafe near the D H Lawrence Birthplace Museum, I chatted to an elderly customer who told me that, when she was a girl, men either worked in the pits or in the bed spring factory, while women were mostly employed at the stocking factory. Now none of these employment opportunities exists.

'There's IKEA and that's it, really.'

What did she think of Lawrence?

'He's not very popular round here. My gran told me she remembered being told by her mum he was 'different' and not to play with him at school. Lawrence said he liked it here but then he couldn't wait to leave and then, once he left, he never ever came back. That about says it all, really.'

Actually, he did return, though not very often – and he certainly continued to write about the area where he was brought up, most famously in *Lady Chatterley's Lover*. After the Chatterley trial it was probably not surprising that his works would generate more interest. Film director Ken Russell made his reputation with the film version of Lawrence's 1920 novel *Women in Love*.

Eastwood may not like Lawrence very much, but, economically speaking, the author's tourist potential is about the only trump card it has in its hand. In the face of local diffidence, and occasional hostility, it has attempted to chisel out a D H Lawrence product to lure visitors. It has created The Blue Line Trail, a D H Lawrence heritage trail which is designed to allow visitors to 'follow in the footsteps of a literary legend'.

The main attraction, though, is the D H Lawrence Birthplace Museum, 'an authentically recreated late Victorian miner's house: 'It almost feels as though the family could come back home at any moment…'

Well, if they do come back, I hope they get a warmer reception than I did. The truth is that they get so few visitors here that the council seems forever to be on the brink of closing it down yet, when somebody arrives full of enthusiasm to inspect their attraction, their response was less than welcoming. From the museum's website, it makes it clear that visits are available through pre-booked timed tours. I may be a cock-eyed optimist but, unable to commit to a specific time in advance, I decided to visit, convinced that seeing I was so keen, they would feel it in their hearts to wave me in. In fact, I was told that it would be impossible for me to have even a quick look as there was a school party in the house at that moment.

I couldn't really wait, I explained.

'Sorry,' I was told in a way that suggested they weren't sorry at all. 'You can look at the rooms on the website,' I was told by way of consolation.

'I didn't get up at six o'clock to drive 200 miles so that I could go home and look at it on the internet.'

'Sorry.'

I gave up, left, and did the 'virtual tour'. Virtually disappointing. Virtually pointless.

What some sort of D H Lawrence museum could be doing is to look at how or why Lawrence became estranged from the place of his birth; it could also look at the question of censorship, which dogged his career. What won't work is what seems to be happening now (based on my virtual internet visit), which is really nothing at all: at the moment the D H Lawrence Birthplace Museum feels as if it is dying a slow death (rather like the death that Lawrence himself suffered with his TB). D H Lawrence deserves better – much better.

Nottinghamshire's other celebrity connections include Robin Hood, Brian Clough and Lord Byron. It was Byron who was once famously described as 'mad, bad and dangerous to know' – though the same description could equally apply to a greater or lesser extent to both Cloughie and Robin Hood.

Some are born with Great Houses, some achieve Great Houses, some have Great Houses thrust upon them. Byron fell into the latter category when, at the tender age of ten, he found that he had inherited the extraordinarily grand Newstead Abbey, near Nottingham, and also took over the baronetcy to go with it. His inheritance came from a flamboyantly mad great uncle – famously put on trial for killing a neighbour in a duel – who ended his days in the attic of a crumbling Newstead with (it is said) a troop of 'tame crickets'. Both the house and estate were in a shambolic state when Byron inherited them, but he came to love the house, and quickly took on the hifalutin attitude of a great lord, even if his situation may be roughly described as 'all fur coat and no knickers'. In any poll of Britain's most eccentric writers, Byron would surely be in the top five. His life – like his poetry – has greatly added to the sum of human happiness; having had the chance to pay homage at his home, I found a genuine treat. But you don't have to be a lover of Byron's writing to find a visit to the house and its gardens a most rewarding experience. Look out for the poet's giltwood bed, which was brought by Byron from his Cambridge student rooms when he moved into Newstead Abbey. You have to admire a student who takes his own bed with him to university – there's a touch of Austin ('Yeah, baby!') Powers to this.

Regarded as one of Britain's greatest poets – the author of long narrative poems *Don Juan* and *Childe Harold's Pilgrimage,* and fine shorter works such as 'She Walks in Beauty', his was the Great Romantic Life devoted to pleasure and excitement. He spent much of his later life in Italy and later joined the Greek

War of Independence fighting the Ottomans – an effort which earned him hero status in Greece. He died aged 36 from a fever contracted while in Greece.

His was a 'live fast, die young' life – a precursor of those Hollywood actors and drug-addled rock stars who never made it as far as middle age. Byron seemed driven to enjoy every moment of his life. 'Life's enchanted cup sparkles near the brim,' he wrote.

※

Fellow Romantic poet Shelley seems to have been rather more rooted. It was he who was moved to verse by the plight of the Manchester protestors in 1819, when a gathering of more than 60,000 people agitating for political reform had gathered at St Peter's Field. This was at about the time when Blake's 'dark satanic mills' were being built across the region, of which Manchester – known as 'Cottonopolis' – was the capital. In an attempt to disperse the protestors, there was a cavalry charge that resulted in the deaths of 15 people and injured between 400 and 700 others. It became known as the Peterloo Massacre, an ironic comparison with the Battle of Waterloo four years earlier. In his 1819 poem 'The Masque of Anarchy', Shelley praised the virtues of the protestors' non-violent demonstration, believing their ultimate victory was inevitable:

> …*Rise, like lions after slumber*
> *In unvanquishable number!*
> *Shake your chains to earth like dew*
> *Which in sleep had fallen on you:*
> *Ye are many—they are few!*

Given its important place in the Industrial Revolution, it is not surprising that Lancashire as a whole, and Manchester, in particular, witnessed a gathering political storm in the 19th century as workers organised and demanded better pay and improved working conditions, It was in Manchester that Karl Marx and Friedrich Engels wrote about working life and jointly produced parts of *The Communist Manifesto* – a book that shook the world.

I was in my twenties when I first visited Manchester and Leeds. It might seem incredible, yet it is surprising how little travelled British people are in their own country. I've seen it suggested that probably just 14% of the UK population, for example, has ever visited Liverpool. We are more likely to have visited Malaga than Manchester, be more familiar with Lloret da Mar than Leeds. Which is a shame because travelling around the UK, especially in the north, is a delight.

These days, Manchester is famous for *Coronation Street*, gobby musicians, extremely rich football clubs and constant rain. It is not a city well known, you might have thought, for either prose or poetry – yet it has several literary claims to fame.

There is Salford's punk poet John Cooper Clarke and current poet laureate Carol Ann Duffy (of Scottish ancestry), who has lived in the city for almost 20 years. Among Manchester's literary landmarks is the International Anthony Burgess Foundation, devoted to the life and works of the Manchester-born author. Its collection of Burgess possessions includes the original manuscript of *A Clockwork Orange* – complete with doodles by the author – as well as correspondence with Stanley Kubrick, who directed its film adaptation, which proved to be very controversial for its scenes of sex and extreme violence.

Its star literary site, however, is Elizabeth Gaskell's house at 84 Plymouth Grove, which, remarkably, has survived despite widespread redevelopment of the area. Mrs Gaskell lived here with her husband William and daughters Marianne, Meta (short for Margaret), Florence and Julia from 1850 to 1865, and this was where she wrote nearly all of her books including *Cranford*, *North and South* and the biography of her friend Charlotte Brontë. Her final novel, *Wives and Daughters,* was nearly finished when she died in 1865. After an expensive programme of refurbishment, the Grade II-listed Regency villa has been made to look as if the family had just popped out and left the table set for dinner (arranging houses to look as if their owners have just popped out seems to have become a bit of a literary landmark trope).

Gaskell's writing covers a significant period in Manchester's development. In 1750, Manchester had a population fewer than 20,000 people – in 1850, when the Gaskells moved to Plymouth Grove, it had become Britain's third-largest city with a population of around 250,000. Rapid industrialisation had resulted in very poor conditions for workers: long working hours, low wages, poor housing and bad sanitation – Engels called it 'Hell upon Earth', adding 'everything here arouses indignation'. Mrs Gaskell wrote about what she saw, courageously addressing the social issues of the day. The refurbishment of the Gaskell house is a brave project by the local authority and deserves to succeed.

❊

It is just 42 miles from Manchester to Leeds via the M62, but such is the mutual antagonism and animosity between the two places (a Lancashire–Yorkshire Red Rose–White Rose enmity which led to the bloody War of the Roses) that you imagine they must be further apart. The trans-Pennine highway links Liverpool and Hull via Manchester and Leeds (apparently, it is part of something calling itself the unsigned Euroroute E20, which, in its imagination, links Shannon with Saint Petersburg. This compares with a construction worker telling me that the cable he was installing along the bottom of my drive was an optic fibre link which directly connects New York with London. I fear he may have been having me on).

It took me barely 10 minutes' rapid driving on Manchester's orbital motorway before I was heading up the Pennines. The motorway signs were full of places familiar from a lifetime's football results: Rochdale, Oldham, Stockport, Huddersfield, Halifax, Barnsley and Bradford. Driving down towards Leeds, there was plenty of industrial architecture to be seen either side of the motorway, before suddenly I was in the city. Who knew that places 'oop North were all so close?

It seems incredible now, but our school trips tended to be approached by the pupils as fidgety Colditz Castle prisoners of war may have anticipated a rare outing to the sports field: it was seen as the perfect opportunity to make a wild bid for freedom. My secondary school was semi-private – it admitted fee-paying pupils and had boarders, but it was also the school you went to locally if you passed the 11-plus. While most of the latter group – including me – were relatively sane (or what passes for sane among adolescent boys), many of the boarders were definitely odd.

A lot of those incarcerated in Colditz in the Second World War said they were able to survive because in many ways life in a prisoner of war camp was indistinguishable from the brutal privations and callous hardships they had already suffered for many years at British public school. A school theatre trip of a couple of dozen 14-year olds being taken to Bristol or Stratford may seem an innocuous exercise; the problem for my school was that the number that was counted out getting off the bus would turn out to be a couple short when counted back on. The police would have to be called and local pubs searched – for 14-year olds, honestly – until the recalcitrant youths had been tracked down. Result: a ban on all school trips for everybody.

So it was an uncommon pleasure to travel to Bristol's Old Vic in around about 1968 to see the stage version of *Billy Liar*, adapted for the stage by Keith Waterhouse and Willis Hall from the novel by Keith Waterhouse. I first saw the play, read the book and then saw the film: *Billy Liar* is one of those rare cases when the film, which stars Julie Christie and Tom Courtenay, is as good as the book. (Julie Christie was to repeat this unusual trick with the film version of Daphne du Maurier's short story 'Don't Look Now').

On Waterhouse's death in 2009, the *Telegraph* described *Billy Liar* as 'one of the great comic novels of the 20th century'; for my money it can be ranked with *Great Expectations* and *Hamlet* as one of the great works of English literature in its depiction of the story of conflicted youth. William Fisher, the eponymous Billy Liar, lives in dull suburbia in a city clearly modelled on Leeds; he lives with his mum, dad and gran, works in a dead-end job at an undertaker's, and all the time dreams of escaping to London, where he will be become a hotshot writer. Keith Waterhouse was that boy with dreams of literary stardom (in another part of Leeds, at about the same time, a young Alan Bennett was likewise planning his own great escape).

Billy Liar tells you all you need to know about the agonies of life in post-war provincial Britain, where young men were expected to know their place and settle for humble goals. When Billy Liar races to the station with his ticket for the midnight train to London and a way out of the humdrum world, the reader sits on the edge of their seat. Whenever I pass through Leeds station I always think of that fictional night 60 years ago, and my heart skips a beat.

I was lucky enough to make Keith Waterhouse's acquaintance and had lunch with him on several occasions. While he had cultivated the 'curmudgeonly old man' persona – it was a pose that admirably served his *Daily Mail* column (he was notably less grouchy in his heyday as a star writer at the *Daily Mirror*)

– in real life he was an entertaining and charming companion, full of stories and anecdotes about his life in Leeds before he boarded his midnight train to Fleet Street. While in later life he lived in Brighton and Bath, he never forgot the pleasures of the life he had left behind in Yorkshire. He spoke of the pleasure of spending weekends tramping across Ilkley Moor or exploring Wharfedale, which served as an extended municipal park for the people of Leeds and Bradford: 'all it lacked was a bandstand and a silver jubilee drinking fountain':

> During my youth it was a rare Sunday or bank holiday when I did not queue in Leeds City Square for the blue single-decker that would take me out to Ilkley, preferably with the girl of my choice, for all that that would double the shilling bus fare. I always set off in high hopes and with a spring in my step, but alas for teenage sex maniacs at that time, it was almost invariably better to travel than to arrive...[39]

※

Travelling further eastwards down the 'unsigned' E20 Euro superhighway to St Petersburg took me beneath the slender limbs of the Humber Bridge to Hull, whose most famous literary scion is Philip Larkin. According to Martin Amis, Larkin was a 'nine-to-five librarian, who lived for thirty years in a northern city that smelled of fish'. It's not clear who this remark is intended to wound most: nine-to-five librarians, Philip Larkin, Hull or the poor fish who are stinking the place up. The essential point is that, while his father Kingsley was living the high life of a celebrity writer in London, boring old Philip Larkin was busy cataloguing books in the dullest – and smelliest – city in the UK. Martin Amis protests too much; truth be told, Kingsley's life seems to have been a procession of failed relationships, publishing disappointments, a diet that included too much alcohol and too many reactionary boozy lunches. It seems to me that it was Larkin who was having the better time in Fish Town. In the foreword to an anthology of Hull poets he wrote:

> When your train comes to rest in Paragon Station against a row of docile buffers, you alight with an end of-the-line sense of freedom...For Hull has its own sudden elegances...People are slow to leave it, quick to return. And there are others who come, as they think, for a year or two, and stay a lifetime, sensing that they have found a city that is in the world, yet sufficiently on the edge of it to have a different resonance.[40]

Larkin loved Hull and Hull, in its turn, loved Larkin. After his death, the city devised one of the most effective tributes ever created for a writer anywhere in the UK, possibly the world. The Larkin Trail – you can download a guide free of charge at thelarkintrail.co.uk – is a walk which takes you around 25 locations in the footsteps of the poet, each stop marked by a nicely informative wall plaque. Larkin wore his success lightly, so it is fitting perhaps that he is formally remembered with this low-key but entirely appropriate celebration for a man who is rated in the front rank of 20th-century poets. Larkin was awarded the Queen's Gold Medal for Poetry in 1965; in 2008, *The Times* chose him as the greatest post-war writer in Britain. Significantly, he never wanted to give up his full-time job, nor to leave Hull. If you see nothing else of the The Larkin Trail, have a drink at the bar of the Royal Hotel – it has an entrance on the station concourse; this lovely wood-panelled bar was a favourite watering hole for Larkin. In the bar, near the lifts, is a photograph of Larkin which shows the poet with Sir John Betjeman, taken at a ceremony in Hull City Hall when

Betjeman received his honorary degree. Until Larkin passed his driving test at the age of 41, he was a busy train traveller. It was on a train journey from Hull that he took the trip he describes in 'Whitsun Weddings' which begins:

> *That Whitsun, I was late getting away:*
> *Not till about*
> *One-twenty on the sunlit Saturday…*[41]

In the station concourse there is a statue of Larkin, hastening to catch a train while at his feet are spread out lines from 'Whitsun Weddings'. It's all very imaginative and cleverly executed. Nearby in Trinity Square, a peaceful space that surrounds Holy Trinity Church, is a statue of Andrew Marvell, the metaphysical poet; Larkin's poetry, incidentally, was first published by the Marvell Press.

It was a pleasant 45-mile drive from Hull up through what might be described as 'South Riding' – the setting for Winifred Holtby's excellent posthumously published novel *South Riding,* set in the area of East Yorkshire where she grew up. Holtby went to secondary school in Scarborough, which has more recently become a major centre for drama. Ben Brown's 1999 play *Larkin with Women* was produced at the Stephen Joseph Theatre in Scarborough; the theatre has become famous for its world premieres of almost all of Alan Ayckbourn's 75-plus plays.

The Brown play dealt with Philip Larkin's tangled relationships with women. Ayckbourn later revealed that he 'despaired' when a London producer came to him to discuss taking *Larkin with Women* to London's West End; the producer confided that, in order to attract a big audience, the London performance of the play would need a big name for the lead role of Larkin. Someone bald and who wore glasses.

'Harry Hill,' suggested the London producer.

The continuing success of the Stephen Joseph Theatre provides compelling and reassuring evidence of the fact that a thriving arts scene can exist in relatively small places far beyond the reach of the M25.

※

York has fewer literary links than you might expect for a city of its size and historical importance. Daniel Defoe, author of *Moll Flanders* and *Robinson Crusoe*, was a frequent visitor to York. He begins *Crusoe* with the words: 'I was born in the year 1632, in the city of York, to a good family...'

Dickens came to York while he was writing *Nicholas Nickleby*. Dotheboys Hall, the awful educational establishment where Nickleby is sent to board, was one of what were known at the time as 'Yorkshire Schools', where unwanted or illegitimate children were dumped for a bargain price: an emphasis being placed on providing much work and no holidays.

The area around York still seems to have plenty of boarding schools – hopefully none like Dotheboys Hall (the publication of *Nicholas Nickleby* had a devastating effect on the 'Yorkshire Schools', with many being forced to close). *Nicholas Nickleby* was set in a period about 15 years before it was published, a pre-railway time when Yorkshire was quite remote – I've seen the description a 'British Siberia'.

The advent of regular fast rail services from London brought London closer to Yorkshire – and Yorkshire closer to London; not such a good thing when vampires are seeking to make their way to the capital...

I took a steam train from Pickering for the first section of my journey to the part of Yorkshire that the local tourist board really should have named 'Dracula Country'. The title would be a gift for posters: 'Dracula Country: love at first bite' or even 'Whitby: bloody brilliant!'

I must confess that I discovered only relatively recently that Whitby and *Dracula* were connected, when I finally got round to reading the Bram Stoker novel (in my defence, I had a morbid fear of novels created out of letters and diaries ever since I had to read the dire *Les Lettres Persanes* and the even direr *Les Liaisons Dangereuses*). My first actual meeting with the vampire myth came at the end of the 1970s when I was invited to Romania on a press trip to Brasov in Transylvania – who knew Transylvania was a real place? The itinerary included a day trip to Bran Castle, home of Dracula, *aka* Vlad the Impaler.

If you were ever taken captive by Vlad, at least you were under no illusion about what the large spikes were for outside in the prison yard. When I visited Transylvania, it was at the height of Ceausescu's communist regime; the country desperately needed tourists and their valuable foreign currency, but officials weren't keen on playing up the whole vampire thing. They apparently thought that people from the West ought to be more interested in a city tour of Bucharest, during which a guide could point out the tractor factories where 'last year they overfulfilled their production quota by 300%'. The 1958 Hammer Horror version of *Dracula*, as far as I can recall, mostly involved Transylvania and not very much Whitby. Not any Whitby, in fact, as Hammer filmed all their Horrors on studio sets – mostly in Bray Studios and the leafy leas of Berkshire.

In Bram Stoker's original *Dracula* novel published in 1897, Whitby, situated about 50 miles northeast of York, plays an important role. Dublin-born Stoker had happy memories of holidaying in the Yorkshire fishing port, and in his book Whitby provides a neat counterpoint: on the one hand you have the very frightening land of Dracula, while on the other here you a have a sweet little Yorkshire seaside town – definitely not the sort of place you are expecting to encounter a vampire.

The steam train ride on the delightful North Yorkshire Moors Railway was a joy (you may well recognise it from ITV's *Heartbeat*; Harry Potter's Hogwarts Express scenes were filmed at Goathland Station, also, which the train passes through – it doubles as Hogsmeade Station.) But when I reached Whitby, the town did have a bit of a supernatural feel. Even when I was enjoying Whitby's famous chips at one of its quayside eateries, I couldn't help noticing the ruined abbey brooding down from a hilltop high above me. It was at Whitby railway station that Mina Murray arrives in chapter 6: '…we drove up to the house at the Crescent in which they have rooms. This is a lovely place…'

Not for much longer, it wasn't – not once the Count arrived from the Black Sea on the Russian ship *Demeter*, which had been driven ashore in a storm with the death of all hands on board. Dracula, however, bounded ashore in the form of a dog; according to the novel he then loped up the famous 199 steps to St Mary's Church, where he found refuge in the outrageously scary graveyard at the top.

'The houses of the old town…are all red-roofed, and seemed piled up one over the other…' observed Mina. Bram Stoker and his family took their first Whitby holiday in 1890, staying at No. 6 Royal Crescent, a guesthouse run by Mrs Emma Veazey; a plaque on the front of the house commemorates this connection. It is believed that the view of Whitby from near the Crescent proved an inspiration to Bram Stoker for the scenes set in the town. This is the location of the 'Bram Stoker Memorial seat' – a seat seems a bit of a disappointingly cheapskate choice when it comes to memorials. However, this spot afforded me an excellent prospect of the harbour, with an impressive view of the abbey ruins, the church and the stone steps. I could also see, down to the left, where the *Demeter* came ashore. Sacked by the Danes, Whitby Abbey, was described by Stoker, via Mina, as 'a most noble ruin, of immense size, and full of beautiful and romantic bits' (I like the word 'bits' here). (S)he continues: 'Between it and the town there is another church, the parish one, round which is a big graveyard, all full of tombstones'.[42]

It was during his holiday visits to Whitby that Stoker discovered the name 'Dracula' during a research trip to the local library. Until his discovery, the title of the book was going to be 'The Undead' – not quite as catchy.

Whitby, while no doubt grateful for the extra income that *Dracula* brings, almost certainly views the whole thing as a bit of a mixed blessing. Bath, for example, has Jane Austen, who attracts a very wholesome crowd of educated, well-behaved people. *Dracula*, on the other hand, brings a rather more alternative following. The town is at pains to stress its other claim to fame: the achievements of local boy Captain Cook, who sailed the world from the port on ships built in Whitby.

But when it comes to tourism, if it bleeds, as they say, it leads. Twice a year, for example, Whitby is the venue for a Goth weekend – the YouTube videos from people attending this event are colourful, to say the least. A newer innovation has been a Bram Stoker Film Festival. Whitby would probably like people to know that there is more to the town than vampires… but in the meantime, however, vampires are OK to be going on with.

After my *Dracula* tour I retired to the Quayside restaurant for chips. I asked the waitress, who had a foreign accent, where she was from.

'You will laugh,' she replied: 'I am from Romania. I am not a vampire, by the way!'

Well, she would say that…

10

Heptonstall to Cockermouth

In which our erstwhile bibliophile heads over to Heptonstall, enjoys the Wuthering Heights and lows of Haworth, potters about at Hill Top and seeks perspective in Dove Cottage.

THE young lad in charge of the car hire desk in Leeds was curious about my travel plans. 'Having a holiday?' he asked, slightly incredulous. After all, it was mid-November in Yorkshire and not exactly sightseeing weather.

'Taking a trip anywhere nice?' he pressed.

'I'm here to visit Sylvia Plath's grave,' I said; then, worried in case he might think this was a gloomy trip to a relative's tomb, I said: 'Sylvia Plath, the writer.'

'Aye, I know who she is. Married to Ted Hughes, killed herself – people used to keep trying to chisel her husband's name off t'gravestone.'

You're well informed, I said jocularly.

He thickened up his Yorkshire accent: 'Folk in Hebden Bridge talk of little else.'

Actually, the subject of Sylvia Plath's gravestone in the churchyard at Heptonstall, near Hebden Bridge, had recently been given new life following its background appearance in BBC TV drama *Happy Valley*. A policewoman, played by Sarah Lancashire, visits the grave of her daughter, who committed suicide – just behind this fictional grave, viewers can pick out the real grave of Sylvia Plath; the shot is presumably designed to send out some sort of subtextual message of existential despair.

'That programme didn't put Hebden Bridge in a very good light, did it?' said my car hire man. Since the drama was largely about rape, kidnap, murder and drug dealing in the happy valleys of Yorkshire, one imagines that Visit Yorkshire was probably more than a bit narked.

If you've never been to this part of England before, however, it's not the rampant crime you notice, but the exquisite wild beauty of the countryside. The few dark satanic mills that didn't fall prey to the wreckers' ball now seem to have been largely restored and repurposed, fitting in harmoniously with the scenery. In the towns that you pass through en route, handsome 19th-century buildings, which must have been imposing banks or company offices, now serve as wine bars, coffee houses and restaurants. If people are turning to towards a life of crime here, it can't be because they lack somewhere nice for a night out or the opportunity to enjoy a decent macchiato.

The switch-back drive to Heptonstall took my car up through wispy morning mist. A road sign invites visitors to park in a relatively remote car park and then walk into the small town. With rain starting to drizzle, I resisted the invitation and drove straight to the church. Plath's grave is in the newer part of the cemetery – surprisingly there are no signs to point the way, so you have to find it for yourself. It doesn't take long. The headstone contains a quote, chosen by Ted Hughes, who thought it was from the *Bhagavad Gita* – but it actually turned out to be a bastardised line from 'Monkey' by Chinese writer Wu Ch'Eng-En: 'Even amidst fierce flames the golden lotus can be planted.' Plans to erect a separate memorial to Sylvia Plath, something more in keeping with her international reputation as a poet, have so far not been realised.

Ted Hughes once compared his first wife Sylvia Plath with Emily Brontë in a poem: both defeated by a quest for something that was beyond mortal reach. You can see how Hughes would have been happy to see his wife's early death as the stuff of destiny. In fact, Sylvia Plath's early demise was as cruel as the largely avoidable fate suffered by the author of *Wuthering Heights*. Emily blamed the poor health of the Brontë family on the inhospitable climate and the poor state of their drinking water, which was contaminated by runoff from the church's neighbouring graveyard. Her end came after she caught a severe cold while attending the funeral of her brother Branwell in September 1848, an infection which is said to have led to tuberculosis. For her part, Sylvia Plath killed herself following Ted Hughes' adulterous romance with Assia Wevill who, with her husband, had taken over the tenancy of the Hughes' London flat after Ted and Sylvia moved to Devon.

It is difficult to write anything about Ted Hughes which paints him in an attractive light. After he took up with Assia, Sylvia gassed herself; some years later, when Hughes began an affair with yet another woman, Assia not only killed herself, but also Shura, her four-year-old daughter with Hughes. To pile on the misery, Nicholas Hughes – one of the two children that Hughes had with Sylvia – killed himself in 2009.

Perhaps the unkindest cut of all was that Sylvia was buried in Heptonstall, near Hughes' childhood home in Mytholmroyd, somewhere which clearly meant much more to Hughes than to the wife he abandoned. Sylvia's grave is modest, which may well have been what Plath would have wanted. (There is some irony, however, in the fact that Hughes himself has several memorials, including one in Westminster Abbey, while the wife he wronged has yet to be so honoured.) Less understandable, and certainly much less forgivable, was that, despite their actual, if not legal, divorce, he was happy to assume control of Plath's literary estate and hand the management of it to his sister Olwyn, even though she and Sylvia had detested each other.

In happier times, Sylvia and Ted had walked together on the moors seeing the *Wuthering Heights* 'sights'; if you have time, you can walk from the cemetery in Heptonstall to Haworth in about three hours. Sylvia wrote a travel piece about this part of Yorkshire for the *Christian Science Monitor*. She also wrote a fairly gloomy poem called 'Wuthering Heights'.

The extraordinarily tempestuous picture of *Wuthering Heights* painted by Emily Brontë creates such a fantastic mental image that it's hard to imagine it's all based on a real place. Yet it really is just a 30-minute drive away. As I drove, I happened to be listening to *The Archers* – driving into *Wuthering Heights* country was as surreal as motoring into *The Archers'* Ambridge. As I approached Haworth through the windswept moors, it was easy to see why this has been such an inspirational place.

Sales of *Wuthering Heights* were reported to have quadrupled in 2010, when teen heartthrobs Edward Cullen and Bella Swan discussed their love for the novel in Stephenie Meyer's bestselling *Twilight* vampire series – but this was by no means its first brush with pop culture. In 1978, 'Wuthering Heights' was the debut release for young singer-songwriter Kate Bush; it's still her most successful single. (It says something of the modern era that the song was inspired not by the book, but by a BBC TV adaptation of which she happened to catch the last 10 minutes. This prompted her to look at the book, where she read a few pages to get the flavour – she was also pleased to discover later that she shared a birthday with Emily Brontë.) Written when she was 18, the song, with Bush's fluting voice, took the charts by surprise – an unforgettable appearance on *Top of the Pops* sent the record storming to the top of the charts.

There are some parallels with *Wuthering Heights'* success as a novel. Emily Brontë's story astonished the English literary scene in 1847 when it first appeared – like all the Brontës' books – published under a pseudonym: Ellis Bell in Emily's case. Brought out in the wake of the success of *Jane Eyre*, by Emily's sister Charlotte Brontë, *Wuthering Heights* was judged by many to be a slighter fictional work. As it was my 'O' level set text, I'm probably not the best person to ask, as all the ghostly hammerings on windows in the middle of the night, wild winds and unharnessed passion struck me at the time as a bit tedious: *Wearying Heights*, we called it.

The achievement of the book, however, is that it came to be written and published at all. For the British public, fed a diet of refined manners by Jane Austen, *Wuthering Heights* arrived from another planet of wild moors and howling storms: how would Elizabeth Bennet, in her high-waisted sprig muslin dress, have coped with a wild wuthering moorland downpour? *Wuthering Heights* is about real passion and actual life and death (people tend not to die that much in Jane Austen). This is a book that could never have been coolly composed on a side table in an elegant Georgian parlour; this was something that was torn from the heart. Emily Brontë barely survived long enough to complete it; she died the year after its publication, aged 30, and her sister Charlotte tidied up the novel for its second edition.

When you learn a little about Emily Brontë and her sisters and their childhood in Haworth, you can't help but want to visit their parsonage home. And one of *Wuthering Heights'* great assets as a novel is that it is set in a fictional farmhouse, but in a recognizable location out on the moors, 'completely removed from the stir of society'.[43]

The Brontë parsonage in Haworth, on the very edge of the wiley and windy Yorkshire Moors, offers a story of literary genius more extraordinary and more wonderful than anything than even the greatest writer would dare to imagine. In this stark, solidly built house grew up three girls who would collectively help transform the English novel in the 19th century. The girls' mother and father, the Reverend Patrick Brontë and his wife Maria, moved to Haworth in 1820 – the year that Anne, the youngest of their six children, was born (Maria died shortly after giving birth, probably from cancer, a year after the family's move to Haworth; two daughters, Maria and Elizabeth, both died from tuberculosis as children). Of the three surviving sisters, Charlotte, the eldest, was born in 1816 and Emily in 1818, two years before Anne; Branwell, the only son, was born in 1817. The children lived relatively short lives: Branwell died of tuberculosis in 1848, Emily died of the same disease later that year, Anne died the following year, while Charlotte survived until 1855. Almost incredibly in these modern times, tuberculosis seems to have been a factor in the deaths of all six of the Brontë children, as well as their father – Emily may well have been right that there's something in the water here, if not the air.

The house has many relics of this tragic past: you can see, for example, the sofa upon which Emily died; upstairs in the bedroom, glass cases hold their small shoes (Charlotte Brontë, it has been estimated, was around 4ft 9ins tall).

I was trying to imagine what it would have been like to visit the Haworth Parsonage 160 years ago when Charlotte was still alive and living here. But as it turned out, I didn't have to imagine; I was able to read *The Life of Charlotte Brontë* by *Cranford* author and Charlotte Brontë fan Mrs Gaskell, who visited her and wrote a fascinating book.

Given that the real lives of the Brontës were every bit as extraordinary and fascinating as their novels, the Brontë parsonage, which has been a museum for almost 90 years, ought to provide a fascinating experience. Ask a crowd of people a question and, according to 'the wisdom of the crowd' theory, collectively they will give you the right answer. This is the process at the heart of the online review sites which cover not just hotels and restaurants, but also tourist attractions. Critics sometimes underestimate the significance of these sites because, at first glance, there often seem to be too many cloyingly enthusiastic reviews ('Exquisite…unforgettable…once in a lifetime'). These shrill soprano trills, however, are nearly always counterbalanced at the other end of the scale by dull nagging bass notes of complaint; on the site these are filed under the categories 'Poor' and 'Terrible'. When researching a place, I often find it more instructive to chew on the gritty titbits served up by the disappointed. All enthusiastic reviews are alike; each unhappy review is miserable in its own way – sometimes in quite extraordinary ways.

It should be causing Haworth's Brontë Parsonage Museum some anxiety that, according to users of one particular site, at the time I visited it ranked as only the fourth best attraction in Haworth: it somehow trailed behind a local walking tour company (Wuthering Hikes!), a heritage railway made famous in the original *The Railway Children* movie, and the derelict remote farmhouse reckoned to be the inspiration for the windswept setting of *Wuthering Heights*. It would be foolish to place too much weight on online review sites, which are based on an algorithm which ranks positive over negative reviews and doesn't take into account the number of visitors – an attraction with just 50 reviews, if they are all positive, can take precedence over one with several hundred more mixed responses. However, the relatively poor performance of the Brontë Parsonage Museum among online reviewers is a significant straw in the wuthering breeze.

Staff at all small attractions such as the Brontë Parsonage Museum can be a problem, since many are volunteers who may be retired and of an age to resist what they may well see as impertinent suggestions about developing their 'interpersonal skills' – why should they have to turn a sunny face to the visitor? Small literary museums are tiny businesses that, unless they're careful, can end up suiting the needs of the employees rather than those of the visitors; in true *Fawlty Towers* style, visitors can quickly come to be seen as nuisances who interrupt the smooth running of an attraction. This was certainly my experience, for example, in Westminster Abbey.

But even Westminster Abbey had nothing to match the sudden squall of unpleasantness that engulfed me shortly after entering the Brontë museum. It had become my usual practice to take photographs where possible, largely as an aide-memoire rather than for illustrative purposes. It is, actually, an interesting exercise to discover which places allow photography throughout their museum (there seems to me to be no compelling reason to ban photography absolutely, certainly not photography without a flash; it's difficult not to see the banning of photography as anything less than an unsympathetic user-unfriendly attitude). I was barely finished with paying for my ticket when the ticket seller spotted my camera and informed me that photography in the museum was banned.

'Can I take photos in the gift shop?'

She said that I could. (Taking photos in the gift shop isn't as daft as it sounds: the way that a museum organises the shop, what it sells and how much it charges for things speak volumes.) In the Brontë Parsonage Museum, the visitor both begins and ends their journey in the gift shop – a neat set up that Disney World and other theme parks would kill for.

But so it was that I began my tour taking photos of books and mugs. I had barely started when someone who called herself 'the retail manager' was at my side clearly in some state of agitation.

'Who are you?' she demanded, 'I understand you're a photographer.'

I'd never claimed to be a photographer; I'd simply asked if I could take a few photos in the gift shop.

'Who said you could take photographs here?' she now demanded.

'The person at the ticket desk,' I said.

'That's X,' (I've omitted her name to protect the innocent). 'She's not in charge.' The Retail Manager was still very agitated. 'I'm a photographer myself. It's polite to ask, you know,' she repeated.

'I did ask,' I said again.

'I'm going to have to report this to the property manager,' she said, hastening to the back office. It all felt distinctly uncomfortable. I told her that I was going to tour the house and that if the property manager wanted to join in the interrogation, this is where I would be.

The front door to the parsonage which in happier days had admitted the Brontë sisters was, on my arrival, opened to reveal no fewer than four members of staff in a bizarre sort of 'welcome to the wedding reception' receiving line. 'Can we help you?' said probably the more senior of the four.

'Who are you?' asked a man, who turned to his neighbour. 'Is he the photographer?'

'We were expecting a photographer,' said another. This suddenly began to resemble a scene from the surreal sitcom *The League of Gentlemen*.

'I'm not a photographer,' I said again. The party fell back in confusion and I was allowed to enter. Nothing further was said on the subject of photographs – and certainly no apology was forthcoming from the Retail Manager, the Property Manager nor anybody else. Just another crazy day at the office, I suppose.

The plot thickened, however: looking online for information about the Brontës at Haworth a little later on, I happened to discover that the Brontë Society, which owns and operates the parsonage, is currently riven by a bitter feud, culminating in

June 2015 in the resignation of its president, author Bonnie Greer. Visitor numbers have declined significantly in recent years, and a new faction has been established with the aim of improving the running of the museum and to make it more visitor friendly. Clearly, there is more to do at the Brontë Parsonage Museum than simply make the staff more visitor-friendly; the presentation of the house and the Brontë artefacts is very 'old school'. There are few writers' houses open to the public these days that have ropes restricting entry into the rooms – Haworth Parsonage is one of this dwindling number. Certainly, the house needs to be opened up and its presentation sharpened – a visit needs to be made a joyous experience; it is a long way from this, sadly, at the moment. When the two feuding sides have settled their dispute about who is best placed to run a literary heritage-type site – the people who love the author best, or the people who know how to do the job – perhaps the Brontë Parsonage Museum will recover its mojo: it is a consummation devoutly to be wished.

The Brontë Parsonage Museum may not be the perfect visitor attraction but, if you love literature, it's a place that you have to visit. The story of the Brontë sisters is perhaps one of the most fascinating in the annals of literature and to see where they lived and wrote is a special privilege. Their home was the combination of very bleak – having a house more-or-less in a graveyard must inevitably generate a certain *weltschmerz*. But having a back door which opens onto the moors? Incredible.

After an oppressive experience in the museum, it really was a heart-soaring joy to step out into the broad Yorkshire countryside, where I could fire off my camera to my heart's content. I took the four-mile walk along the clearly marked trail from Haworth to Top Withens, a route which took me past the Brontë waterfall. Top Withens, the property known as 'the *Wuthering Heights* house', is now little more than a shell; but you really haven't come to enjoy the interior design or the period furniture. You've come to pick up a Heathcliff vibe, the sense that this is where great drama and powerful passions unfolded. I admit that, despite the presence of a surprisingly large number of visitors who had bravely plodded their way here across the moors, the property had a palpable atmosphere. *Wuthering Heights* was a work of fiction which may have been inspired by the place in which I was standing.

I was uplifted – until I read the sign on the wall; the dead hand of the Brontë Society had worked mischief here too. The Society has placed an engraved stone on the wall of the farmhouse with this inscription:

> This farmhouse has been associated with 'Wuthering Heights', the Earnshaw home in Emily Brontë's novel. The buildings, even when complete, bore no resemblance to the house she described.

So if you've bothered to come all of this way in the hope of a *Wuthering Heights* experience, it's more or less saying that you've wasted your time: this is the subtext of the message. Then, perhaps overcome with guilt at displaying quite so much naked negativity, the plaque continues:

> But the situation may have been in her mind when she wrote of the moorland setting of The Heights.

It then signs off:

> This plaque has been placed here in response to many inquiries.

Just in case we thought they were being mardy for no reason. Well, while Top Withens may have no particular literary merit, it is, however, a splendid hike across the moors and as a tourist attraction it appears to be better liked by online reviewers than the Brontë Society's 100%-proof Haworth Parsonage Museum. Think on, as they say in these parts…

⚌

From Haworth, it was the A65 almost all the way up to Kendal. Near the beginning of the drive I passed through Ilkley, a place made famous in dialect song 'On Ilkla Moor Baht 'at', literally 'On Ilkley Moor Without Thy Hat'. The song is the story of what happens to a young man who goes courting on the moor without the required warming headgear. This is one of those songs of Olde Englande – very *Wuthering Heights*, in fact – that you imagine must be hundreds of years old, yet it appeared in published form less than a century ago.

I stopped at Kirkby Lonsdale – the name suggests a fifties heartthrob – and took a quick look at the lovely Norman church of St Mary the Virgin. I followed the signs pointing the way to 'Ruskin's View' from the far corner of the churchyard. The path led into Church Brow, which overlooks the River Lune; from here I had a glorious prospect of the Lune Valley. This is the famous Ruskin's View.

Turner painted here in 1822; his picture made such an impression on all-round 19th-century achiever John Ruskin that he wrote that he knew of nowhere in Britain, France or Italy which was 'more naturally divine'. In his opinion, it was one of the finest sights in England – and 'therefore in the world': well, obviously. I left Ruskin's View (shouldn't it really be Turner's View?) and wandered down the Radical Steps to the river and followed the path to the three-arched Devil's Bridge.

Ruskin knew a thing or two about natural beauty: he owned Brantwood, one of the most attractively sited properties in the Lake District, overlooking Coniston Water. Ruskin was a Renaissance man: the foremost art critic of his time, a patron of the arts, a water-colourist, draughtsman, an eminent thinker on social matters and a philanthropist (he was probably also a useful plumber and an occasional cake-decorator). Unhappily for him, however, he is probably best known today for the failure of his marriage to Effie Gray because, it is said, he was shocked by the sight of his new wife when he saw her naked for the first time on their wedding night. Robert Brownell's 2013 Ruskin biography, *Marriage of Inconvenience*, claims that this is untrue; unfortunately one imagines that, true or not, this is what people are always likely to believe.

Beatrix Potter also had her struggles growing up in Victorian England. The qualities that made her a brilliant artist and imaginative storyteller were not the characteristics likely to make her a sought-after partner for marriage – and so, as she remained resolutely unmarried well into her thirties, she proved to be a big disappointment to her mother; she would rather have had a well-connected son-in-law than an unmarried daughter who wrote books about the strange adventures of rabbits and hedgehogs. Potter's mum would no doubt be amazed that her daughter made her mark on the world in a way which few others have managed to achieve. (She did, eventually, marry, at the age of 47; better late than never, Mrs Potter might well have thought.)

Much of children's literature is strange and disturbing, a world where sometimes violent punishment and occasionally death are meted out to both the righteous and unrighteous. In the tales of Beatrix Potter, as with much of Dahl, humour disguises a surprising amount of strange, random cruelty. A lot of the *Grimm Fairy Tales* are, well, grim, but I can understand that in the Victorian era where children had to be seen and not heard, and were probably beaten a lot, they liked their children's literature with a dose of terror. In the 21st century, I would have thought that children are happier to imbibe the more benign world of *Spongebob Squarepants* or the *Teletubbies* where the sun shines most the time and nothing bad ever really happens. And yet Potter still seems to strike a chord with children. (The other big constituency for Potter are the Japanese: it is said that the reason the house receives so many Japanese visitors is that Potter books are a favourite method of teaching children English in Japan.) I suppose a Peter Rabbit toy looks cuddly as long as you don't have think about Peter's dad, who ended up as the main course in Mr McGregor's tea – and there is little in children's literature that can be as chilling as Tom Kitten being turned into a pudding by Samuel Whiskers. It's a fine balance between the macabre and the humorous, one I confess I shall probably never understand fully, but Potter's enduring popularity suggests that she has the formula spot on.

Hill Top, Beatrix Potter's home at Near Sawrey, lies about six miles from Ruskin's Brantwood. Bought in 1905 with proceeds from her first book, *The Tale of Peter Rabbit*, entrance to the property is controlled by timed ticket. The National Trust says that the 17th-century farmhouse is designed to appear as if Beatrix Potter 'had just stepped out for a walk,' (what's the matter with these writers? They're forever just popping out...).

Eager to get the full Beatrix Potter experience, I was there before official opening time; but it was school half term and already the smallish car park was nearly full. I stood outside the house's entrance some 10 minutes before my official entry time, hoping that, as it was raining, the house staff might take a more relaxed attitude to ticket control. Due to the downpour there was no opportunity to enjoy what is described as 'the lovely cottage garden' with its assortment of herbs, flowers, vegetables and fruit, including Peter Rabbit's infamous vegetable patch. I was cold and wet, and anxious to get into the warm and light.

Happily, I was blithely waved in, but once inside the house I quickly discovered that it could hardly be described as a sunlit haven. This, alas, is the price of authenticity – bright light is the enemy of conservation work, so the National Trust preserves the fabric of the interior by keeping the lighting dim at all times. House stewards can lend you a wind-up LED torch to help you find your way around, which can give the visit something of the feel of a treasure hunt.

To add to this, each room has a reference to a picture in a 'tale', so youngsters can compare the book illustrations to the real-life counterparts Potter drew them from. Tom Kitten and his family, Samuel Whiskers and Jemima Puddle-Duck all lived in a house recognisable as Hill Top – the National Trust even suggests *The Tale of Samuel Whiskers* as an 'alternative' guide book. Plenty of the other visitors (and there were lots of them) appeared to find this experience charming; I just wanted to be able to see better. Perhaps the problem is that I am becoming a grumpy old man these days.

For anyone who loves Beatrix Potter books, however, a visit to Hill Top will be delightful, even in its permanent crepuscular gloom. Bear in mind that at busy times you may have to wait a while for your timed ticket to let you in – and that, once you are in, you can expect it to be busy inside. You are, however, allowed to spend as long as you like in the house once you're through the door. My advice: come at least half an hour before official opening time and get in line.

For more Potter, you can also visit the Beatrix Potter Gallery, run by the National Trust and situated in a 17th-century stone-built house in Hawkshead. It is dedicated to presenting original book illustrations by Beatrix Potter. The World of Beatrix Potter in Bowness-on-Windermere has a Peter Rabbit garden and some interactive exhibits: an alternative if you can't get into Hill Top. I have to confess I visited neither: it was time to Potter on.

From Beatrix Potter, the journey to Wordsworth lies via the ferry across Windermere; there is no trip so good it can't be improved by a short trip on a small car ferry. This great little ferry, a service which in various forms has been operating for 500 years – thankfully the operators are no longer required to row passengers across – takes you to Bowness.

As an alternative to the ferry, however, I made a 15-minute detour southwest to St Paul's Church, Rusland. *Swallows and Amazons* author Arthur Ransome is buried here with his second wife Evgenia; she had been Trotsky's secretary and they had met when Ransome was covering the Russian Revolution for the *Daily News*. Fans of *Swallows and Amazons* can have a treat visiting the places described in the book. You can even stay at his former house, Hill Top, which is now a holiday home; I stayed here shortly after it opened for business in 2013 and found it entirely delightful.

I took a further side trip to Kendal to visit the interesting Abbot Hall Museum. I enjoyed the fascinating permanent exhibition devoted to Arthur Ransome – and was equally taken by the display devoted to *Postman Pat*, who is the creation of Lake District author John Cunliffe. The *Postman Pat* village of Greendale was apparently inspired by the village of Longsleddale, near Kendal, while Beast Banks post office in Kendal, now closed, is said to have inspired Greendale post office. A plaque marks the building.

※

'A man who has not been in Italy is always conscious of an inferiority, from his not having seen what it is expected a man should see', said Dr Johnson.

In my opinion, the same stricture should apply to the Lake District: how many British have yet to gaze on the majesty of Skiddaw? Shame on you! That first glimpse of the high fells you get from the M6 reminds me of that first time you spot the Alps on a drive south. Are they clouds or mountain peaks? When you get into the heart of the Lake District beyond Kendal, the heart skips a further beat. And reaching Grasmere, the home of Wordsworth, has its own special delight, particularly if you can find somewhere to park (parking has become a bit of an issue in the Lake District. Wordsworth, who opposed the coming of the railways to Kendal and worried about the effect of tourism, must be saying: 'I told you so…').

'You know what I hate about these writer places?'

Two young American girls dressed for an assault on the South Pole, even though in Lake District terms this was a balmy autumnal afternoon, were waiting for our Dove Cottage tour to begin.

'What don't you like?' enquired her friend.

'All the bad stuff gets edited out. It will be 'Wordsworth… what a great guy…blah, blah, blah…when really he was probably not very nice at all. You think: "Get some perspective, guys!"'

A Lake District museum devoted to the Lake District's greatest poet is probably not the place to come for that sort of perspective. But she had a point. Visitors, generally speaking, would prefer a 'warts and all' portrait rather than a hagiography. Nobody is perfect, not even great poets. To be fair, the young Canadian who conducted our Dove Cottage tour was happy to impart information about the Wordsworth home that offered a less flattering slant. The best story is about when Sir Walter Scott came to stay – he presented the Wordsworths with a dog, 'Pepper' – and had to escape through a bedroom window to get a decent meal at a local hotel. At Dove Cottage, he is said to have reported, 'they had three meals a day and two of them were porridge'.

The Dove Cottage tour is in many ways a model of excellence that other writer museums would do well to imitate. First of all, the house has been handsomely restored to how it might have looked when the Wordsworths were in residence (amazingly, the Wordsworths haven't 'popped out' here, at least); visitors have full access to all the rooms, and there are no rope barriers. The guides are bright, enthusiastic and well informed. Best of all, the tour is quick – less than half an hour. If you want more information you can find all you need to know in the adjoining Wordsworth Museum, which claims to hold the world's largest collection of the Wordsworths' letters, journals and poems. To help understand Wordsworth's 'journey', the museum has maps, pictures and interactive displays – all of which are thoughtful and very informative. In 1936, John Masefield, then Poet Laureate, opened the first Wordsworth Museum; it was housed in a converted barn near the Cottage. In 1950, the collection of manuscripts and books was removed to a converted smithy a short distance away; this in its turn was upgraded in 1981. Wordsworth, it seemed, had become big business in the Lakes.

Of course, if you're interested in Wordsworth, then you'll be keen to walk the paths up and down the fells that he was wont to wander in the company of his sister and any transient guests (the Wordsworths always seemed to have a houseful – the porridge diet didn't seem to put many off). 'I wandered lonely as a cloud', *aka* 'Daffodils', seems to have been inspired by a walk around Glencoyne Bay, Ullswater, taken by Wordsworth and his sister Dorothy, who wrote in her journal on 15 April 1802:

> When we were in the woods beyond Gowbarrow park we saw a few daffodils close to the water side, we fancied that the lake had floated the seed ashore & that the little colony had so sprung up – But as we went along there were more & yet more & at last under the boughs of the trees, we saw that there was a long belt of them along the shore, about the breadth of a country turnpike road. I never saw daffodils so beautiful they

grew among the mossy stones about & about them, some rested their heads upon these stones as on a pillow for weariness & the rest tossed and reeled and danced & seemed as if they verily laughed with the wind that blew upon them over the Lake, they looked so gay ever dancing ever changing.

With this flowery description, Dorothy had all but written her brother's poem for him.

It's certainly a fairly easy walk of about two miles from Dove Cottage to Rydal Mount House, a later Wordsworth home which now belongs to descendants of the writer. I confess, I enjoy Wordsworth as a tourist attraction slightly more than I like his poetry; I particularly liked Rydal Mount, which has an atmosphere that the guidebook describes as 'lived-in'. A highlight was the dining room, with flagstone floors and beams of oak, clearly a part of the original Tudor structure. They offered a marked contrast with the more elegant drawing room and library that were added to the house in 1750. Wordsworth's study up in the attic was where he carried out his correspondence as Poet Laureate.

Wordsworth was offered the laureateship on the death of Southey; at first he refused, claiming that he was too old to take on the job – he was then in his early seventies. Prime Minister Robert Peel told him he wouldn't have to write anything, so Wordsworth accepted, becoming the only Poet Laureate never to have written any official verses. Given the rubbish that most Poet Laureates have churned out, this must be counted as a blessing.

※

The journey from Rydal Mount to the Wordsworth House and Garden, the poet's childhood home in the Cumbrian town of

Cockermouth, was a fairly long haul: a trip by car of about 30 miles. It was well worth making, however, for the picture it offered of William's childhood – again, this was another surprisingly fascinating slice of Wordsworth life, served up by the National Trust – back to top form after that slight lapse in the Beatrix Potter house. Wordsworth and Dorothy, with their parents, three brothers and servants, lived here in the 1770s. On selected dates, National Trust staff posing as 'the maid' or 'manservant' are ready to spare time (the Wordsworths, yes, have popped out) from their 'hard work' to chat to visitors. This is that 'immersive experience' again, which I have to admit I rather liked. There was, for example, real food on the dining table, a real fire burning in the working kitchen and a recipe that William and Dorothy might have eaten available for visitors to taste. 'Ink and quill pens are ready in the clerk's office and, if you play the piano, you might like to try our replica harpsichord.'

I gave it my party piece: 'A Whiter Shade of Pale'.

'Don't give up your day job,' opined a fellow visitor.

The lovely small market town of Cockermouth is one of the most interesting places in the Lake District, boasting a fine Norman castle. Despite a family tragedy which eventually forced the Wordsworths to leave, the poet had only happy memories of his childhood here spent near the River Derwent, which he describes in 'The Prelude' as 'the fairest of rivers'.

I left with only happy memories, too, though my own journey was about as far away from its prelude as it was possible to be. It was time for the final leg of my literary trip around Britain and to head north of the border for Scotland.

11

Burns Cottage to Muckle Flugga

In which our intrepid reader discovers a Burns Cottage as it says on the shortbread tin, discovers many great Scots and one great Scott, enjoys and endures the journey to Jura, before touching down on his final Treasure Island.

ONE of the first significant accounts of literary tourism in Britain came in July 1818, when John Keats set off on a walking tour of the Lake District and Scotland with a friend. Having walked 170 miles from Lancaster to Alloway in Scotland, they stopped off to visit the childhood home and grave of his hero Robert Burns.

While Keats was excited to experience his first trip 'abroad' – he was delighted to discover that in Scotland people spoke to each other in Gaelic – the Burns part of the trip was largely a disappointment. He was able to talk to people who had known Burns, and they painted a rather less flattering picture of the Scotsman than the one that Keats had conjured up in his imagination. Disappointingly, Scotland turned out to be a poverty-stricken nation where most people struggled to make a hard living – not quite the romantic world of Burns' poetry.

Visiting Burns Cottage was the worst part of the trip. At that time, it was still surrounded by the fields which Robert Burns had worked with his father. To his horror, however, Keats discovered that this famous literary shine was now a 'whisky-shop'. As he recounted to his friend John Hamilton Reynolds:

> We went to the Cottage and took some Whisky. I wrote a sonnet for the mere sake of writing some lines under the roof: they are so bad I cannot transcribe them.

They found that the caretaker – 'The Man at the Cottage' – was a 'great bore with his anecdotes': 'I hate the rascal', wrote Keats. In a series of remarks, which might have been made for Twitter, he went on to observe that the caretaker's anecdotes concerning Burns were lacking in definition:

> …his life consists in fuzy, fuzzy fuzziest. He drinks glasses, five for the quarter, and twelve for the hour; he is a mahogany-faced old jackass who knew Burns: he ought to have been kicked for having spoken to him. He calls himself 'a curious old bitch'– but he is a flat old dog.[44]

Keats had already discovered the potential disappointments involved in literary tourism. Earlier on his walking tour he had been to the Lake District to call on Wordsworth at his famous Dove Cottage, but he discovered that the great poet was not at home (well, one imagines the person who had answered the door had said that Wordsworth wasn't home). Keats had also earlier made a special trip to Stratford-upon-Avon to visit Shakespeare's Birthplace, to join the 'numbers numberless' who 'literally blackened the walls' of Shakespeare's half-timbered home on Henley Street. As Keats discovered, Shakespeare's birthplace was already firmly established as a tourist attraction – a process which began with a huge Jubilee staged by David Garrick in 1769 to mark the bicentenary of Shakespeare's birth (-ish – they were five years late, but that clearly didn't stop them) – although, disappointingly, while there was much merrymaking, none of his plays were actually performed.

Tempting as it was to follow in Keats' footsteps and walk from the Lake District up into Scotland, I decided, on reflection, that driving might be preferable. But I did want to echo his journey: having already been to Stratford and Dove Cottage, Burns Cottage seemed the only place I could begin my own literary visit to Scotland.

Burns has now been dead for more than 200 years, but he still looms large in Scottish cultural life. 'How would Robert Burns vote in the Scottish referendum?' asked a major feature in the *Guardian* in the run up to the big vote in 2014. The article decided that the radical Burns would have opted for independence – the writer concluded that the poet wasn't a natural supporter of the status quo. (Actually, while during the referendum debate the SNP leader Alex Salmond was quick to annex him for the purposes of his ill-fated referendum, there was plenty of evidence to suggest that Burns – who, after all, had worked for His Majesty's Customs and Excise department – would probably have been quite happy with the status quo. Burns is one of those Lucky Eight Balls whose writings come up with just the answer that the questioner is keen to hear, it seems.)

The question of how to create a museum around Burns and turn him into a literary tourist attraction in 2010 was clearly a tricky issue: this was tampering with greatness. Opinions on this still relatively new museum are mixed.

'Oh my Gawd,' exclaimed the woman peering into a carefully ordered display cabinet, whose precisely arranged exhibits attempted to untangle Burns' troubled love life: 'I cannae see a bloody thing,' she wailed. She was holding her iPhone ready to take a snap, but just as she was about to press the virtual button, the lights went out, leaving us all in virtual darkness. 'Has the bloody bob dropped?' she cried: 'Why have the stinking lights gone out completely now?'

Alloway's still-shiny new Robert Burns Birthplace Museum, which opened in December 2010, is an impressive effort to tell the story of the poet's life and work. There are two clear problems, however. One, the general lighting in the main part of the museum lies somewhere between 'atmospheric' and 'total darkness', a situation not helped by the fact that, for reasons best known to the museum's designer, the lights in particular areas go on and off unexpectedly – occasionally plunging the visitor into rather more than semi-darkness.

The second problem is that the thematic nature of the exhibition means that you don't follow the life story of the poet from cradle to grave in a continuous timeline. And suddenly Burns poems start to be recited from hidden speakers, provoking a general feeling of chaos. According to a contemporary article in the local paper, the intention was not to offer 'the definitive or authoritative account of Burns' life'; rather they were seeking to 'question perceptions'. The idea was for visitors to be provided with a few undisputed facts – including the date of Burns' birth in 1759 and death in 1796 – but then to leave it to visitors to transport themselves back to Burns' time, 'walk in Burns' buckled shoes and live his often chaotic and complicated life'. The exhibition invites the visitor to dip in and out of Burns' life and legacy: you put in your thumb and hopefully, if the lighting allows, you pull out a plum.

There are lots of fascinating facts to be had about Robert Burns. For example, it seems that, apart from Queen Victoria and Christopher Columbus, Robert Burns is said to be commemorated in more statues than any other non-religious figure. Nobody is sure of the exact number of Burns monuments around the world, but the best estimates suggest that Scotland boasts fifteen, America has fourteen, Canada and Australia tie with seven each, while England has six (including a bust in Westminster Abbey's Poets' Corner), New Zealand has four and Northern Ireland has a statue in Belfast – to name but a few.

Burns' poetry and lyrics are supped with mother's milk in Scotland, while many people outside Scotland and around the world are largely familiar with his greatest hits: 'Auld Lang syne', 'A Man's A Man For A' That', 'Address To A Haggis', 'Ae Fond Kiss And Then We Sever', and lines from his songs and poems have echoed down the centuries: 'The best-laid schemes o' mice an 'men Gang aft agley' (part of which was used by Steinbeck as the title of his novel *Of Mice And Men*) and 'Comin' Thro' the Rye' which inspired the title of J D Salinger's classic cult novel *The Catcher in the Rye*.

Burns' problem, unfortunately, is that he is probably less well-known today for his poetry than as a symbol of a certain sort of Scottishness: his is the face on souvenir shortbread and celebratory whisky. The souvenir shop at the Birthplace Museum is unashamedly full of this sort of thing: Tam o'Shanter Single Spey Malt Whisky or Robert Burns Blended Whisky £22.99 a bottle, a snow globe of the Burns Cottage or a Moorland Pottery 'A Man's A Man For A' That' mug for £13.99 – or who fancies a tin of Burns Cottage Haggis, Neeps & Tatties? In his poem 'A Drunk Man Looks at the Thistle', Scottish poet Hugh MacDiarmid says that he loves Burns but has come to loathe the cult that has grown up around him and threatens to suffocate his art; MacDiarmid says that more nonsense has been uttered in Burns' name 'than in ony's barrin' liberty and Christ.'

Impressively, the Robert Burns Birthplace Trust prominently displays MacDiarmid's cautionary words near the museum entrance right next to the souvenir shop – as if to say, we know much of what we sell here can be described as 'tat', but there you are. This might be postmodern irony.

The actual Burns Cottage itself, about a 10-minute walk from the museum, has been kept pretty much as it was when Burns was born and brought up here. As Keats discovered when he walked all the way here from Lancashire, it's just as it says on the tin – in this case, a souvenir shortbread tin. Unlike the museum, the cottage was reasonably well lit and incredibly quiet (not many people who visit the museum seemed prepared to take the walk to the cottage).

There was much else to see nearby: the famous Brig o'Doon as featured in the poem 'Tam o'Shanter', the Auld Kirk where Burns' father and sister are buried, and the Burns monument. Back at the museum, it was time for something to eat and a cup of tea; the museum's restaurant seemed about the most popular place in town. Afterwards, I had my picture taken with 'Robert Burns' and his wife, 'Jean Armour'. At this point, the attraction had become less a museum and more a theme park – but then, Burns has been a brand as big as Disney, but for 200 years.

The man himself, you feel, would be delighted. Never well off in his life, in death Burns is a millionaire. Poetic justice?

A famous painting by Charles Martin Hardie, painted in 1893, shows *The Meeting of Robert Burns and Sir Walter Scott at Sciennes Hill House* in Edinburgh. This was the one occasion on which Scott and Burns actually met and had a conversation. Scott was 15, Burns was 12 years older; they met at the Edinburgh home of his good friend, Adam Ferguson. Scott described how self-confident Burns seemed in the presence of the city's literati. An old school friend and business partner of Scott's, James Ballytyne, once asked Scott how his own genius compared to Robert Burns. It was clear that Scott worshipped Burns: 'We ought not to be named in the same day,' he said, with impressive modesty.

Interestingly, the two biggest writers' museums in the UK are both in Scotland, some 100 miles apart. From the substantial Burns museum to Sir Walter Scott's mighty Abbotsford was about a two-and-a-half-hour drive, a journey from the slightly stark scenery of Ayrshire to the lusher valleys of the Scottish Borders.

Writers and reputations rapidly go in and out of fashion; authors who evoked great passion 100 years ago are today sometimes barely recognised. When *Sherlock Holmes* creator Arthur Conan Doyle first came to London, he raced to Westminster Abbey to pay homage to a man he placed ahead of all other writers. Dickens? Chaucer? Keats? Actually, it was the grave of essayist Thomas Macaulay: 'It was the one great object of interest which London held for me.'

The other great writing love of Conan Doyle's life was Scott, whose novels, he wrote, 'started me on to rhapsody'. However, he does admit that 'there is an intolerable amount of redundant verbiage in Scott's novels'.[45] He's certainly right about that.

If I'd put my mind to it, there was a lot about Sir Walter Scott and his grand home Abbotsford which I was ready to dislike quite intensely. I'm not a big fan of his books. I've started a few Scott novels but never finished one: as Conan Doyle pointed out, the man has logorrhoea – verbal diarrhoea – never finding one word sufficient if he can use a hundred instead. Most 19th-century writers seem to have had this problem – though those writing for serialisation, such as Dickens, clearly had an interest in padding out each instalment. (Interestingly, Frank Richards – real name Charles Hamilton, author of the Billy Bunter books – was apparently paid by the line, which may account for his preponderance for short lines: 'Oh Lor', 'Ha! Ha! Ha!', 'I say you fellows!', 'Fat Owl!'. It's estimated that Frank Richards wrote 72 million words in 7,000 stories. Oh Lor…)

Scott's problem is not really the number of words he used, but his subject matter. Not so much what he was writing about, but what he wasn't writing about. He was writing at a time of enormous social upheaval in Scotland, when smallholders were being forced off their crofts by brutal landlords in the shameful Highland Clearances. Yet Scott chose to ignore all of this – an odd decision, you might have thought, given its dramatic potential. Scott's literary focus was directed elsewhere; writers such as Hugh MacDiarmid have described his subject matter as presenting 'a hopelessly false and anachronistic image of Scotland'.[46] He was almost single-handedly fashioning the sort of White Heather Club view of Scotland – all kilts and tam'o'shanters – that has launched a thousand shortbread tins.

Scott made Scotland enticing enough to lure Queen Victoria and Prince Albert on a rare journey across the border to 'North Britain'. When they decided to remodel the house at Balmoral, they unapologetically had the enlargement built in the style now known as Scottish Baronial, with clear inspiration taken from Scott's Abbotsford; when Victoria wanted a monument built to Prince Albert opposite the Albert Hall – wasn't the Hall memorial enough, you wonder? – it seems that they copied the steepling Scott Monument in Edinburgh. Dickens was a tireless campaigner, using his books to highlight terrible social wrongs; Scott, however, was unashamedly on the side of the toffs. For him, as for so many of the 19th century, he was quite happy with the way that life had turned out: the rich man in his castle, the poor man at his gate, God made them high and lowly, and ordered their estate. All things were bright and beautiful if, like Scott, you were the rich man in his castle; not so wonderful if you were the hapless soul starving at his gate.

There is a twist in the Scott tale, however. In 1825, when he was 54 and at the height of his wealth and fame, he was ruined by a phenomenon which has become rather more familiar to us in recent years: a banking crisis. This led to the collapse of the Ballantyne printing business in which Scott had a significant financial interest; he immediately became liable for massive debts. This was a disaster. Had he declared himself bankrupt, he risked losing his beloved house, so he announced that he would pay back his crippling debts through a prodigious effort of writing, saying that his 'right hand shall work it all off'.

He not only had to suffer the loss of his fortune, but – at the same time – also the death of his wife. But he saw no alternative than to buckle down and embark on a punishing programme of writing, turning out not just more fiction, but a staggering amount of non-fiction – including, for example, a biography of Napoleon Bonaparte. Scott died exhausted in 1832 still owing money – but, as his novels continued to sell well after his death, his debts were quickly discharged.

Despite Scott's huge reserves of pluck and his tireless energy, I still can't summon up much enthusiasm for either him or his vast literary output. Given the massive following that he attracted, not only in Scotland or the UK but all around the world, I am clearly in the minority. But I did enjoy visiting Abbotsford, which is not only a fascinating house, all the more interesting for being built entirely to Scott's specifications, but also extremely well managed and presented. The visitor centre, which I had to pass through to buy my ticket en route to the house, is one of the best of its sort – clearly arranged, easy to read and understand, assiduously placing Scott in his historical perspective and explaining how and why he built Abbotsford. If you pop upstairs to the excellent restaurant, you have the perfect view of the house before you start your visit – as I gazed out through the huge floor-to-ceiling windows, Abbotsford had the look of a carefully constructed stage set, created simply to look beautiful in its glorious Tweed valley setting. Of course, the property has been very artfully designed and arranged to impress – but the interior of the property was just as fabulous as the outside.

It was not just the grandness of the rooms, their rich decor and the intricacy of the lay-out – Scott had a secret staircase to enable him to escape if unwanted visitors came calling – it was the number of extraordinary things he managed to accumulate in his lifetime. The amount of weapons and armour suggests an unhealthy interest in violence – I could imagine Blofeld here with James Bond.

'Ah, Mr Bond, I see you are admiring my medieval halberd which could slice a man in half with a single blow.'

'I've heard of cutting remarks, Blofeld…'

Also here were Rob Roy's gun, dirk and sword; the house did have his sporran, but it was stolen in September 2014.

The striking thing about Scott's house was that it has its original contents – other writers, such as Dickens and Hardy, for example, made provision to dispose of their houses and their contents after their death. So at Abbotsford I could enjoy a visit to the huge library, which held over 9,000 books, including many rare volumes. Around the building I could walk through the handsome gardens and take in the wider landscape, which was designed and planted to Scott's plans. I could even have holidayed here – a wing of Abbotsford has been extensively refurbished to allow self-catering.

※

For final proof that Scotland truly loved Scott, reflect on the fact that the original estimate for building the massive Scott Monument in Edinburgh was £10,175 and ten shillings – but it actually cost £16,154 seven shillings and 11 pence. Extra money was raised by a door-to-door collection throughout the City. Greater love hath no Scotsman than this…

Based on my own experience – admittedly fairly limited – the Scott Monument isn't as rigorously managed as it might be. The monument's website advises prospective visitors to check its Twitter feed – the Scott Monument has a Twitter feed? – which lets you know when they have 'unexpected closures'.

There is so much wrong with this, I barely know where to start...although the Scott Monument's gross over-optimism regarding my technological prowess might be one. Here's another suggestion: don't keep closing the monument at short notice. I tried to gain admission on three occasions and, despite the fact that it should have been open, it was closed.

In truth, there are probably more interesting and more exciting treats in Edinburgh than the Scott Monument. Its main attraction is its size: at 61m high, it is the world's largest monument to a writer. It's worth noting that Edinburgh is the only city in the world to have a railway station named after a novel: *Waverley* (Sir Walter Scott again). And the only city with a football team named after a novel: Hearts, from *The Heart of Midlothian*, also by Sir Walter Scott – the novel is centred on the Old Tolbooth prison which was situated in the heart of Midlothian. One presumes the football team was inspired by the book's title rather than from the wider reference to the gaol...

There are certainly other literary delights. Edinburgh has a dedicated Writers' Museum, located in Lady Stair's House a 17th-century residence in a close off the Lawnmarket. Makar's Court, a paved area next to the Museum, commemorates Edinburgh's famous writers, each with a phrase evocative of their works. A sign reminds visitors that Edinburgh is a UNESCO City of Literature (according to Google there are 11 cities of literature: an eclectic choice which also includes Norwich, Iowa City and Granada).

Lady Stair's House is a fascinating property containing displays devoted to the careers of three Scottish writers: Robert Burns, Sir Walter Scott and Robert Louis Stevenson. The implicit suggestion is that these are the only three writers which matter; in fact the museum accidentally grew up around collections linked to these three men. It was a nice place to visit – the staff were cheerful and helpful far above and beyond the call of duty. I was able to see portraits, rare books and an interesting selection of original items, including Burns' writing desk from the time that he was a Dumfries resident. I also saw a stool apparently used by Burns in 1787, from the printing office of William Smellie when the Edinburgh Edition of his poems were proofed: it's just a stool, really. A little more exciting was the swordcane with an engraved head that Burns owned when he worked as an exciseman. Did he get involved in sword fights? It would have been interesting to know. This is a Scottish TV series waiting to happen: *Robert Burns: Exciseman* – arresting whisky smugglers by day, poet by night. James Bond with a rhyming dictionary...

The collection also has letters from Burns, plus 'Scots wha hae' in manuscript, on which you can see the poet's crossings-out and notes. More macabrely, I saw Robert Burns' skull, one of three plaster casts made. Scott possessions on display included a chessboard and the press on which his *Waverley* novels were printed. Also on display is the ring given to Robert Louis by a Samoan chief; it carries the inscription 'Tusitala' – 'teller of tales'.

If your literary tastes are more contemporary, you can find connections out in the city itself. *Trainspotting* author Irvine Welsh, for example, set most of the action of his best-known novel in late-1980s Leith, painting a lurid picture of a world of drug addiction, crime and urban poverty. The Leith of the 1980s, then an impoverished suburb, is dramatically juxtaposed against Edinburgh's thriving, culturally-orientated city centre. Some 30 years on, however, the historic port of Leith has been wonderfully transformed into a successful vibrant community with lots of good eating places and interesting shops. I had a drink at the Central Bar at the foot of Leith Walk, which once stood next to the platform of Leith railway station. *Trainspotting* fans have argued that the novel's ironic title alludes to the fact that trains no longer run to Leith; the derelict station was instead used by drug addicts.

Favourite Edinburgh spots for fans of the *Inspector Rebus* novels written by Ian Rankin include The Oxford Bar in Young Street, in the New Town of Edinburgh – a hostelry patronised by both Inspector Rebus and Rankin himself. It was after his flatmate got a job at the bar that he discovered the Oxford, says Rankin; he has described the pub – which only has two rooms, one with church pews for chairs – as 'small and homely': it is. I also took a look at St Leonard's police station on St Leonard's Street, which is the real-life Edinburgh station where Rebus worked; it is situated at the bottom of Arthur's Seat and the Salisbury Crags. (David Nicholls' 2009 novel *One Day* begins and ends with principal characters Emma and Dexter climbing Arthur's Seat.)

J K Rowling fans pay homage to The Elephant House on George IV Bridge, which was the cafe where Rowling would push baby Jessica – named after the literary Mitford sister – and sit at a table while she worked on her first *Harry Potter* book. The wall inside the ladies toilets is covered with Potter fan graffiti. The cafe has also been frequented by Ian Rankin – it features in a *Rebus* novel.

Fans of local resident Alexander McCall Smith's *44 Scotland Street* books, meanwhile, can download a tour which allows them to walk 'In the Footsteps of 44 Scotland Street'. This will lead you, for example, to Drummond Street Gardens; it was here where Cyril the dog had his short-lived love affair which resulted in six puppies; not far away is the place where Scotland's First Minister Jack O'Connell stopped Bertie from being run over.

✼

About two hours' drive north of Edinburgh was the National Trust for Scotland's J M Barrie's Birthplace on Brechin Road in Kirriemuir. The house was where Barrie spent his formative years – events which supplied the genesis of the *Peter Pan* story.

It was in Kirriemuir that the defining moment of Barrie's childhood took place when his older brother David died in a skating accident. Barrie's mother seems never to have got over this, remaining permanently grief stricken. Barrie began to realise that, even when he had achieved adulthood, as far as his mother was concerned David would always be 'the boy who wouldn't grow up'.

As Barrie's family were of humble origins, the family house didn't really have that much to see. There was some interesting memorabilia: the christening robe made of silk – shared between Barrie and his nine siblings (and also available to other families in the area). Outside the house, I saw the communal wash-house which was where Barrie, at the age of seven, staged his first dramatic performance. In his dedication in *Peter Pan*, Barrie says that it was his Kirremuir home which inspired the Never-Never Land house built for Wendy – the original Wendy House – in Never-Never Land.

Kirriemuir isn't the only Scottish place with a J M Barrie connection: Barrie moved to Dumfries in his early teens and was a pupil at Dumfries Academy, where he was an active member of the newly formed Academy Dramatic Club. It was said that here he first developed a love of theatre.

The Dumfries location that seems to have had the biggest effect on him as a teenager is the large Georgian town house, Moat Brae, on George Street, where his close friends the Gordon brothers lived. Barrie was a regular visitor; he and his friends would amuse themselves for hours in the garden climbing trees and playing at pirates; many years later, he said that this experience helped inspire him to write *Peter Pan*, calling the garden an 'enchanted land' where the 'genesis of that nefarious work' took place. Plans are in hand to create the Scottish Centre for Children's Stories at Moat Brae House.

※

Treasured Island

While it is easy to imagine Neverland being born in sweet, unspoilt Dumfries, it is harder to imagine a dystopian view of the future being created on a lovely Scottish island. On its website, the Jura Hotel bills itself as 'the' place to get away from it all on Jura. Actually, once you're on Jura – anywhere on the island – you're pretty much as away from it all as you can reasonably expect to get. When I began planning my tour of literary places, the island of Jura was one of the first names pencilled into my itinerary. I first visited here over 20 years ago, and it was such a happy visit that I immediately began looking forward to going back.

Jura's isolation clearly appealed to Orwell. For the old Etonian author of *Down and Out in Paris and London*, who had lived rough in the city – and suffered immense physical hardship fighting in the Spanish Civil War – the inevitable lack of comforts was no deterrent. Indeed, Orwell seems to have nurtured dreams of self-sufficiency, happy to supplement his meagre income from writing with home-grown vegetables and the comforts of farm eggs and milk. (Orwell seems to have had a lot in common with Richmal Crompton's Just William: like Orwell, William was keen to be a tramp when he grew up and lived life with anarchic energy – he would, no doubt, have loved Jura.)

Orwell travelled here for an extended stay for the first time in spring 1946. Jura is a small island, about 30 miles from end to end. While the southern half of the island is a relatively close-knit community, linked by a single metalled road, the top part is remote – served by a rough track unsuitable for ordinary cars. The house that he rented, Barnhill, is a very isolated farmhouse on a very isolated island.

From the moment he arrived, Orwell must have sensed that here on Jura he would find the peace he was looking for. His reputation as a writer had finally been established with the publication of *Animal Farm*, and now he was preparing to start work on what would be his greatest novel.

The first glimpse down to Barnhill from the high point of the road is stunning: the lonely farmhouse framed by a dark sea. Orwell quickly settled into life here, accompanied by Richard, his adopted son, and a variety of friends who came and went throughout his time there: digging vegetables, hay-making, putting up shelves (Sonia Brownell, who became his second wife in October 1949, just three months before his death, described him as the only intellectual she knew who could mend a fuse), fishing and shooting – yet still finding time to work on his book. He wrote to his friend, George Woodcock, in 1947, during his second extended summer on the island that he could work there with fewer interruptions. The islanders' most vivid memory of Orwell was of him bouncing up and down the unmade road on an old motorbike that frequently broke down, leaving him tinkering with its engine, hoping some passer-by would lend mechanical assistance.

Orwell was thought by some to have been foolish to travel north when he was suffering from TB, but Jura, washed by the Gulf Stream, has a mild climate and in winter rarely sees a hard frost. A lack of easy access to expert medical advice was a greater problem – but, if Jura killed Orwell, it was not the climate, nor the absence of medical expertise – rather, it was the lack of typists. Ill in bed after completing the manuscript of his latest book at a time when he needed complete rest, Orwell was unable to secure the services of a stenographer he was willing to trust; he undertook the retyping of the novel himself.

It is generally agreed that, if the effort involved in typing the final draft did not actually kill him, it certainly hastened his death (although the continual heavy smoking of roll-ups and the presence in his bedroom of a smoky paraffin heater did little to improve his health). But Orwell did at least have a title for the new book. He rejected his working title, *The Last Man in Europe*, and instead took the year in which he completed the novel – 1948 – and reversed the last two digits: *1984*.

One of the great watchwords in travel is: 'Never go back!' If it's true that you can't step into the same river twice, it is certainly almost impossible to repeat the experience of a much-enjoyed holiday. You won't be the same person you were on that happy original visit – and the place itself will also probably have changed.

Frank Sinatra sang that love is 'lovelier' the second time; sadly Jura was not. The first time around, Jura was enveloped in a heatwave, with temperatures in the eighties. I had planned a visit to do something with the fact that Orwell had written *1984* on Jura, and that at the time I visited it was approaching 1994 – a sort of ten year anniversary (terrible idea, I know).

Everything came together in the way that sometimes things can when the travel gods are smiling. Not just the most perfect weather – but by chance the Jura Hotel was running a Land Rover safari while I was there up to the Corryvreckan whirlpool. (This is holy ground for Orwell fans because the writer managed to row into the middle of it one day and almost drowned – the things which we wish to commemorate are, I confess, sometimes odd.) It was a bonus that the trip was passing the road to Barnhill.

We had barely begun this trip to the north of the island when we encountered the then-owner of Barnhill coming south. He invited us to Barnhill to visit the house and see the very room in which Orwell had written *1984*. So it was that we stood in the bedroom where the ailing Orwell sat in bed, with a paraffin stove belching out choking fumes, as he clattered away on his typewriter; sucking in not only the fumes of the heater, but also his chain-smoked cigarettes. So this is where the magic happened...

Of all the literary places I have visited, this was the most affecting experience.

I was crazy to try and repeat it. It was, however, a return journey with a great start: a fairly rapid journey to Jura (Flybe plane from Glasgow to Islay, then car hire at Islay airport followed by a short drive to the ferry port and then a quick crossing to Jura). I began to realise that Jura second time around wasn't such a good idea when I walked up the path to the Jura Hotel – in the sort of fine drizzle that soaks you right through – and was greeted by the prospect of a stout man in hiking gear elaborately cutting his toenails on a bench. (Call me old-fashioned but, back in my day, this is one of those things we did in private.) My Orwell plans on this second visit were as unshaped as they had been on my original trip: this time, however, the travel Gods were not smiling.

I thought about risking a drive up the long unmade road to the north of the island in order to take in at least a distant view of Barnhill – but realised that, with a hire car, and not wishing to replicate Orwell's lengthy waits for mechanical assistance in the likely event of a mishap, this would be unwise. There were no safaris to be had today, even if one did wish to take the trip in the rain. I had travelled to Jura to revisit past delights which were now no longer so easily available. I could, of course, have arranged to rent Barnhill – the property's owner makes it available via the escapetojura.com website from £800 a week – perhaps I shall during the next heatwave. I returned to Islay airport to await the flight back to Glasgow, a sadder but wiser literary traveller.

※

Orwell mined literary treasure on one Scottish island. Robert Louis Stevenson (RLS) struck storybook gold on another. For, while *Treasure Island* reaches its climax in the fictional Caribbean, its actual starting point, it is suggested, lies far north of the Scottish mainland.

Shetland is a group of about 100 islands, just 15 inhabited, which lie about 110 miles north of the Scottish mainland.

Treasured Island

Shetland is 600 miles north of London and just 400 miles south of the Arctic Circle; it is as far north as St Petersburg or Anchorage, Alaska. The island's capital Lerwick is actually closer to Bergen in Norway than it is to Edinburgh. It was in this remote spot that the road to *Treasure Island* begins.

After he left full-time education, his ill-health and constant lack of money caused RLS to lead the nomadic life of a hack writer. He had disappointed his father by rejecting a career in the family business of building lighthouses – the Lighthouse Stevensons, as they were known. He had also made it clear that he was an atheist and had rejected their religious beliefs. The writing of *Treasure Island,* which began when RLS was temporarily back in Scotland, was an opportunity for a *rapprochement* between father and son. An adventure story involving sailing ships and pirates, it was bound to appeal to RLS's father Thomas.

The story began with the 'X' marks the spot' treasure map; possibly drawn by RLS on a trip to Unst with his father to look at Muckle Flugga lighthouse – it is generally agreed that the outline of the eponymous treasure island is that of Unst, the most northerly part of the UK. What's undisputed is that Stevenson did, indeed, walk these shores.

There is a regular ferry service to the Shetland Islands from Aberdeen; however, I flew from Edinburgh – a journey of just 90 minutes. But such was the unique world of the Shetland Islands I felt I had somehow travelled further than when I'd visited Australia or New Zealand.

Time was of the essence: I'd landed at Sumburgh airport at about 1pm and needed to reach the northern coast of Unst to see the Stevenson lighthouse before the sun set at about 5pm. The journey was complicated by the fact that it involved two separate ferry crossings – the actual crossings themselves were short, but the ferry service is infrequent – a missed connection could mean that I was driving up to Muckle Flugga in total darkness. At about 3.30pm, however, I was driving off the ferry at Belmont and starting the final section up through Unst. I had a nagging feeling I was lost, but there aren't many people around on Unst to help with directions – eventually I struck lucky: here was a native. Is this the road to Muckle Flugga?

The lad standing at the bus stop in the middle of nowhere slowly removed his earphones and narrowed his eyes as I asked again.

'Muckle Flugga? Aye, keep going straight until you're about to fall off the end of the island, that's Muckle Flugga.'

My satnav was behaving as if we were about to drop off the end of the world: the car symbol, which was supposed to show me where I was – and where I was heading – began a dad dance of restless gyrating, one minute pointing north, the next south. But there really was only one way to go: straight ahead. And as I looked at it, the satnav image of Unst suddenly offered an extraordinary and marvellous prospect: I realised I was on the *Treasure Island* map.

The sun was beginning its descent towards the horizon, filling the world with a golden blaze. Minutes, however, were fast ticking by, and the sun was sinking ever lower when the car climbed the last hill towards a disused military base. And there, suddenly, across the sea, was the clear white stack of Muckle Flugga lighthouse, gloriously bathed in the final rays of the setting sun. If I had set my foot on the North Pole, I could scarcely have felt a greater sense of achievement.

The north Unst lighthouse dates back to 1851, when fears of war with Russia in the Crimea concentrated government minds on safeguarding their northern approaches. It was decided that they needed a lighthouse at Muckle Flugga, one of the most northerly rocks in the British Isles, and the Stevensons were instructed to build it. Work began with the construction of a temporary lighthouse building, which was apparently finished in just 26 days. The temporary structure was 50ft high, standing on top of a rock 200ft above the level of the sea.

This structure was so high it was assumed that it would only have to resist the wind and the rain. However, the onset of the winter gales generated waves high enough to wash over the temporary lighthouse, causing anxieties that they could topple the structure – the Scottish weather, clearly, should never be underestimated. Work was begun on a permanent lighthouse in 1855: this was a 64ft brick tower which had foundations that were sunk ten feet into the rock. A permanent light appeared on 1 January 1858; Stevenson was to visit the following year.

If this sounds simple and easy, you only need to look at the precarious situation of the highly exposed rock on which they had to build the lighthouse to realise what a terrifying enterprise the construction here was. In fact, nearly all of the Scottish lighthouses built by the Stevenson family were an exercise of unbelievable courage and phenomenal ingenuity in the face of the most awful physical and meteorological perils. Particularly when you bear in mind that, in the 19th century, they had little but brute force and relentless optimism to see them through. It's not hard to see why Robert Louis Stevenson might have opted against a career in lighthouse construction and chose writing instead.

I lingered until the sun had dipped over the western horizon and then made my way back to Sumburgh, pausing only to dine at the celebrated Frankie's Fish and Chips – the most northerly chippy in the UK.

I was booked to stay at the Sumburgh Head Light House on Mainland, at the southern end of the Shetland Islands – another Stevenson production. Recently lavishly refurbished, it boasts a range of luxuries which would have seemed incredible to those Lighthouse Stevensons: there was an Aga and underfloor heating. At night I lay in my bed watching the lighthouse's giant lamp flash its signature beam to ships at sea and listened to the wind howling (the lighthouse is in such an exposed position, I'm not sure the wind has a setting which dips below 'howling' here). During a really bad storm, the building must vibrate like a 747 plane preparing to charge down the runway.

There was just one more thing I felt I had to do. After unpacking my bag I got out my cherished copy of *Treasure Island* and, in the pirate spirit, poured myself a tot of rum and raised a glass to my uncle and to RLS. Together, they had taken me on the greatest journey of my life.

Fin.

'IT'S ironic, isn't it?' said the man at the ticket desk, 'This is a literary attraction and we're literally about to close.' He laughed; I glowered.

Alanis Morissette has driven me nuts since her 1996 song 'Ironic'; this lists a huge number of supposed examples of irony – the fly in your chardonnay or the death row pardon that arrived two minutes too late – yet not one of these instances can be properly described as ironic. Annoying? Certainly. Badly timed? Probably. Ironic? Definitely and utterly not.

So I have taken a solemn and binding oath never to turn a blind eye to irony abuse. Some people get angry about the 'greengrocer's apostrophe'; me, I've drawn a line in the sand on supposed examples of 'irony'.

'It's not ironic,' I told the ticket desk man: 'It's lots of things: it's annoying; it's disobliging; it's unaccommodating. It's not ironic. Is it really, really not possible to take just a very quick look around, I promise I won't be long at all, it would save me a difficult journey tomorrow…'

The man smiled and shook his head. We have rules, he was admitting ruefully: his non-verbal gestures were meant to convey the impression that if it were up to him he would happily keep the doors open until 2am but, you see, it's not up to him…

'Do you want to know what's 'ironic'?' I said, 'It's you having a badge on your lapel saying 'How can I help you?' and then you not wanting to help me at all. That's ironic.'

A few of Britain's literary attractions are run as totalitarian regimes, apparently inspired by Honecker-era Communist East

Fin.

Germany: lots of notices banning things – photography, use of mobile phones, eating, drinking, chewing gum, pets, umbrellas – now 'selfies' have been added to the list. There was even one place I visited where they were unhappy at people coming in with muddy shoes. They have my sympathy; if I ran a nice museum I would find most visitors very annoying. But if you're in a business where your livelihood depends on welcoming the public, here's a tip: welcome the poor bloody saps!

Britain is in transition. As an economy increasingly dominated by service industries, new generations have had to adopt the 'have a nice day' customer contact skills that we used to find so amusing whenever we went to America. Time was when you went into Boots and had to wait 10 minutes before two 16-year old girls finished a discussion about their stuttering romantic life before they would deign to acknowledge your existence and sell you some athlete's foot cream. That doesn't happen so often now. Actually, the problem has flipped in the other direction – too many hotel receptionists, car hire staff, waiters, hairdressers and retail therapists continually asking 'How was your journey here today?' or 'Are you planning anything nice tonight?'

If there is one place where this service revolution has yet to make much headway, it is in our museums and allied tourist attraction trades (if there's one place that ought to be stuck in the past, then I suppose it really ought to be a museum). This is because: a) the majority of staff you meet at these places are generously providing their services free of charge, b) they have not been trained, or c) they really do find members of the public annoying.

But, in truth, these are but small shadows on an otherwise bright and sunny picture. The world of literary tourist attractions in the UK is in many ways a showcase for the Best of Britain. Forget the 2012 London Olympics, every day in the UK (well, many places close during the off-season – so most days in the UK) lovers of the written word can not only visit locations that celebrate our national literary achievements but enjoy a list of places that are international gold medal winners. From the Jane Austen museum in the south to Walter Scott's Abbotsford in the north, we offer exemplary attractions that tick all the visitor boxes: well presented, friendly staff, imaginatively conceived with thoughtful gift shops and top-class pots of tea.

Most of the National Trust properties I visited were outstanding: I dare you to enjoy a day out better than that offered by Monk's House, Bateman's, Thomas Hardy's cottage, T E Lawrence's Clouds Hill or Carlyle's House, for example. But there were lots of equally good 'small' places: the Pepys Library in Cambridge is magnificent; I loved the Boathouse in Laugharne, Dr Johnson's house in London, Burns Cottage in Scotland, the Larkin Trail in Hull and Dove Cottage in the Lake District. I look forward to returning to the Brontë Parsonage Museum in Haworth when they, as they surely will, eventually get their act together.

My long-abiding pleasure from this book, however, will be the trip to Shetland to follow Robert Louis Stevenson to the probable genesis of *Treasure Island* on the wonderful island of Unst, and a hell-for-leather trip to see the superbly named Muckle Flugga lighthouse before the sun set. I regret that it took me such a long time to get to the Shetland Islands – I'm hoping to make a quick return.

Several years ago, passengers arriving by train at London Paddington station were greeted by a piece of enigmatic graffiti which read: 'Far away is close at hand in images of elsewhere' (surely an Arts Council grant should be furnished to get this restored!). *Treasure Island* paints pictures of far away, but its inspiration is surprisingly close at hand in the northernmost point of the UK. You can travel to the furthest place on earth, but I guarantee you will not find anywhere more truly exotic than Muckle Flugga.

Isn't it ironic?

Notes

The author and publisher would like to thank the following for allowing or not raising objections to the use of copyright material: p21 'Annus Mirabilis' taken from *Collected Poems* © Philip Larkin (Estate) and reprinted by permission of Faber and Faber Ltd; p59 *Rogue Male* by Geoffrey Household (Copyright © Geoffrey Household, 1939). Reprinted by permission of A.M.Heath & Co Ltd; p90 'An Arundel Tomb' taken from *Collected Poems* © Philip Larkin (Estate) and reprinted by permission of Faber and Faber Ltd; p91 *The Day of the Triffids* by John Wyndham (Penguin Books, 1969) © John Wyndham; p194–5 *Such, Such Were the Joys* by George Orwell (Copyright © George Orwell, 1952). Reprinted by permission of Bill Hamilton as the Literary Executor of the Estate of the Late Sonia Brownell Orwell; p167 *The Nine Tailors* by Dorothy L Sayers (Hodder & Stoughton, 1959) © Dorothy L Sayers; p169 'Dreaming of Spires' by Philip Pullman (first published in the *Guardian*, 27 July 2002) © Guardian News & Media Ltd; p207 'A Writer's Britain: On England's Roof' by Keith Waterhouse (first published in the *Independent*, 16 January 1994) © Keith Waterhouse; p208 *A Rumoured City: New Poets from Hull* ed. Douglas Dunn (Bloodaxe Books, 1982) © Philip Larkin and reprinted with the permission of the Society of Authors as the Literary Representative of the Estate of Philip Larkin; p209 'Whitsun Weddings' taken from *Collected Poems* © Philip Larkin (Estate) and reprinted by permission of Faber and Faber Ltd.

1 See Larkin, Philip, 'Annus Mirabilis' in *Collected Poems*, ed. Anthony Thwaite (Faber & Faber, 2003)

2 See Sibley, Brian, *The Thomas the Tank Engine Man: A Biography* (Heinemann, 1995)

3 See Du Maurier, Daphne, *Vanishing Cornwall* (Gollancz, 1967)

4 See Du Maurier, Daphne, *Rebecca* (Virago, 2003)

5 See Fowles, John, *The Journals, Volume 2* (Vintage Classics, 2007)

6 For all quotations see Household, Geoffrey, *Rogue Male* (Penguin, 1949)

7 See McEwan, Ian, *On Chesil Beach* (Vintage, 2008)

8 See Forster, E M, *Two Cheers for Democracy* (Mariner Books, 1962)

9 See Kipling, Rudyard, 'The Janeites', in *Debits and Credits* (Macmillan, 1926)

10 See Larkin, Philip, 'An Arundel Tomb' in *Collected Poems*, ed. Anthony Thwaite (Faber & Faber, 2003)

11 See Wyndham, John, *The Day of the Triffids* (Penguin Books, 1969)

12 For all quotations see Gibbons, Stella, *Cold Comfort Farm* (Penguin Classics, 2006)

13 From a letter to Ka Arnold Foster, 12 August 1919; see *The Letters of Virginia Woolf*, ed. Nigel Nicolson and Joanne Trautmann, 6 vols (Hogarth Press, 1975–80)

14 See Carrington, Charles, *Rudyard Kipling: His Life and Work* (Penguin, 1955)

15 From a letter to Vivian Burnett, 28 February 1898; see Gerzina, Gretchen, *Frances Hodgson Burnett: The Unpredictable Life of the Author of* The Secret Garden (Chatto & Windus, 2004)

16 From a letter to Edith Jordan, 25 September 1908; see Gerzina

17 See Dickens, Charles, *Great Expectations* (Penguin Classics, 2004)

18 See Forster, John, *The Life of Charles Dickens* (Cecil Palmer, 1872–74)

19 See Wodehouse, P G, *P. G. Wodehouse: A Life in Letters* (Arrow, 2013)

20 See Gallagher, Donat, *The Essays, Articles and Reviews of Evelyn Waugh* (Little, Brown & Co, 1984)

21 See de La Rochefoucauld, Francois, *A Frenchman in England 1784: Being the Melanges sur l'Angleterre of Francois de la Rochefoucauld*, ed. Jean Marchand, trans. S C Roberts (CUP, 1933)

22 Both quotations from an essay entitled 'Great Men's Houses', originally published in *Good Housekeeping*, March 1932

23 From a letter written to Eliza Savage, November 1884

24 Quoted in the inside flap copy of Carlyle's *On heroes, hero-worship, and the heroic in history* (Macmillan, 1918)

25 See Orwell, George, 'Such, Such Were the Joys', in *Essays* (Penguin Classics, 2000)

26 See Treglown, Jeremy, *Roald Dahl: A Biography* (Harcourt Brace, 1994)

27 See Sayers, Dorothy L, *The Nine Tailors* (Hodder & Stoughton, 1959)

28 See Carter, Humphrey, *J. R. R. Tolkien: A Biography* (Houghton Mifflin, 2000)

29 See Pullman, Philip, 'Dreaming of Spires' (*Guardian*, 27 July 2002)

30 See Crompton, Richmal, 'William and the Lost Tourist' in *William the Conqueror* (George Newnes, 1926)

31 Study conducted by market research company Vision Critical in 2012

32 See Seymour-Smith, Martin, *Robert Graves: His Life and Work* (Bloomsbury, 1995)

33 See FitzGibbon, Constantine, *The Life of Dylan Thomas* (Dent, 1965)

34 For all quotations see Llewellyn, Richard, *How Green Was My Valley* (New English Library, 1982)

35 See, for example, Kilvert, Francis, *Kilvert's Diary, 1870–79* (Penguin, 1977)

36 See Housman, A E, *A Shropshire Lad* (Mitchell Kennerley, 1908)

37 See Housman, A E, *The Letters of A.E. Housman*, ed. Archie Burnett (Clarendon Press, 2007)

38 Several Lawrence biographies recount his difficulties growing up; see, for example, Worthen, John, *D. H. Lawrence: The Life of an Outsider* (Penguin, 2006)

39 See Waterhouse, Keith, 'A Writer's Britain: On England's Roof' (first published in the *Independent*, 16 January 1994)

40 See Larkin, Philip, *A Rumoured City: New Poets from Hull* ed. Douglas Dunn (Bloodaxe Books, 1982)

41 See Larkin, Philip, 'Whitsun Weddings' in *Collected Poems*, ed. Anthony Thwaite (Faber & Faber, 2003)

42 For all quotations see Stoker, Bram, *Dracula* (Penguin Classics, 2004)

43 See Brontë, Emily, *Wuthering Heights* (John Murray, 1910)

44 All quotations from an 1818 letter to John Hamilton Reynolds; see Keats, John, *Letters of John Keats to his Family and Friends*, ed. Sidney Colvin (Macmillan, 1925)

45 For all quotations see Conan Doyle, Arthur, *Through the Magic Door* (McClure, 1908)

46 See MacDiarmid, Hugh, *Selected Essays of Hugh MacDiarmid* (Cape, 1969)

Select bibliography

Bathurst, Bella, *The Lighthouse Stevensons: The Extraordinary Story of the Building of the Scottish Lighthouses by the Ancestors of Robert Louis Stevenson* (Harper Collins, 1999)

Booth, James, *Philip Larkin: Life, Art and Love* (Bloomsbury, 2014)

Clark, Peter, *Dickens: London Into Kent* (Armchair Traveller, 2013)

Daiches, David, *Literary Landscapes of The British Isles: A Narrative Atlas* (Paddington Press, 1979)

Dickens, Charles, *A Christmas Carol* (Longman, 1987)

Du Maurier, Daphne, *Vanishing Cornwall* (Gollancz, 1967)

Gaskell, Elizabeth Cleghorn, *The Life of Charlotte Bronte* (Smith, Elder, 1871)

Gibson, Anthony, *With Magic In My Eyes: West Country Literary Landscapes* (Fairfield Books, 2011)

Hardyment, Christina, *Literary Trails: Writers in Their Landscapes* (National Trust, 2000)

Harper, Charles George, *The Hardy Country: Literary Landmarks of the Wessex Novels* (A&C Black, 1904)

Hill-Miller, Katherine C, *From The Lighthouse To Monk's House: a Guide to Virginia Woolf's Literary Landscapes* (Duckworth, 2001)

Hutton, Laurence, *Literary Landmarks of London* (Harper & Brothers, 1892)

Leader, Zachary, *The Life of Kingsley Amis*, Jonathan Cape, 2006

Morley, Frank, *Literary Britain* (Hutchinson, 1980)

Nicolson, Nigel, *The Letters of Virginia Woolf 1929–1931* (Hogarth Press, 1975)

Orwell, George, *The Collected Essays, Journalism and Letters of George Orwell* (Secker & Warburg, 1968)

Thomas, Edward, *A Literary Pilgrim in England* (Jonathan Cape, 1928)

Tomalin, Claire, *Charles Dickens: A Life* (Viking, 2011)

Tomalin, Claire, *Samuel Pepys: The Unequalled Self* (Viking, 2002)

Tomalin, Claire, *Thomas Hardy: The Time-Torn Man* (Viking, 2006)

Watson, Nicola J, *The Literary Tourist: Readers and Places in Romantic and Victorian Britain* (Palgrave Macmillan, 2006)

Selected reading

The following works are just a few of those which helped to inform the writing of *Treasured Island*, and may be of further interest to readers:

Amis, Kingsley, *Lucky Jim*, 1954

Austen, Jane

—— *Northanger Abbey*, 1817

—— *Persuasion*, 1817

—— *Pride and Prejudice*, 1813

Barrie, J M, *Peter Pan*, 1911

Bennett, Alan, *Forty Years On*, 1968

Benson, E F, *Mapp and Lucia*, 1931

Blackmore, R D, *Lorna Doone*, 1869

Bronte, Charlotte, *Jane Eyre*, 1847

Bronte, Emily, *Wuthering Heights*, 1847

Brown, Ben, *Larkin with Women*, 1999

Buchan, John, *The Thirty Nine Steps*, 1915

Burgess, Anthony, *A Clockwork Orange*, 1962

Burnett, Frances Hodgson, *The Secret Garden*, 1911

Christie, Agatha

—— *Dead Man's Folly*, 1956

—— *Five Little Pigs*, 1942

—— *Ordeal By Innocence*, 1958

—— *Towards Zero*, 1944

Coleridge, Samuel Taylor and Wordsworth, William, *Lyrical Ballads*, 1798

Conan Doyle, Arthur, *The Hound of the Baskervilles*, 1902

Cordell, Alexander, *Rape of the Fair Country*, 1959

Crompton, Richmal, *William the Conqueror*, 1926

Dahl, Roald

—— *Charlie and the Chocolate Factory*, 1964

—— *Danny, the Champion of the World*, 1975

Defoe, Daniel, *Robinson Crusoe*, 1719

Dickens, Charles

—— *A Christmas Carol*, 1843

—— *David Copperfield*, 1850

—— *Great Expectations*, 1861

—— *Oliver Twist*, 1837

Du Maurier, Daphne

—— *Jamaica Inn*, 1936

—— *Rebecca*, 1938

—— *Frenchman's Creek*, 1941

Eliot, T S

—— *Four Quartets*, 1943

—— *The Waste Land*, 1922

Falkner, J Meade, *Moonfleet*, 1898

Fleming, Ian, *Goldfinger*, 1959

Fowles, John, *The French Lieutenant's Woman*, 1969

Gaskell, Elizabeth

—— *Cranford*, 1851

—— *North and South*, 1854

Gibbons, Stella, *Cold Comfort Farm*, 1932

Golding, William, *The Spire*, 1964

Grahame, Kenneth, *The Wind in the Willows*, 1908

Greene, Graham, *Brighton Rock*, 1938

Hardy, Thomas
—— *Far From the Madding Crowd*, 1874
—— *Jude the Obscure*, 1895
—— *Tess of the D'Urbervilles*, 1891

Household, Geoffrey, *Rogue Male*, 1939

Housman, A E, *A Shropshire Lad*, 1896

James, Henry, *The Golden Bowl*, 1904

Kingsley, Charles, *Westward Ho!*, 1855

Kipling, Rudyard
—— *Debits and Credits*, 1926
—— *Puck of Pook's Hill*, 1906
—— *Stalky & Co*, 1899

Klickmann, Flora, *The Flower-Patch Among the Hills*, 1916

Larkin, Philip
—— *Collected Poems,* 2003
—— *The Whitsun Weddings*, 1964

Lawrence, D H, *Lady Chatterley's Lover,* 1928

Lawrence, T E, *Seven Pillars of Wisdom*, 1922

Lewis, C S, *Alice's Adventures in Wonderland*, 1865

Llewellyn, Richard, *How Green Was My Valley*, 1939

McCall, Alexander, *44 Scotland Street*, 2004

McEwan, Ian, *On Chesil Beach*, 2007

Milne, A A
—— *The House at Pooh Corner*, 1928

—— *Winnie-the-Pooh*, 1926

Nesbit, E H, *The Railway Children*, 1906

Orwell, George, *1984*, 1949

Osborne, John, *The Entertainer*, 1957

Peters, Ellis, *One Corpse Too Many*, 1979

Potter, Beatrix, *The Tale of Peter Rabbit*, 1902

Ransome, Arthur, *Swallows and Amazons*, 1930

Rowling, J K, *Harry Potter and the Philosopher's Stone*, 1997

Sayers, Dorothy, *The Nine Tailors*, 1934

Scott, Walter
—— *The Heart of Midlothian*, 1818
—— *Waverley*, 1814

Shakespeare, William
—— *Macbeth*, 1611
—— *Richard III*, 1633

Stevenson, Robert Louis, *Treasure Island*, 1883

Stoker, Bram, *Dracula*, 1897

Thomas, Dylan, *Under Milk Wood*, 1954

Waterhouse, Keith, *Billy Liar*, 1959

Waugh, Evelyn
—— *Men at Arms*, 1952
—— *Brideshead Revisited*, 1945

Welsh, Irvine, *Trainspotting*, 1993

Williamson, Henry, *Tarka the Otter*, 1927

Wodehouse, P G, *The World of Jeeves*, 1967

Woolf, Virginia
—— *Mrs Dalloway*, 1925
—— *To the Lighthouse*, 1927

Wyndham, John, *Day of the Triffids*, 1951

In addition, the poetry of:

William Blake
Rupert Brooke
Robert Burns
George, Lord Byron
Samuel Taylor Coleridge
T S Eliot

Thomas Gray
John Keats
A E Housman
Ted Hughes
Rudyard Kipling
Philip Larkin

Wilfred Owen
Sylvia Plath
Percy Bysshe Shelley
Dylan Thomas
Edward Thomas
William Wordsworth

Acknowledgements

WHEN the sages of Victorian literature were considering which of literary contemporaries Edward Bulwer-Lytton and Charles Dickens would still be read in the future, it was widely assumed that it would be the work of Bulwer-Lytton that would endure. Bulwer-Lytton, who wrote wordy historical novels in the Sir Walter Scott style, has, alas, become something of a latter-day music hall joke, famous for supposedly writing the worst opening paragraph in the whole of literature: 'It was a dark and stormy night; the rain fell in torrents, except at occasional intervals, when it was checked by a violent gust of wind which swept up the streets…'. There is an annual Bulwer-Lytton prize for the worst opening paragraph to a novel.

Actually Bulwer-Lytton had a very sharp turn of phrase (his greatest hits include: 'the pen is mightier than the sword', 'the great unwashed', 'pursuit of the almighty dollar' and 'Talent does what it can: Genius does what it must'. He had a decidedly unusual life: Bulwer-Lytton was once offered the Greek throne (he declined it); and he is said to have lived in the original Craven Cottage, now better known as the home of Fulham Football Club. Bulwer-Lytton is an author crying out for his own museum – but alas, pilgrims have to make do with a memorial in Poets' Corner (something which he had said that he really didn't want – the sad fate of several reluctant inhabitants of this dismal Westminster Abbey demesne).

When I was writing this book, I thought often of EBL. Literary reputations are strange and unpredictable: writers go in and out of fashion just as surely as boybands. Sir Walter Scott, for example, is now largely famous for being famous: who picks up one of his works these days for reading pleasure? Several other distinguished writers have expensive and extensive memorials which far exceed the measure of their modern reputation. Their flame however is busily kept alive by bands of devoted volunteers convinced that the tide of fashion will surely turn and once again their literary hero or heroine will reclaim their rightful place in popular estimation.

We have an abundance of literary museums of various sorts in the UK: many exceedingly good, some dismal – all of them, however, are never less than interesting. In the several months I spent visiting them, I can honestly declare that I had the time of my life. When I was quite small I loved it when we visited other people's houses because I had *carte blanche* to snoop into our hosts' private lives (you can cut five year olds a lot of slack in this respect). It didn't take me long to suss out that people's home life is intensely fascinating: what books do they read, what's in the fridge, what board games do they play, what's in their bedroom drawers (yes, I crossed a line there)? Journalists, after all, are nosey parkers who make a living out of nosiness. Imagine, therefore, the pleasure I had in poking around Agatha Christie's drawers or rooting in Dylan Thomas' cupboards.

A further unwonted delight derives from the fact that writers are blessed with a mighty opinion of their own efforts and a raw rancorous dislike for anything produced by anyone who might be regarded as a rival (Charles Dickens and William Thackeray seemed often on the point of fisticuffs in their bitter feud).

My regret is that I didn't get the chance to visit everywhere: I failed, for example, to accommodate G B Shaw this time – though I visited many years ago and can recommend it; Churchill's home Chartwell regrettably proved beyond reach (but was he a writer who dabbled in politics or a politician who dabbled in writing?).

Wernher von Braun, the inventor of the V1 and V2 rocket programmes which rained death and destruction on the UK –

who evaded prosecution at the Nuremburg war trials to become director of the US space effort – wrote a self-serving autobiography coyly titled *I Aim at the Stars*; American humourist Mort Sahl suggested an extension: 'I aim at the stars; sometimes I hit London…'

With this book, I aimed at the stars – I hope I hit the target; apologies to anyone who feels slighted in any way. I salute everybody who gets up everyday and attempts to satisfy the needs and interest of tourists – generally a fickle lot. A character in E M Forster's *A Room With A View* asks what memorable sights they had encountered during their stay in Rome:

'Rome?' muses his companion: 'Guess that was where we saw the yellow dog.' Forster was poking fun at the package tourists flooding into Europe at the end of the 19th century; people who visited St Peter's and the Colosseum, yet their abiding memory of the Eternal City was of a yellow dog.

To some extent, I'm on the side of the yellow dog tourists. My heart warms to people who visit the home of Kipling and wonder whether he had anything to do with baking cakes; blessed are the meek, for they will enjoy the museum cafe.

I am meekly grateful to everyone in the literary landmark business who helped me in the writing of this book – thank you also to the obstructively unhelpful who probably pushed me towards taking the way less travelled, and my journey was the better for it.

In the actual creation of this book I must express the warmest appreciation to my agent Cat Ledger; Tom Bromley, Helen Brocklehurst and Rebecca Needes of AA Publishing; and the unwavering support of my wife Sheila ('We are all travellers in the wilderness of this world, and the best we can find in our travels is an honest friend,' said the author of my inspiration for this book, Robert Louis Stevenson.)

Back to my old chum Bulwer-Lytton for the last word: 'Laws die. Books never.'

Index

44 Scotland Street 246
221B Baker Street 141–3
1984 249, 250

A
Abbot Hall Museum 229
Abbotsford 240, 242–3
Ackroyd, Peter 79
Alexander the Great 13
Alice in Wonderland 168
The Ambassadors 108
Amis, Kingsley 42, 90, 176, 180, 207
And Then There Were None 54
Andersen, Hans Christian 115, 158
Arthurian legend 28
'An Arundel Tomb' 89–90
Ash Farm, Exmoor 34–5
Ashdown Forest 99
Auden, W H 153
Austen, Jane 15, 26, 57, 64–6, 80–4, 213
Awdry, Revd W 27
Ayckbourn, Alan 209

B
Barchester Chronicles 79
Barnhill 248–9, 250, 251
Barrie, J M 17, 75, 136–40, 144, 158, 246–7
Bateman's 100, 102–3, 258
Bath 15, 64–6, 213
Beerbolm, Max 108
Belaney, Archibald Stansfeld ('Grey Owl') 186

Bell, Vanessa 94
Belloc, Hilaire 108
Belmont House 56
Bennett, Alan 85–6, 98, 153, 206
Benson, E F 108
Betjeman, John 26–7, 89, 91, 197, 208–9
The BFG 161
Billy Liar 206
Blackmore, R D 26, 39
Blackwell's bookshop, Oxford 167–9
Blackwood 187–8
Blake, William 17, 29, 152
Bleak House 120, 128
Bloomsbury Group 94
Blyton, Enid 156, 158
Boathouse, Laugharne 181–2
Bockhampton 71–2
Bodmin Moor 45
Bowerchalke 79
Bredwardine 189, 190
Brideshead Revisited 168
Brighton 94–5
Brighton Rock 94
Bristol 23–5, 26
Broadstairs 118–20
Brontë, Charlotte 10, 218, 219
Brontë, Emily 15, 216, 217–18, 219, 224
Brontë Parsonage Museum 218–23, 258
Brooke, Rupert 162, 165–6
Brown, Ben 209
Buchan, John 118–19

Buckfastleigh 49, 50
Bulwer-Lytton, Edward 266, 268
Burgess, Anthony 203
Burgh Island 54
Burnett, Frances Hodgson 105–7, 108
Burney, Fanny 79
Burns, Robert 234–5, 236–9, 244, 245
Burrington Combe 35
Burton, Richard 178
Bush, Kate 217, 218
Butlin's 30–1
Byron, Lord 162, 201–2

C
Cadfael Chronicles 195
Cambridge University 161–5
Camden Town 126, 131
Canterbury 117
Carlyle, Jane 147–8
Carlyle, Thomas 17, 146–9
Carroll, Lewis 159, 168
Cats (musical) 61
Chandler, Raymond 124
Charlie and the Chocolate Factory 159–60
Chartists 187
Chatham 113
Chatterley obscenity trial 21, 198–9
Chatterton, Thomas 26
Chaucer, Geoffrey 14, 116–17
Chawton 80, 82–3
Cheddar Gorge 35

Index

Chesil Beach 59–60
Chesterton, G K 108
Cheyne Row, London 147–9
Chichester 88, 90–1
children's literature 97–8, 158–61, 226–7
Christian legend 28, 29
Christie, Agatha 17, 52–3, 54, 153
A Christmas Carol 15, 126, 129–33
Churchill, Winston 121–2, 267
Clarke, John Cooper 203
Clarke, Sir Arthur C 31
A Clockwork Orange 203
Clouds Hill 53, 76–8, 258
Clun 194
Clunton 194
Cockermouth 232–3
Cold Comfort Farm 93–4, 97
Coleridge, Samuel Taylor 12, 15, 17, 33–5, 36–8, 162
Coleridge Cottage 36–8
Collins, Wilkie 16
Combe Florey 26
Communist Manifesto 203
Conrad, Joseph 108
Cook, Peter 153
Cooling 110–12
Cordell, Alexander 85, 187
Cornhill 129–30
Cranford 204
Crompton, Richmal 16, 170, 248
Cunliffe, John 229

D

Dahl, Roald 17, 156–7, 158, 159–61, 176, 226
Daniel, Samuel 26
Danny the Champion of the World 156, 161
Dartmoor 49–50
Dartmoor Prison museum 49
Davenant, William 169

David Copperfield 109–10, 120, 126
Day of the Triffids 91–3
Dead Man's Folly 53
Defoe, Daniel 24, 210
Desperate Remedies 72
Dickens, Charles 15, 16, 88, 109–15, 119–20, 125–33, 145, 147, 148, 152, 171, 175, 210, 240, 241, 243, 267
Dilton Marsh Halt 26–7
Dittisham 53
Dorchester 70
Dove Cottage 230–1, 235, 258
Doyle, Sir Arthur Conan 49–50, 140–3, 240
Drabble, Margaret 153
Dracula 210–13
du Maurier, Daphne 26, 45–9
du Maurier, Gerald 47, 136, 138
Duffy, Carol Ann 203
Dulwich College 124
Dumfries 247

E

ebooks 20
'East Coker' 61–2
Eastwood 197–8, 199–200
Edinburgh 243–6
'Elegy in a country churchyard' 155
Eliot, T S 26, 61–3
Engels, Friedrich 203, 204
The Entertainer 95
Eton College 154–5
Evil Under the Sun 54
Exmoor 26, 38–9

F

Falkner, J Meade 59
Fantastic Mr Fox 156
Far From The Madding Crowd 68, 69, 76
Felpham 17

First World War 41, 85–6, 87, 101, 166
Five Hundred Acre Wood 99
Five Little Pigs 53
Fleet Street 133–4
Fleming, Ian 116, 118, 120–1, 152, 153, 155
Ford, Ford Madox 108
Forster, E M 77–8, 94, 96, 162, 268
Fowey 43–5, 47–8
Fowles, John 55–9
Fox Tor Mires 50
Foy Boat pub, Ramsgate 1120
The French Lieutenant's Woman 57–8
Frenchman's Creek 48–9

G

Gad's Hill Place 113–15
Galsworthy, John 153
Gaskell, Elizabeth 203–4, 219
George & Vulture pub, London 130–1
Georgeham 39–40
Gibbons, Stella 93–4, 97, 153
Glastonbury 28–9, 30
Glastonbury Thorn 30
Gloucester 67
The Golden Bowl 108
Golden Valley 188
Goldfinger 116, 117–18, 120, 121, 153
Goldfinger, Erno 152, 153
Golding, William 26, 78–9
Grahame, Kenneth 156, 158
Grant, Duncan 94
Grantchester meadows 165–6
Grasmere 230–1
Gray, Thomas 15, 154, 155–6, 162
Great Expectations 110, 111, 112, 113
Great Maytham Hall 105, 106–7
Great Missenden 156–7, 159–61

Great Ormond Street Hospital, London 139–40
Greene, Graham 94
Greenway 50–3

H

Halliwell, Kenneth 143
Hampstead 150–3
The Hand of Ethelberta 79
Hardy, Thomas 15, 17, 53, 68–76, 79–80, 88, 144, 243
Harrogate 54
Harry Potter novels 15, 32, 212, 246
Haworth 218–23
Hay on Wye 188–9
The Heart of Midlothian 244
Heptonstall 215–16
heritage railways 30, 31–2
Hill Top 227–8
His Dark Materials trilogy 169
The Hole in the Wall, Bristol 25
Holmes, Sherlock 17, 27, 140–3
Holtby, Winifred 209
Holy Trinity Church, Stratford 9, 172
Hopkins, Gerard Manley 152
Horsham 94
The Hound of the Baskervilles 49–50, 142
The House at Pooh Corner 97, 98, 100
Household, Geoffrey 58–9
Housman, A E 162, 191–4
How Green Was My Valley 183–5, 187
Hughes, Ted 26, 41, 86, 89, 146, 159, 214, 215–17
Hull 207–9
Huxley, Aldous 153

I

Ilkley 225
Ingrams, Richard 195
Inspector Rebus novels 246

Islington Local History Centre 143–4

J

Jamaica Inn 45–6
Jamaica Inn 45
James, Henry 106, 108–9
The Janeites 80–1
'Jerusalem' 17, 29
Johnson, Samuel 17, 134–6, 229
Jonson, Ben 145–6
Jude the Obscure 68, 73, 79
Jura 248–51
Just William stories 16, 139, 170, 248

K

Keats, John 150–2, 234–6
Keighley & Worth Valley Railway 32, 107
Kendal 229
Kensington Gardens, London 137, 139
Keynes, John Maynard 96
Kilmarth 48
Kilmersden 67–8
Kilvert, Francis 189–90
Kings Cross Station, London 15, 32
Kingsbere 76
Kingsley, Charles 15, 42, 162
Kipling, Rudyard 17, 42, 75, 80–1, 100–4, 108, 268
Kirkby Lonsdale 225
Kirriemuir 246–7
Klickmann, Flora 190–1
Knockholt 32
Kubla Khan 34–5

L

Lady Chatterley's Lover 198–9
The Lady in the Van 153
Lake District 229–232
Lamb House 108–9
Landmark Trust 56

Lane, Allen 54–5
Larkin, Philip 21, 88, 89–91, 198–9, 207–9
laudanum 36–7
Laugharne 181–2
Lawrence, D H 17, 26, 88, 145, 197–200
Lawrence, T E 17, 53–4, 76–8, 149
le Carre, John 26
Leadenhall Market 133
Lee, Laurie 26
Leeds 204–5, 206, 207
Leith 245
Lewis, C S 188
Lichfield 135
literary tourism 9–11, 13, 18, 70
Little Dorrit 126
Llandoger Trow pub, Bristol 24–5
Llewellyn, Richard 183–5, 186
Llewelyn Davies family 137–8, 139
London 13, 15, 92, 123–53
Longsleddale 229
Look Back in Anger 194
Lorna Doone 26, 39
lost and destroyed manuscripts 148, 149
The Loving Spirit 47
Ludlow 193–4
Lyme Regis 55–9
Lyrical Ballads 12

M

McCall Smith, Alexander 246
McEwan, Ian 59–60
Mackenzie, Compton 108
Manchester 202–4
Manning, Marie and Frederick 128–9
Mansfield, Katherine 153
Mapp and Lucia 108, 109
March 166–7
Marlowe, Christopher 15, 162

Index

Marvell, Andrew 209
Marx, Karl 203
Matilda 160, 161
Max Gate 71, 73–4
The Mayor of Casterbridge 68, 70, 73
Medway 112–13
Mells 67
Menabilly 47–8
Mill, John Stuart 148
Miller, Jonathan 153
Milne, A A 97–100, 153
Milton, John 15, 162
Minehead 30–1
Monk's House 95–6, 258
Moonfleet 59, 60
Mosley, Oswald 41
Mr Potter's Museum of Curiosities 46
Mrs Dalloway 95
Muckle Flugga 252–4, 258
Murder in Mesopotamia 54

N

National Trust 11, 17–18, 38, 52, 71, 73, 76, 96, 102, 103, 108, 152, 227, 233, 246–7, 258
Nesbit, Edith 107, 158
Nether Stowey 34, 36–8
New Quay 182–3
Newport 187
Newstead Abbey 201
Nicholas Nickleby 133, 210
Nicholls, David 246
The Nine Tailors 166–7
North and South 204
North Chideock 59
North Yorkshire Moors Railway 212
Northanger Abbey 66
nursery rhymes 66–8

O

Oare 39
The Old Curiosity Shop 16

Old Possum's Book of Practical Cats 61
'The Old Vicarage, Grantchester' 165–6
Oliver Twist 127–8
On Chesil Beach 59–60
One Day 246
One Hundred and One Dalmatians 12–13
Ordeal by Innocence 53
Orton, Joe 143–4
Orwell, George 102, 153, 154–5, 248–51
Osborne, John 95, 194
Owen, Wilfred 166, 195–6
Oxford 70, 167–9
Oxford Bar, Edinburgh 246

P

Painted Rooms, Oxford 169
A Pair of Blue Eyes 72
Pantisocracy 37
Parker, Dorothy 97
Penguin Books 54–5, 198–9
Pepys, Samuel 16, 162–5
Pepys Library 164–5, 258
Persuasion 57, 65
Peter Pan 136–7, 138, 139–40, 246–7
Peterloo Massacre 202
Peters, Ellis 195
Plath, Sylvia 162, 214–17
Poets' Corner, Westminster Abbey 75, 144–6, 178–9, 266
Polridmouth Cove 48
Pope, Alexander 15
Portsmouth 115
Postman Pat 229
Potter, Beatrix 17, 226–8
Potter, Dennis 192
Poundbury 68
Pride and Prejudice 15, 64, 82, 84
Priestley, J B 153
Puck of Pook's Hill 103–4
Pullman, Philip 169

R

racism 102, 157–8, 159–60
The Railway Children 32, 107, 158, 220
Ramsgate 120
Rankin, Ian 246
Ransome, Arthur 229
Rape of the Fair Country 187
Reading Station 149
Rebecca 48
Reculver 117–18
Rewards and Fairies 103
Richards, Frank 240
The Rime of the Ancient Mariner 33–4, 36
Robinson Crusoe 24, 25, 210
Rochester 113
Rock 'n' Roll 161
'Rock of Ages' 35
Rodmell 95–6
Rogue Male 58–9
Romney Marsh 121
Rowling, J K 12, 15, 26, 32, 80, 246
Royal Exchange, London 132–3
Royal St George's golf club, Sandwich 120–1
Ruskin, John 123, 225–6
Ruskin's View 225
Rusland 229
Rydal Mount 232
Rye 108–9

S

St Enodoc's Church, Padstow 26
St Giles Church, Stoke Poges 155–6
St Leonard's Police Station, Edinburgh 246
St Margaret's Bay 116
St Mary the Virgin Church, Oare 39
St Michael and All Angels, East Coker 62

Treasured Island

St Wendreda's Church, March 166–7
Salisbury 78–9
Salter, Martin 64–6
Sandwich 120–1
Sassoon, Siegfried 67, 166, 196
Sayers, Dorothy L 166–8
Scarborough 209, 210
scattering ashes 31–3
Scott, Sir Walter 175, 230, 239–244, 245, 266–7
Scott Monument 243–4
The Secret Garden 105, 106–7
Selborne 81
Seven Pillars of Wisdom 77, 149
Shaftesbury 68
Shakespeare, William 9, 14–15, 16, 169–75, 192–3, 235–6
Sharpe, Tom 162
Shelley, Percy Bysshe 155, 202
Sherlock Holmes pub, London 142–3
Shrewsbury 195–6
A Shropshire Lad 191–2, 193–4
Slad 26
Smith, Dodie 12–13
South Riding 209
South West Coast Path 34, 35–6, 58
Southey, Robert 26, 30, 37
Southwark 126
The Spire 78–9
staff and volunteers 11, 52, 82, 200, 220–3, 244, 256–8, 267
Stalky & Co 42
Steep 86
Stevenson, Robert Louis 22, 24, 153, 244, 245, 251–5, 258, 268
Stinsford 75
Stoke Poges 155–6
Stoker, Bram 211–13
Stonehenge 79–80
Stoppard, Tom 161

Stratford-upon-Avon 9, 170–5, 235–6
Sussex Downs 92–3, 94
Swallows and Amazons 229
Swansea 179–80
The Sword of Honour 31

T

The Tale of Peter Rabbit 227
A Tale of Two Cities 113, 148
Tarka the Otter 39–41
Tennyson, Alfred, Lord 17, 162, 175
Tess of the d'Urbevilles 68, 69, 73, 79–80
The Thirty Nine Steps 118, 119
Thomas, Dylan 17, 146, 149, 176–83, 185
Thomas, Edward 86–7
Thomas the Tank Engine 27, 32
Tintern Abbey 12
Tolkien, J R R 168–9
Toller Down 76
Top Withens 223–5
Toplady, Augustus 35
Towards Zero 53
Trainspotting 245
Treasure Island 21, 22–3, 24–5, 251, 252, 253, 255
Trelowarren House 48–9
Trollope, Anthony 79
Twain, Mark 83–4, 175

U

Under Milk Wood 149, 177, 178, 182
Under the Greenwood Tree 72
Unst 252–4, 258

W

Watchet 31–2, 33–4
Waterhouse, Keith 206–7
Waterston Manor 76
Waugh, Evelyn 26, 31, 67, 93, 125, 153, 168
Wells 28

Wells, H G 108, 153, 153
Welsh, Irvine 245
Welsh Valleys 183–9
West Bagborough 31
West Highland Railway 32
West Somerset Railway 30
Westward Ho! 15, 42
Westward Ho! 15, 42
Whitby 211–13
White, Gilbert 81
'Whitsun Weddings' 209
Wilde, Oscar 16, 145, 149
Williamson, Henry 39–41, 54, 78
Willow Road, Hampstead 152
The Wind in the Willows 98, 156
The Wings of the Dove 108
Winnie-the-Pooh 97, 98–100
Wives and Daughters 204
Wodehouse, P G 16, 68, 124–5
Woolf, Virginia 17, 26, 94, 95–7, 147
Wordsworth, William 12, 16, 17, 26, 36, 37, 162, 230–3, 235
Writers' Museum, Edinburgh 244–5
Wuthering Heights 15, 216, 217–18, 220, 223–4
Wye Valley 12, 190–1
Wyndham, John 91–3

Y

York 210